SEX 3rd EDITION
CRIMES

To all our students past and present
Thanks for all you have given us

SEX CRIMES
3rd EDITION
CRIMES
Patterns and Behavior

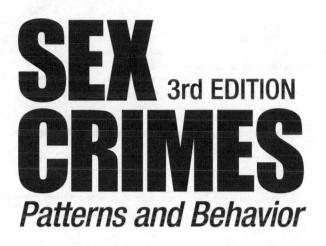

Stephen T. Holmes
University of Central Florida

Ronald M. Holmes
University of Louisville, KY

SAGE Publications
Los Angeles • London • New Delhi • Singapore

For information:

SAGE Publications, Inc.
2455 Teller Road
Thousand Oaks,
  California 91320
E-mail: order@sagepub.com
	SAGE Publications India Pvt. Ltd.
	B 1/I 1 Mohan Cooperative
	  Industrial Area
	Mathura Road, New Delhi 110 044
	India

SAGE Publications Ltd. 1 Oliver's Yard 55 City Road London EC1Y 1SP United Kingdom	SAGE Publications Asia-Pacific Pte. Ltd. 33 Pekin Street #02-01 Far East Square Singapore 048763

Printed in the United States of America.

Library of Congress Cataloging-in-Publication Data

Holmes, Stephen T.
Sex crimes: patterns and behavior/Stephen T. Holmes & Ronald M. Holmes.—3rd ed.
    p. cm.
Ronald Holmes' name appears first on previous ed.
Includes bibliographical references and index.
ISBN 978-1-4129-5298-9 (pbk.)
    1. Sex crimes—United States. 2. Sex offenders—United States. 3. Sexual deviation—United States. I. Holmes, Ronald M. II. Title.

HV6592.H65 2009
364.15'30973—dc22   2007023144

This book is printed on acid-free paper.

09   10   11   12   13   10   9   8   7   6   5   4   3   2   1

Acquisitions Editor:	Jerry Westby
Editorial Assistant:	Eve Oettinger
Copy Editor:	Geof Garvey
Typesetter:	C&M Digitals (P) Ltd.
Proofreader:	Scott Oney
Indexer:	Rick Hurd
Cover Designer:	Candice Harman
Marketing Manager:	Jennifer Reed Banando

7/09

Contents

Preface

F ew topics arouse more attention of people than sex and sex crimes. The sex offender is viewed by many as a moral degenerate and one who preys upon moral citizens at an alarming rate with relative impunity. The crimes committed, such as rape, lust murder, and child molestation, appall and disgust, but they attract and fascinate at the same time. Rapists, serial killers, lust murderers, frotteurs, and others galvanize the concerns of those who are victimized and those who experience their actions secondhand through the media.

In lecturing throughout the United States on sex crimes, psychological profiling, and ritualistic crimes, we are constantly being told stories about the brutal, sadistic, and appalling sex crimes that have come to the attention of the criminal justice system. Realizing this fact, we set about gathering information to add to the original first edition of *Sex Crimes*. In the first edition, we gathered information from various sources, which served as a framework for the original work. We research professional journals, academic books, and other reliable sources. We also interviewed and exchanged correspondence with a variety of sex offenders, some unknown to the public and others whose names are household words, such as Ted Bundy, Douglas Clark, and John Wayne Gacy. We especially were enlightened with the thoughts, words, and letters from our own "Hannibal Lector," a killer and sex offender in prison in the Great Northwest. They all gave us insight into the world of the sexually violent, their fantasies, ritualisms, fetishes, and compulsions. We also maintained contact with practitioners in the field who come in daily contact with the sexually deviant and the sexual criminal.

Our research into the second edition yielded a great many new bits of information, which added many new citations in a deliberate attempt to bring the reader up to date. The Internet and other media outlets had also added many sites to gather information on sex crimes. When the first edition was published in 1991, actually written in 1989 and 1990, such information was relatively sparse, and many of the citations were classical works. The second edition was able to add a great deal of information that had amassed in the previous 5 years. The third edition was prompted by the greater attention now being paid to sexual offenders across the country. It adds a chapter on internet crime and sexually motivated homicides.

Of course, there are many whom we wish to thank as colleagues and friends who understand and appreciate the work we are doing. Hesitant to list, but choosing to do so anyhow because of the risk of leaving someone out, we would like to thank a few: Drs. Robert Langworthy and Joyce Dorner, University of Central Angela West, and Tad Hughes, University of Louisville; Thomas Harris, author and friend; Sgt. David Rivers (Ret.), Metro-Dade (FL) Sheriff's Office; Sgt. Marty Bloom, Metro-Dade (FL) Sheriff's Office; James Massie, Kentucky Probation and Parole; Lt. George Barrett, Louisville Police Department; Dr. Eric Hickey, University of California at Fresno; Dr. Steve Egger, Illinois State University at Springfield; Dr. Jack Levin, Northeastern University; Drs. Ed Latessa and James Frank, University of Cincinnati; Detective Jay Whitt, Greensboro (NC) Police Department; Tom Harris, author; Dr. Suzette Cossette, University of California at Sacramento; Dr. George Rush, University of California at Long Beach; Dr. Neal Haskell, forensic entomologist; and Dr. Joseph Davis, University of California at Davis. We are certain there are others. Please accept our sincere apology for any slight; it was not intentional.

We would also like to thank our wives, Amy and Tootie. Bless them.

1

Sex Behaviors and Crimes in the United States

❖ ❖ ❖

S ex crimes have for many years occupied a position of high interest in American society. Rarely a day passes without some type of sex crime or scandal being reported on the evening news. Whether it be a report of a missing child, a famous person, or a politician, we are deluged with information by the media on the sexual indiscretions of others. Whether it be from the involvement of a former president with an intern, a former member of the U.S. House of Representatives chatting on-line with current and former male congressional pages, or the abduction of a child, it is big news and typically results with a lead story from the news anchorperson.

Some sexual acts involve willing partners, others are solitary events, and others are perpetrated unfortunately on unwilling and helpless victims. Some result in no or minor physical damage, yet others result in death. During an interview with serial killer Ted Bundy, he related, "He (the unknown killer) entered her vaginally from the rear, pulled her head back by the hair, and slit her throat. The most powerful orgasm this person had ever had" (authors' files). Accounts such as these fascinate the public and scare them at the same time. But what is it about these offenders that captivates the public? Is it a willingness to try to understand what these offenders are about or is it just plain curiosity that drives our compulsion to know more about these offenders and what makes them tick? The answer to this and other questions of this kind are difficult to answer and most likely are specific to the individual.

Even without having a firm understanding of why this information fascinates the public, it is clear that everyone wants to know more about sex, sexuality, and the sexual indiscretions of others. Newspaper publishers know that a scandal will sell papers. Television news channels (especially cable news networks) will devote weeks of programming to the topic because of the boost in ratings that will follow. And magazine publishers understand that many of their annual sex surveys sell more magazines than any other issue.

The accounts of the criminally sexually deviant are so compelling that many students who enter colleges and universities want to study these individuals, and classes on profiling violent crime and serial and mass murder are often filled during the first week of registration. These accounts are moving and often very explicit. Take, for instance, an account of another serial predator who murdered two 12-year-old girls.

I woke up that morning knowing I was going to kill like I had killed many mornings before. I showered, ate breakfast, and drove to work. All morning I shifted papers from one side of my desk to the other. Finally, at lunch, I told my secretary that I was signing out to the field. I drove downtown, and there she stood. Blond haired, blue eyes, unmistakably very definitely female, cheerleader type. But before I could get to her, a car came from the side street and she got in. The feeling was so strong inside of me that I decided that the next person I saw I would kill. I got out of my car in the parking lot of the junior college and started to walk across the field by the football stadium. Two young girls were walking toward my direction. As they walked to my side, I grabbed each by the arm and forced them into the stadium itself. We walked up the steps to the second floor dressing room. I forced each into a stall separated one from the other by a half wall of concrete block. To the first I said do this, and she would not. Say this, and she would not, perhaps too shocked to hear my demands and obey them. I killed her almost immediately because she would not do as I had commanded. To the second young girl, I said do this, and she did. Say this, and she did. I told her to get her clothes back on. As we walked out of the stadium, she asked about her friend, not knowing that her friend was already dead. I told her not to worry about her friend. As we approached my car, a campus security officer stood by the sidewalk. We had to walk by him to get to my car. My pace quickened but the young girl grabbed my arm and said, "Please mister, slow down." Why she didn't tell the officer I don't know, and she will never be able to tell.

I took her home and for the next eighteen hours I brutally ravished her. Her body weighed more than seven pounds more when she was found the next day. [He inserted rocks into her body's orifices.] (authors' files)

These statements reveal a personality that has made a vital connection between violent and fatal violence and sexual pleasure. In no society can such actions be deemed either permissible or tolerable despite the attention such celebrated killers as Bundy, the Menendez brothers, Charles Ng, or other such killers have received. These individuals commit crimes judged to be despicable and well beyond the normal range of acceptable behavior that we demand of our nation's residents. While it is true that we must study these individuals (their fantasies and compulsions) to better understand the etiology of their behavior, we must also be careful to condemn their behavior and work hard not to glorify it or the individuals who commit these despicable acts.

Clearly no society would expect or support its elected representatives propositioning young adults into a sexual liaison the way Representative Mark Foley did. When the transcripts and allegations of his indiscretions were made public, Representative Foley resigned, and some have even claimed that the residual effects of this scandal is one of the main factors that cost the Republicans control of the U.S. House and Senate.

———— ❧ ————

Maf54: ok. .i better go vote. .did you know you would have this effect on me

Teen: lol I guessed

Teen: ya go vote . . . I don't want to keep you from doing our job

Maf54: can I have a good kiss goodnight

Teen: :-*

Teen: <kiss>,

Excerpt from Rep. Mark Foley's online chat with a teenage, male congressional page in 1993.

SOURCE: Weisman, J. and J. Eliperin (2006, October 6) "Lawmaker's Intentions Appear Clear In Exchanges" The Washington Post. Retrieved October 17, 2007, from http://www.washingtonpost.com/wp-dyn/content/article/2006/10/05/AR2006100500008.html.

Within each society there is a culture. This culture can be seen as a normative system of behavior instructing persons on the proper way to behave. Obviously, some standards preserve the society and others are merely "nice" to have. These imperative standards allow all to live and grow as a people. These norms of behavior are called rules, regulations, and laws. In sociological terms, these standards are termed folkways, mores, laws, and institutions.

Classification of Sex Offenders

Sexual Predator

is defined as a person who has been convicted of, or pleaded guilty to, committing a sexually oriented offenses and who is likely in the future to commit additional sexually oriented offenses

Habitual Sex Offender

is determined by the sentencing court to have previously convicted of or plead guilty to one or more sexually oriented offenses.

Sexually Oriented Offender

is a person who has been convicted of, or pleaded guilty to, committing a sexually oriented offense

---

SOURCE: Adapted from Stark County Ohio Sheriffs Office, 2008.

Folkways are those normal, habitual ways of behaving. Often it is simply a matter of good manners. For example, even in contemporary American society, many consider it good manners to permit one gender to exit from a door before the other. In addition, it is viewed as a sign of chivalry that a man walks next to the curb when walking alongside a woman. The original purpose for the male to walk next to curb and the female to walk away from the curb has disappeared over the years. In times past, garbage and human waste were often thrown from a second-story window or doorway into the street, and in that age it was preferable for the male to be the recipient of the thrown debris. In our time, garbage is collected, and human waste is disposed of, in a more sanitary fashion. Thus, the original intent has disappeared; it is now just "good manners."

— ⚘ —

Folkways

The normal, habitual ways of doing things; often matters of good manners

Most parents take great pains in preparing their children for the world in which they will someday become independent citizens. The children are taught responsibility, dependability, and manners. These behaviors are inculcated by socially responsible agents such as parents and teachers into the value system of the child. Thus, parents and other social institutions become involved in the teaching of folkways. The educational system is one such an institution. Schools teach children the various ways to channel their behaviors: politeness, punctuality, neatness, orderliness, for example. Recently at an elementary school, the children were instructed by teachers the proper way to march to the lunchroom, to remain silent while they ate, to dispose of their lunch trays, and other institutionally approved behaviors. They are taught to cooperate with one another and become "good citizens" as well as to enhance the smooth operation of the school itself and eventually to become contributing members of the society. Violations of folkways, such as eating with one's mouth open, walking on the wrong side of the street, or talking in class, will not result in the destruction of the community or society but will or should result in some type of sanction by those in power. Only in the last two years have both authors of this book made it a classroom rule that all cell phones and beepers be turned off once class commences. And, lately, each of us has also required students to shut down their laptops during instruction periods. It is only good manners that these electronic devices be silenced for the good of the class as a whole. Only a couple years ago only a few students carried cell phones, MP3 players, laptops, or other portable electronic devices. Now it appears that everyone has one and, without these rules, it is nearly impossible to hold the students' attention for the duration of class.

There is, however, another set of folkways that are termed mores. The mores are those behaviors that, if violated, would result in the destruction of society. The mores certainly carry more serious repercussions for their violation. Violations of them are thought to be of such seriousness that society has created laws that forbid them because such actions would destroy the moral fabric of society.

Mores

Those behaviors or customs that must be followed to prevent the destruction of the common culture of a society

We do not, for example, allow people in our society to kill indiscriminately. The multiple and continuous killings depicted in television shows would be harshly dealt with by the criminal justice system and the courts. Recently a 15-year-old boy, Charles Andrew Williams, entered his own school in California and killed 2 fellow students and wounded 13 others. He was tried as an adult by the court and was eligible for the death penalty. Even the demonic Hannibal Lecter of *Red Dragon, Silence of the Lambs, Hannibal,* and *Hannibal Rising* would be viewed differently if he were an actual killer rather than a fictional murderer from the mind of author Thomas Harris.

Of course, under special circumstances we do permit the taking of another person's life. For example, one is permitted to protect one's own life if the killing of another is necessary to protect your body or those in close proximity to you. In war, killing is often encouraged. Even on such occasions, however, killing is still sometimes seen as atrocious and wrong. Witness the recent disclosed case of civilian men and women killed by the U.S. Army in Iraq. Apparently in all wars innocents have been slaughtered along with the enemy. Some would call this collateral damage; others (including the authors) would judge it to be murder.

Many states in our country permit legal executions. A few of them allow the convicted to choose the method of death; for example, the prisoner may choose between lethal injection and hanging. In Kentucky, on the other hand, there is only one choice, lethal injection, for those condemned to die. We will not debate states' or society's right to execute; it is sufficient to say that a legal execution is generally seen as a way to terminate a life that is consistent with our mores.

Clearly there are exceptions to the taking of a human life. Factually, the legal definition changes the term to homicide, not murder. Homicide could be termed as the unlawful taking of another human life while murder is simply the taking of another human life. Most, though, use the terms interchangeably (Holmes & Holmes, 2001a, 2001b).

In sexual behaviors, there are acts surrounded by social definitions that are encouraged or discouraged. In some marriages, the minister of a particular faith may inform the parties of their divine obligation to procreate the species. It was their right to copulate but their responsibility to populate. So the act of intercourse may be for some couples a recreational experience; but for others this same act may be conceived as their responsibility to populate the species. So while the act itself may physically be the same, it is often consummated for different purposes. Moreover, when sexual intercourse is forced upon an unwilling victim by a rapist, society defines this same act as criminal and heinous. On one level, the act is the same, sexual intercourse. But social and legal codes define it very differently. The social setting may define one set of circumstances as good and the other bad. Within marriage or a relationship when no force or coercion is used, sexual intercourse is often viewed in a positive fashion. But when rape occurs, either by a stranger or a partner, the act is judged criminally.

Teacher's sex with student taped, say police

Babysitter allegedly arranged, filmed woman's liaison with 12-year-old boy

---

Posted: December 22, 2006
    3:00 A.M. Eastern
    A 24-year-old first-year female teacher has been arrested on charges of molestation and indecent behavior with a 12-year-old male student—and police say they have a videotape to prove it.
    A former teacher at a middle school in Metairie, La., was taken into custody on Wednesday along with an 18-year-old friend.
    According to the *New Orleans Times-Picayune*, police say that friend allowed the teacher to come to the home where he was babysitting the boy. She, allegedly, wanted to have sex with the student.
    Prior to her arrival, the friend set up a video camera in the living room. When she came to the boy's home, she and the student went into another room. No information has been released about any activities that occurred there.
    Afterward, the teacher brought the boy back to the living room, where the friend gave him a Xanax tablet he had taken from the woman's purse. She disrobed to her underwear, performed a suggestive dance for the boy, and performed oral sex on the friend in front of him.
    According to police statements, the friend admitted to the sex acts.

SOURCE: 2006 WorldNetDaily.com http://www.worldnetdaily.com/news/article.asp?ARTICLE_ID=53479

*All names removed by the author to protect the innocent.

It appears, upon some scrutiny, that the act of sex is the same, but the social standards surrounding the acts are important, because it is the norm that is applied by society that accounts for its deviancy.

❖ WHAT IS NORMAL SEX?

We are then left with a simple question about human sexual behavior. What is normal? The answer to this apparently simple question is a complex one. When one asks "what?" there is a demand to the receiver of the question to respond in a very simple way. But to answer such a question with a simple answer is akin to opening Pandora's box. What is normal to one person may be quite offensive or even bizarre to another. Even as one ages from adolescence to older adulthood, private sexual standards may change. What is offensive or practiced may change. For example, one subject we interviewed in this book had changed dramatically in his sexual practices. As a young man, he married a woman who refused to have sex with him once they had their second child. Before his marriage with her, he was a virgin and believed that sex should be confined to the marriage bed.

—————————— ❧ ——————————

Vampirism

Sexual gratification from the drinking of blood

Once she refused to have sex with him, he found numerous paramours while he was in the military. After his retirement, he came back to his hometown and developed a relationship with another woman that lasted more than ten years. During that time his relationship with his wife was nonsexual. After a decade of the adulterous relationship, the woman called off the relationship. The man then started frequenting pornography stores and was introduced to homosexuality, which he now actively pursues.

—————————— ❧ ——————————

Crurofact

Leg fetish

He said in this interview that he would never have tried that in his younger years because he thought it was an abomination. Nonetheless, at this time he engages in homosexual relationships with a group of three friends at least weekly. He says that he feels there is nothing wrong with this current sexual life. He further rationalizes his behavior by remarking that if his wife had not treated him as she had in the years past he would not have become involved in relationships with men.

Homosexuality as a Sexual Behavior

Attitudes toward homosexuality are changing. In years past, no professional athlete would admit to being homosexual for fear of the repercussions in the locker room and on the field. While there have always been rumors about the sexual orientation of many of our athletic role models, few would come out and openly admit to their true sexual orientation. Those that have, especially those in recent years, have found that despite engaging in a lifestyle that is considered deviant to most, the announcement did not affect the way their fans reacted to them. The same can be said constituents reactions to their congressional representatives. While the sexual orientation of our elected officials and role models may matter to some, it is increasingly of little importance in public opinion. Despite the strides than many in the homosexual community have made over the past 20 years, society in the aggregate still views the gay lifestyle as a sexual aberration (Holmes, 1991, p. 46). This, however, no longer means that homosexuals cannot be trusted or are wonderful persons, it just means that their lifestyle is considered deviant and perhaps inconsistent with the majority's core religious or moral values.

There are reasons for the society and social prohibitions regarding homosexuality. Many mistakenly believe that AIDS is spread only by gays practicing unprotected sex. AIDS is a medical problem as well as a social and personal concern for those who are possibly affected. But it must be kept in mind that those from varied sexual orientations including heterosexuality spread AIDS. This lack of social tolerance is not limited to the United States. In July 2005, two teenage boys, Mahmoud Asgari (16) and Ayaz Marhoni (18), were tortured and then hanged in Iran for being gay. Other religious leaders have also issued "death to gays" fatwas such as the one that Shiite Muslim leader Grand Ayatollah Ali al-Sistani issued in Iraq in October 2005.

What is homosexuality? Homosexual is a term derived from the Greek word *homos*, which means "the same." Homosexuality has existed from the time that man began to record history. For example, in both the Old and New Testaments, homosexuality was condemned. In many instances, the punishment was death. In other instances, the punishment might be exile, incarceration in convents (for females), or castration for males.

Homosexuality

Sex drive oriented toward personal and sexual gratification with the same sex

In the early 1950s, Dr. Alfred Kinsey alerted the world about the practices of sex among Americans. This, of course, included the sexual practices of homosexuals. For example, the two volumes of *The Sexual Behavior of the Human Male* and *The Sexual Behavior of the Human Female* reported that approximately 37% of the white male population had had at least one homosexual experience to the point of orgasm sometime during their lifetimes. The volume on female homosexuality reported that somewhere between 13% and 17% of the white female population had had a similar experience. When this report was released, people were shocked. Since this was one of the first mainstream publications in America reporting on the prevalence of homosexuality in this country, it generated much discussion and, of course, doubt. It was not until the gay liberation movement that started with the Stonewall Inn Riot in 1969 that homosexuality became a topic to be seriously discussed and debated. The gays became open with their sexual orientation and defied the police in particular and society in general.

Table 1.1   Important Dates in the Gay Liberation Movement

Date	Event
1948 and 1953	Kinsey's volumes on male and female homosexuality appear.
1950s	Mattachine Society and Daughters of Bilitis are founded.
1969	Stonewall Inn Riot takes place in New York City.
Early 1970s	Gay pride parades occur in New York and San Francisco.
1973	National Gay Task Force is founded.
1975	Leonard Matlovich is discharged from Air Force as a result of his personal declaration of homosexuality.
1977	Dade County, Florida, ordinance prohibiting discrimination based on sexual orientation is successfully revoked.
1980	The New York State Court of Appeals strikes down the state's sodomy laws. Other states followed, including Maryland in 1998 and Texas in 2000.
1986	Supreme Court upholds states' right to restrain sodomy legally.
1987 and 1989	Militant gays march on Washington and New York.
1989	5,000 demonstrators march in front of St. Patrick's Cathedral in New York City to protest the Roman Catholic Church's opposition to homosexuality.
1990	President George W. Bush signs the Hate Crime Statistics Act.
1994	Delegates of the American Medical Association declare their opposition to medical treatment to "cure" homosexuality.
1996	The U.S. Episcopal Church declares that there is no core doctrine that prohibits a gay man as a deacon; San Francisco approves a bill that requires all companies doing business with the city to offer gays and lesbian employees domestic partnership benefits.
2003	U.S. Supreme Court rules Sodomy laws unconstitutional.

Types of Homosexuals

Being a homosexual is only one part of a person's public and private life. This same statement is as true for heterosexuals as for bisexuals. They have social lives, business lives, and personal lives as well. But if we are to move to an understanding of any group of people to examine their similarities as well as their differences, a typological examination may be the best method to use (for a list or examination of the types of homosexuals, see Table 1.2).

Tea Room

Public rooms used for impersonal sex

In the past, most states prosecuted homosexual acts under their state sodomy laws. That was until 2003, when the U.S. Supreme Court ruled 6–3 that sodomy laws are unconstitutional. Instead, states that wish to prosecute homosexuals for their acts must do so under the laws under the general title of "unnatural and lascivious acts." In Florida, those that are convicted of violating this statute commits a misdemeanor of the second degree punishable by 60 days in jail and/or a $500 fine. But no person has gone to court under this statute since 1980.

Lesbianism

Female homosexuality

Regardless of the cause or etiology of homosexuality, there are some who believe those who practice sex with members of their same sex are sinners and destructive to the moral fiber of our society. With many, the debate over nature versus nurture and the causation of homosexuality will continue. There is no known reason for someone to be homosexual. This same statement can be said of those who are heterosexual. It is probably a unique combination of nature and nurture, the biological inheritance coupled with the experiences of the person. It may be years before we have some clear understanding of the etiology of the sexuality of any individual.

This does seem to deter some from fearing and loathing those who are different, in this case, homosexuals. But the rejection of society and the frightening epidemic of AIDS in the gay community (not ignoring others affected by the epidemic, such as drug users who contract the disease from a contaminated needle or those who do from a blood transfusion), homosexuality will continue to be a sexual practice that will attract a large number of people.

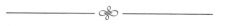

Sodomy

Sexual penetration of any orifice other than the vagina

All societies attempt to regulate the sexual behaviors of their members. All

Table 1.2   Types of Homosexuals

Secret Homosexual	A homosexual who prefers to keep his or her sexual orientation hidden from others, e.g., family, employer. Sometimes the person may even attempt to keep his or her orientation a secret from himself or herself. Naturally, a certain amount of perspicacity is necessary in practicing homosexuality. For example, if one is a schoolteacher, minister, or youth leader, certain traumatic events may occur simply because one is a homosexual.
Blatant Homosexual	A homosexual who, in dress, speech, mannerisms, etc., makes no attempt to disguise her or his orientation. By frequenting places where known homosexuals gather, e.g., gay bars, parks, cruising areas, the blatant homosexual deliberately invites identification and labeling. Homosexual male and female impersonators make up one group of blatant homosexuals. (This is not to say that all male and female impersonators are homosexual.)
Adjusted Homosexual	A homosexual who is quite content to be gay. Adjusted homosexuals accept their sexual orientation and thus do not suffer over their choices of sexual partners. Adjusted homosexuals may readily admit being gay when the question arises, but they do not flaunt their homosexuality in the same fashion as the blatant homosexual.
Institutional Homosexual	A homosexual who does not have a self-image as being gay. Institutional homosexuals become involved in homosexual experiences because of the situation in which they find themselves, e.g., prisons, jails, military, seminaries, convents—that is, anywhere there is no access to the other sex. When an institutional homosexual is removed from such a situation, the individual reverts to heterosexuality.
Homosexual Prostitute	A male who offers his sexual favors to other males for pay. Most are between the ages of 15 and 17. In our research we have found them to be as young as 7. Interviewing juvenile prostitutes in Louisville, Kentucky, we have found that they start their prostitution career usually at about the age of 14. Many come from lower socioeconomic classes and suffered physical abuse as a child; the basic motivation is economical.
Homosexual Pedophile	A homosexual who desires to have sex only with same-sex children. More details will be discussed later.

societies judge what is appropriate and what is inappropriate, standards that allow for some sexual practices and forbid other sexual practices. This does not mean, however, that everyone abides by the same set of laws and standards. Some behaviors, nevertheless, most societies find totally unacceptable, deeming them repugnant. For example, in the United States, incest is against the law.

Sexual Standards

There are at least four sexual standards used to determine normalcy. Naturally, not everyone agrees on which standard is the most important and which one is best suited for their own purposes of rationalization and explanation. The decision of what is normal depends not only on the person but also on the general and particular circumstances. The four standards are the *statistical, cultural, religious,* and *subjective* standards.

The Statistical Standard

The statistical standard is quite simple and makes numbers the deciding criterion. For example, if more than 50% of the population practice a certain sexual behavior, it is then considered normal. This statistical standard, then, validates normalcy for a person or a group of persons who practice that particular act.

Roman shower

Vomiting on partner, usually after drinking urine or wine

For example, the divorce rate among couples married for more than 10 years in the United States is slightly more than 50%. The argument would follow that divorce is a normal part of the institution of marriage. Is it normal to be divorced? If we use the statistical standard as the only standard, then we would call it normal. For another example, it has been estimated that in more than 80% of marriages, one partner will have an adulterous affair. Is it normal then for married couples to commit adultery? Further, if we agree with the Kinsey study's statistics, 95% of males masturbate; is it therefore abnormal for a male *not* to masturbate? If we use only this one standard, all the above behaviors would be considered normal.

Using the statistical standard can be quite dangerous because it can define lawbreaking as normal. For instance, many teenage girls shoplift makeup or jewelry—perhaps even the majority. Does this make it normal to steal? We see advertising claiming that one form of detergent cleans better than the others, using the statistic that 75% or 85% of the people asked agree. After all, if more than half the population buys a certain Toothpaste X, and if we use Toothpaste Y, does that mean there must be something wrong with us. Many parents are confronted with their teenagers who ask to stay out later than they are usually permitted. Their first defense for their request is to inform their parents that "all the other kids are allowed to stay out until. . . ." So, if their peers are allowed to stay out later, why should they not be permitted the same curfew? They are playing the numbers game.

The numbers game is dangerous if for no other reason than that it is devoid of any sense of social right or wrong. This rightness or wrongness is not to be considered a moral judgment but rather a sense of what is functional and socially good for the society. Numbers are simply that, numbers. When one places values solely on statistical results, social functioning and social well-being can be circumvented or even destroyed.

The Cultural Standard

A society has structures that transmit to its members what is considered to be appropriate behavior. In other words, any society has a set of normal of rules and regulations with changing sanctions that accommodate transgression of its rules, which often take the form of laws, statutes, and ordinances. Transgressions or violations will also likely invoke some type of punishment or sanction. Sanctions will vary from one transgression to another. Some transgressions—for example, loitering or littering—may result in a fine. More serious transgressions may result in prison sentences or even death. Armed robbery accompanied by the murder of the storekeeper in many states is punishable by the death sentence or life without the possibility of parole.

It may be the quality of the transgressor that accounts for how serious the act is considered or the manner in which the offender is punished. In Louisville, Kentucky, for example, two previously well-respected citizens, husband and wife, Jim and Patti Hearn, were found guilty of bilking the local board of education of more than $300,000. Their sentence was restitution, 9 months in jail, and 500 hours of community service. When they were released on parole, they served the remainder of their sentence in a resort area of North Carolina. Jim was a former member of the local board of education, and Patti was a high-level administrator for the local school system. On the other hand, Jim Hennessy, age 50, was sent to prison for 10 years. His crime was that he stole a wallet containing $60 from a man who was eating in a McDonald's restaurant. Hennessy was a persistent felony offender, and his sentence was a reflection of that achieved status. In other words, it appears that if a person of a lesser social status commits a crime, the potential punishment and possible sentence is more severe than crimes committed by the rich and powerful. Are we all equal before the law? We think not or at least not all the time. Often it depends on other factors than the violation of some socially and sometimes legally prohibited action.

Folkways, mores, laws, and institutions control behavior. Laws are legally sanctioned folkways and mores. As codified folkways and mores, some laws are more serious in their nature than others because some laws are reflected in their base as folkways while other are reflected in the base as mores. For example, in many cities it is against the law for a person to jaywalk. Simple assault is also against the law. Society will not crumble and die if we permit citizens to jaywalk, although there are sure to be more injuries and even fatalities if this behavior is not sanctioned to some extent. Simple assault also may be hazardous to the victim, but again, society will not be a terminal victim as a consequence of this behavior. But we will not permit people to arbitrarily murder one another. There are laws that prohibit the voluntary killing of another person. First-degree murder is punishable in some jurisdictions by execution. The murder offense is reflected in the more base. If we permit a person to take another person's life without just cause, society may certainly be in danger of disintegrating. This same argument is used in the case of assisted suicide. It may be that we will change our societal attitude toward assisted suicide in the scenario where the victim freely chooses to end life when she or he is suffering from a terminal and painful illness. Certainly this argument was brought to bear in the trial of Dr. Jack Kevorkian. We, as a society, will certainly permit one to place one's own life at risk in certain circumstances. Each society has its own set of such circumstances. For example, the kamikaze pilots in Japan in World War II flew their planes into Allied ships to certain death. Even suicide bombers such as Mohamed Atta and others who took their lives in the fatal events of September 11, 2001, are considered martyred heroes in some parts of the world. Heroes on both side of a war or conflict offer their lives for their country or cause. Still, our common culture looks down upon those who deliberately and with unimpaired forethought take their own lives. This judgment can depend on where one's allegiances fall.

In World War II, a young soldier, Roger Young, drew enemy fire by running from a foxhole toward the German soldiers while his comrades retreated by another route. He in effect offered his own life so his comrades could escape with their own lives. Young was called a hero; he was awarded posthumous medals for his bravery and valor.

Americans spoke his name with pride and patriotism. At the same time, when men from other countries place themselves in harm's way as Roger Young did, but against their enemy the American government, they are called fanatics and deranged.

There are other expected behaviors. Although it may be slowly changing, most adults marry. The only socially acceptable form of marriage is monogamy. We do not permit people to have plural spouses, either in polygyny or in polyandry fashion. We strongly discourage and make it unlawful for people to practice these forms of marriage. This also includes group marriages. There may be good arguments for any of these three forms of married life, but we cling to monogamy as the desired form despite the high divorce rate and the precariousness of a marital form that may be ruined by death, illness, divorce, or other calamities.

Community rules and state laws limiting the actions and behaviors of its members often arise from the needs of the society at the time. A culture then arises to meet those needs and ensure that the members obey those rules, regulations, and laws. For example, at one time in American society, children were seen as an asset. They were a free form of labor for the family. As time has progressed, children no longer served as assets, and many see children as economic dependents. The cost of medical care, educational experiences, and so on, incur large costs in raising children at this time. So, the average size of the American family has decreased over the past century. It may be that society still wants couples to have children, but the desired number of offspring has decreased dramatically.

How do we learn these expectations? Certainly the family is the first cradle for this valuable learning experience. Then friends, peers, the educational enterprise, religious institutions, and other sources provide the fountain for dispensing critical cultural information. The words, ideas, customs, and beliefs of the culture for the behavioral expectations of its members are transmitted to those members at an early age. These lessons become a part of the personality and identity of the member. Then we all judge the person according to the standards that become a part of the society through the culture. The concept of what is appropriate behavior and what is deviant behavior is relative. What is appropriate and expected behavior at one time, in another time may be judged to be deviant and inappropriate.

This concept of deviancy will then depend on the needs of the society. In ancient Greece, the sexual relationship between an adult male and a young boy was more than a simple sexual affair. The adult served as a sexual mentor and also as a source of educational experience for the child. It was not a clandestine relationship with the child and was not deemed inappropriate. Today sex with a child, pedophilia, is seen as a sexual paraphilia (perversion), and penalties are severe.

Religious Normalcy

The third standard is the religious standard. Historically, religion has played an important and vital role in developing the value systems of societies and individuals. Only a few years ago, many Christians were guided by strong and absolute guidelines. Certain acts constituted grievous or mortal sins. If one committed a mortal sin and died without the opportunity to confess those sins, one was assured of the inevitable punishment, eternal damnation in the fires of hell. Less grievous sins were venial sins. The penalty for these transgressions was not as serious as the fires of hell. Instead, an individual may be forced to spend a little more time in purgatory before joining their maker in heaven.

For many people, the religious standard is the most important, if for no other reason than because religious beliefs play an important part in their lives. Those commandments of the faith have in the past been dogmatic and many placed behaviors into categories of wrong or right, sin or not. This leaves the religious person with a comfortable position of knowing how a particular behavior is judged.

This traditional sexual philosophy of traditional repressive asceticism certainly has an effect even today. Sex is something that many feel is a duty of one spouse for the other, not to be enjoyed but endured. The religious standard, then, has evolved into something that has proscriptions against appropriate sexual acts. These acts, in many religions, belong only to those who are legally and spiritually married and then only under specific conditions. This has had an effect upon the sexual mentality of the citizens of any country. Many people, especially those of a religious bent, will judge sex acts and their appropriateness by this third standard.

There is still another standard that is the most important of all standards in determining what is normal.

The Subjective Standard

The subjective standard is perhaps the most important in any person's life. This standard legitimizes behavior in the same fashion as statistical, cultural, and religious standards, but at a personal level. For instance, take the last time you drove slightly above the speed limit on an interstate highway. Chances are there were many drivers passing you as you drove along. Even though you were violating the speed limit, others were doing the same thing, and you may have rationalized your lawbreaking, saying, "They were driving much faster."

Talking with students in our classes, a question we often ask is, "When was the last time you stole something?" Many students will admit that the pens they are taking notes with were indeed stolen. If a pen came from the students' workplace, the story quickly follows that the boss was a jerk, the student was not paid enough, or some other excuse is often concocted for their petty theft. The students offer a multitude of subjective rationalizations for their acts of thievery, as many people will do for an act of sexual deviance.

Even rape can be legitimized. Susan Brownmiller (1975) states that rape has been historically viewed as permissible for a victorious army victimizing the vanquished by raping the women of the conquered. The soldier who rapes a village woman would not be viewed as a criminal and the act as a sexual crime, but something he deserves as a conquering hero (Brownmiller, 1975). Moreover, there are more than a few states where a husband cannot be criminally charged with the rape of his wife.

It is not enough simply to legitimize the acts that may be judged deviant by some other members of the society; we must feel that what we are doing is not only normal, but "really not that bad." The interview one author had with the serial killer, Ted Bundy, on death row before his execution vividly illustrated the subjective standard to us. When Bundy talked about the killings that this "man" had done (he did not admit to us that he had victimized anyone, only admitting this shortly before his execution), the vividness of the killings and the relish he took in explaining some of the actions illustrated how proud this person was of his accomplishments, none of which was "really wrong." Bundy's lack of guilt demonstrates how the subjective norm is the most important one. It defines for the person the appropriateness of the actions and how these actions fall within the normal range of behaviors for this person at this specific stage in his or her life. It justifies her or his acts and behaviors so the deviancy is not interpreted as really inappropriate or evil, but rather quite normal.

❖   NORMAL SEXUAL BEHAVIOR

So the question to be adequately addressed is, "What is normal sexual behavior?" Those acts that threaten the public morality must be effectively deterred and those who violate them must somehow be punished or rehabilitated. Recognizing that norms and values are not static but will change over time necessitates that society and the common culture must continually define and redefine what behavior is acceptable and what is not.

For this reason, might it not be better to use the terms *acceptable* and *unacceptable* behavior rather than *normal* and *abnormal*? Of course, using these terms implies that the acts will be judged by a social standard. We can still rationalize the choices we make, but these choices are restricted unless the person is mentally ill and cannot individually recognize what is acceptable or unacceptable. So this social definition of sexual behavior would rely on the social demands and the necessity of the functional relationship between the social values and the actions by predators as well as other, normal people. Regardless, there would be no longer an artificial morality that has been violated.

Elements of Sexual Behavior

There are four elements of sexual behavior. These elements are true in either normal or deviant sexual behavior. The elements are fantasy, symbolism, ritualism, and compulsion.

Fantasy

To be sexual, one must have a sexual fantasy. It is impossible to be sexual without some form of fantasy. Of course, not all fantasies are sexual. Some take the form of revenge, love lost, hatred, or what have you. But for our purposes in this discussion, we will say the fantasies discussed here are sexual. It is true that a male can have an erection without a sexual thought. Also, a woman may experience intercourse without being "sexual," for example when she is a victim of rape. But to be sexually involved, whether with another person or with oneself (as in the case of autoeroticism), fantasy is necessary. It is the living out of the fantasy that many report makes the sexual experience extraordinary.

The forms of sexual fantasy vary from one person to the next. Some are extremely simple; others are quite complex. For example, a man in a southern state frequented a department store, selected his ideal victim type—a young mother wearing a denim skirt shopping with a child— and would spray household oil on the back of her skirt and would finally culminate his sexual act fulfilling his fantasy by masturbating within arm's reach of her. He admitted to investigators that he had done this same act more than a score of times in the same store with the same victim type. He later escalated his sex crimes to include rape.

The following fantasy was related by a pedophile. Having interest in 12-year-old girls, he thought about the kidnapping, rape, and finally the murder and cannibalism of young girls:

After an earthquake, two 16-year-old boys were exploring a cemetery near their own home. Noticing a hole in the ground where there had not been one before, the boys decided to explore. They discovered a cave, and their eyes slowly became acclimated to the darkness. Looking at one wall, they saw a skeleton chained to the wall. At the foot of the skeleton was clothing that belonged to the victim, an apparent 11- or 12-year-old female. Looking around the cave, they discovered another skeleton chained to the opposite wall. Again, clothing was at the foot of this skeleton. Frightened, the two boys started to flee the cave.

As the boys were climbing out of the cave, an adult blocked their passage, and in a loud voice demanded to know what the boys were doing in the cave. Effectively intimidating the boys, the adult instructed the boys to fetch him a 12-year-old girl for his pleasure. The two boys went to a local drugstore and awaited a young girl venturing outside the store. Abducting the first one they could get, they took her back to the cave. The two boys were instructed by the adult to rape and sodomize the young victim while he watched. After repeatedly abusing the young girl, they chained her to the wall, the same wall where they had already taken down the skeleton.

Repeating this abuse for several days, the man demanded that the two boys go back to the drugstore for another girl. They abducted a second girl, and the victim was taken to the cave, where she was raped as the first young girl was forced to watch.

After several days, the first girl said she was hungry. Building a fire, the second girl was torn apart and her arms and legs were roasted over the fire. The chained victim was forced to eat the roasted parts of the second victim. Immediately after, the first young victim was strangled to death.

The parting remark made by the man was, "You two boys meet me here tomorrow. I need two more young bitches!" (authors' files)

Such is the fantasy of an aggressive and sadistic child offender, a mysoped. Most persons do not share the aggressive component that is an integral part of this pedophile's fantasy. Westley Dodd had a fantasy of performing exploratory surgery on his young male victims. We will explore Dodd's fantasy in a later chapter dealing with the deadly sadistic child killer, the mysoped. Jerry Brudos wanted his female victims kept in cells on his property so he could victimize each one until they were almost dead and then wait until they physically were well again and then start the cycle of victimization again. His plan was to have seven cells in his backyard. In each cell would be a captive woman, one for each day of the week. On a Monday, he would retrieve a woman in a cell, assault and rape her and then put her back into the cell. He would return to her the next Monday after she had the time to physically recoup. He would then start the cycle of abuse over again. Brudos never had underground cells, but when he moved to Salem, Oregon, he turned one side of his two-car garage into his dungeon.

If I were to kill a man . . .

The following was a note from a college coed who sought counseling from a psychologist at her university for thoughts she was having about personal violence. In the interviewing sessions, she admitted she fanaticized about killing her ex-boyfriend, who had rejected her for another.

I would pick a time that he would be very happy so that the contrast would destroy him mentally as well as I would destroy him physically. The tool I would use to execute the act would be a knife. The use of a knife would be messier perhaps than poison, suffocation, or strangulation, but if I were to kill a man, I would want to revel in the sight of his life's blood flowing like a crimson tide from his body. The knife would also give complete control to me as to how much I applied and therefore how much damage was done to his body and how much pain he suffered. A knife would allow the pleasure of feeling the resistance of muscle and sinew to the blade as it slices through his flesh. The thick sweet smelling blood pours onto the floor in a celebration of red color like wine, and I would control the flow. If I wish to see a fountain, I would cut an artery or just watch it seep from veins. I would skin his chest so that he could watch his own muscles at work as he struggles to be free. I would then press a towel to the wounds to stop the blood flow and elongate his life of pain. When the flow had stopped and the blood dried I would tear the towel away to watch the blood swell to the surface again in a fury or pain and cherish the sound of his scream echoing in my ears. Whenever he lost consciousness I would wait and let him heal enough to revive before I continued the torture before I choose to end his life. I would not release him until both his body and mind were full of pain that even hell could dole out in eternity. His final release in death would be obtained by the stabbing of my knife through the heart. There would be an explosion of blood, life, and death. His final scream of horrifying pain would be my reward for the hours I would have spent and would spend mopping and putting the garbage out. Good night, sweet dreams. Me.

In an interview with a serial killer in a western prison on death row, he admitted that he had cut off the heads of several of his victims and would then place the heads in his freezer. He would retrieve the heads when his sexual fantasy demanded some relief. At one time, he had six heads in his refrigerator (authors' files).

Thankfully, not everyone has fantasies that are so heinous, violent, or destructive. But everyone does have sexual fantasies if they are sexual or wish to be sexual. Most people's fantasies center on willing partners in normal sexual acts. Soft lighting, nice music, and other elements contribute to an ambience that one feels is conducive to good sex.

Symbolism

Sex is very visual. Sex sells. Look at the manner in which sex used to sell automobiles, beer, and even household appliances. When one speaks of sexual symbolism, fetishes and partialisms are evident. A fetish is an inanimate object to which one has attached sexual feelings. It appears that most all males have at least one fetish, and most have several. Bras, panties, stockings, garter belts, high heels, and negligees are all common male fetishes. Jerry Brudos, a serial killer currently in prison in Oregon, had a shoe fetish (Holmes & Holmes, 1997; Rule, 1983). One rapist told us in an interview that he was erotically aroused whenever he climbed through a window to burglarize a home and, in that sexually excited mode, would look for someone in the home to rape. He added that by climbing through the window he would experience an erection leading to a spontaneous orgasm. Since he believed that it was unnatural to have an orgasm in that way, his fantasy would take the form of raping a woman in the home. It was strange: For him, rape was normal and acceptable behavior, but experiencing an orgasm climbing through a window was not.

Albutophilia

Sexual arousal from water

Altocalciphilia

Sexual attraction to high-heeled shoes

Alvinolagnia

A stomach partialism

Similar to a sexual fetish is a partialism. A partialism is an isolated part of the body to which sexual feelings had been attached. Breasts, legs, and buttocks are all classic examples of partialisms. Both men and women have partialisms. One serial killer presently in prison in the northwest would talk with his wife when she visited him only if her feet were bare. Another serial killer in California stated in an interview that he had a fantasy about having sex with a decapitated head. He went on to say that he kept several heads in his freezer and would retrieve a head when he felt like having a sexual encounter. Another serialist stated that his ideal victim was "blond-haired, blue-eyed, unmistakably young, very definitely female." He constantly trolled for victims matching his ideal victim type.

Almost all people have partialisms. This is a natural part of our sexual being. When the fetish or the partialism must be part of a sexual encounter, it often is a sign of an unhealthy attraction to that symbol.

Sex is also visual, for we are all stimulated by visual sexual symbols. Some people may prefer to view unclothed or nearly naked models while another may prefer to view hard core pornography. Common periodicals cater to people of different interests. Those that prefer soft porn may subscribe to magazines such as *Maxim* or *Muscle*; while others may prefer harder material such as that found in *Penthouse* or *Hustler*. Internet sites also cater to the visual appetite of their surfers. For instance, one site commonly visited by college students caters to scantily clad nonmodel men and women who often volunteer have their pictures taken. This site (Priceless 420) invites viewers to send in pictures of their wives, girlfriends, or ones who have been part of their sexual past. These pictures are updated daily and then archived for paying members. Other sites rely on professional models on whom bodily augmentation has surely occurred.

Ritualism

Sex offenders are as ritualistic in their sexual predations as others who are sexually active. For example, couples who have been together for some time almost intuitively know when their partners are sexually receptive. The manner in which certain words are spoken or certain gestures are made, or the way in which any of a great many words or deeds are committed or omitted, can carry sexual messages.

Even in our everyday life we are ritualistic. Think of yourself and the rituals that you follow every morning when you rise out of bed. Typically the order in which you proceed will vary little day in and day out. For instance, when you get in the shower, you typically will wash one part of our body first and then another part last. Even when putting on your socks, notice that right-handed individuals will typically put the right sock on first and the left sock on second.

With many sex offenders, however, the element of ritualism is one that has increased almost to the point of addiction. One serial sex offender stated that when he was 9 years old he read a book of pornography that depicted a sadistic rape:

> The history of my own rise to serial murder cannot be told or understood without first mentioning the person and the deeds of someone I met a very long time ago. For it can be said of this person—this man to be exact—that he was the one who planted within me the seeds of what would later bloom into full-scale sexual violence. This is not to say that he was directly responsible for my becoming a serial killer, as there were many other factors that would also come into play, and no single thing "made" me into a man of violence. Nevertheless, it remains true that this man would play a very large role in starting me on the long and twisted course that would ultimately lead to murder.
>
> For what I can recall of him, he was very tall and exceptionally thin, a stooped-over figure who was always given to wearing a heavy black coat that dragged along the floor as he walked. He made his home in a large, somber, and foreboding castle that had many cheerless rooms within its thick, stone walls. And, in keeping with the gloomy character of his ancient castle residence, he himself was a sullen and very sinister-looking man. Indeed, he had a face that could easily pass for a clean but living skull, were it not for the barest layer of flesh and skin that stretched tightly over his bony features.
>
> The first time I ever met this man, he was shuffling into one of the torch-lit chambers beneath his castle, a menacing expression on his ugly face as he made his way toward a large, odd-shaped table in the middle of the room. On the top of the wooden table there was a frightened young actress whom he had kidnapped earlier in the same day. He had already stripped away all of her clothing, so the woman lay nude and sprawled on her back, her limbs strapped down in a helpless, spread-eagle position. When the man reached the table, I recall that he lowered his hand and started caressing the young woman's face, telling her that she had nothing to worry about, in spite of her very terrifying predicament. After all, she was "guest" in his house, he said to her, and this she would receive only "the very best of treatment" while she remained under his care.
>
> After feeding her this line of phony reassurance, however, the man started torturing the young actress by wrapping his fingers around one of her breasts and slowly tightening his grip. As he gradually increased the pressure of his squeezing fingers, he scanned up and down the length of the woman's body, his eyes

waiting to see the first signs of struggle that she would make against the pain he was causing her. And, when she finally jerked against the bonds encircling her ankles and wrists, the man responded to this movement by stepping on a lever that activated a small motor underneath the table. To the woman's horror, a pair of slats beneath her lower limbs started spreading open automatically, forcing her legs to stretch even wider and more painfully apart. And, as the muscles in her legs began to strain and knot up from this new ordeal, the man continued closed his bony fingers, digging them deeper and more cruelly into her naked breasts.

The young actress screamed. Yet even as the chamber reverberated with the sound of her piercing shrieks, the man was not the least bit moved by his captive's terror or her cries of pain. Indeed, each time the woman was overcome by pain to the point where she slipped away into unconsciousness, the man simply revived her and started up the torture again. He tortured her until she could scream no more—until her mind, like her body, was a broken shell—and then he triumphantly proceeded to rape her where she lay. After assaulting her, he killed her on the spot. Finally, then, being satisfied with the job that he had done, the man cleared the table of his victim's corpse and began thinking ahead to the next young woman who would lay there strapped down on its surface.

The man and the deeds I've just described are actually the ghosts of a paperback novel that came into my hands a little over 25 years ago. Quite clearly, as should be gathered from the brief but highly sanitized dungeon scene that I've recounted here, the story of this fictional castle-dweller was both sadistic and obscene. Indeed, from the opening page to its closing chapter, this book seemed to have no other purpose than to depict sexual violence in the most painstaking detail and as the kind of treatment that women generally deserved. In short, this paperback novel was violent pornography as its worst—a perverse and graphically written tribute to the sexual brutalization of female human beings.

Nine years later, as a college freshman, he raped his first victim. He forced her to say words that he believed were important to the script (fantasy) he had prepared for his victimization of his victim. With each subsequent rape, he impelled his victims to repeat those same words, often in the same sequence.

In ritualism, the sexual acts have to be performed in the same fashion and often in the same sequence. If not done as "the script provides," the act has to be either abandoned or restarted. Some serialist sex offenders, rapists or child molesters for example, may force their victims to repeat certain phases or even call them by a different name. This may become very important when investigators question the victims. The first name used may be the offender's mother's, wife's, or girlfriend's name.

Compulsion

"I woke up one morning knowing I was going to kill, like I had woken up many mornings before," one serial sadistic sex offender said. "It is an awful, gnawing feeling deep down in my stomach which impels me to rape and kill."

"There is something deep inside of me, something I can't control." So said Ted Bundy to Don Patchen when being interrogated in Pensacola, Florida, in 1978. "There's something wrong with me," he continued. "I don't give a shit about those people" (D. Patchen, personal communication, November 1986). These compulsive feelings well up inside the serial sex offender and launch him into action.

In an interview with Bundy on death row, he remarked that this feeling he had within himself was "so strong" that is could not be placated without the fatal victimization of a female. He said from a third-person perspective that the time this "man" was in prison he could not satisfy this feeling but once the man was free it welled up inside him and demanded that it be satiated. That was one reason, Bundy continued, that the attacks at the Chi Omega sorority house had been so vicious and so unlike the ones he had committed in the northwest. In other words, the feeling inside him altered the manner in which he sexually predated upon his victims. Then, only three weeks later, the man killed in a manner similar to the way he had killed earlier. There was an abduction and a disposal site for the victims, both of which were missing at the Chi Omega house on Super Bowl Sunday, 1978.

A rapist who was attracted to young girls told us that when he was feeling the need to rape, he drove to a corner where he had picked up several women in the past. He waited for his ideal victim type, but when none appeared and the feeling got strong, he saw two young girls, one 12 and the other 14, walking toward him. He and his partner told the girls they were police officers, showed them badges, "arrested them," and took them to their home. There, they sexually abused both and finally murdered them.

Acrotomophilia

Sexual preference for amputees

Apotemnophilia

Sexual fantasies about losing a limb

❖ COMBINING THE ELEMENTS

It is true that all normally sexually active persons have the four elements described above. What differentiates these elements in perverse sexual practices? This is a difficult question to address properly. The following scenarios are certainly indicative that the sex involved is not typical, normal sexual functioning:

- when an individual is sexual only when a certain fetish or partialism is present
- when compulsivity is so overwhelmingly potent that emotions and caring for the partner are missing
- when certain scripts must be followed, and any deviation from them is fatal to sexual functioning
- when fantasies center on the dehumanization, torture, or murder of hapless and helpless victims

❖ CONCLUSION

Sex is a very part of most people's lives. Certainly there are those who are celibate by choice, dedicating himself or herself to God, believing that celibacy is one way to get special graces for a heavenly reward. There are others who have some type of mental condition, physical impairment, or personality affliction that makes it difficult for them to locate a willing sexual partner. Others simply have no desire or need for any type of sexual partnership.

Whatever the reason, there is a need for sexual beings to legitimize their sexual urges, preferences, and lifestyles. We use the mentioned standards for legitimizing our behaviors and making them palatable and thus desirable for personal expressions. The combination of the elements provides us with a framework for our own behavior as well as a subjective method for the legitimizing of behavior, including our sexual behaviors and lifestyles.

The following chapters will deal with several sexual behaviors, most of which society has deemed to be deviant, inappropriate, and prohibited. We will first, however, discuss some theories of sexual expression and a historical analysis of the development of sexual philosophies that influence our behaviors.

❖ DISCUSSION QUESTIONS

1. Considering the various types of sexual standards, what standard do you consider the most important for you? Why?

2. Explain the differences between folkways and mores. Gives examples of both. Explain how they function in your daily behavior.

3. Give examples of normal sexual behavior. How do you identify them as normal? What criteria do you use? Would others agree with your examples?

4. Explain how Ted Bundy could legitimize his acts of sexual aberrations. Could he consider some of his own sexual acts normal?

5. How important is sex to an individual? To society?

❖ REFERENCES

Brownmiller, S. (1975). *Against Our Will: Men, Women, and Rape.* New York: Simon and Schuster.

Holmes, R. (1991). *Sex Crimes.* Newbury Park, CA: Sage.

Holmes, R., & Holmes, S. (1997). *Serial Murder* (2nd ed.). Thousand Oaks, CA: Sage.

Holmes, R., & Holmes, S. (2001a). *Mass Murder.* Englewood Cliffs, NJ: Prentice Hall.

Holmes, R., & Holmes, S. (2001b). *Murder in America* (2nd ed.). Thousand Oaks, CA: Sage Publications.

Rule, A. (1983). *The Lust Killer.* New York: Signet.

Stark County Ohio Sheriffs Office. (2008). Frequency asked questions about sex offenders. Retrieved March 15, 2008, from http://www.sheriff.co.stark.oh.us/pr01-questions.htm#q4

Weisman, J. and J. Eliperin (2006, October 6) "Lawmaker's Intentions Appear Clear In Exchanges" The Washington Post. Retrieved October 17, 2007, from http://www.washingtonpost.com/wp-dyn/content/article/2006/10/05/AR2006100500008.html.

2

Theories of Sexual Deviance

UNDERSTANDING THE CAUSAL NEXUS

❖   ❖   ❖

E xactly what causes deviant or violent offenders to behave the way they do is a question that has perplexed the medical and social sciences for years. As the previous chapter showed, the topic and offenses under the rubric of sex offenses is wide and varied. Almost any sexual behavior can and may in some societies or cultures be considered a forbidden act or one that deserves a criminal sanction. Looking at pornography, engaging in premarital sex, exhibitionism, kleptomania, prostitution, sexual assaults, rape, erotic hanging, bondage, sadomasochism, necrophilia, and even homicide all can in some cases be construed to have a sexual dimension. Individuals who engage in these prohibited behaviors may be called neurotics, sexual variants, psychopaths, or even criminals. The negative connotation associated with the label of sexual deviant is devastating despite the context in which the event, actions, or even the attraction occurs

In contemporary society, those convicted of a sexual offense are often required to register with the state, and certain restrictions may be placed on where they can live and the people with whom they associate.

Almost every state now has a list of sex offenders or predators who can be tracked on the Internet. On these pages, not only is their personal information available, but their physical addresses, their pictures, and a list of their previous offending behaviors.

While society does have a need to protect itself and its children from falling victims to sexual offenders, the listing of offenders' names often inhibits their ability to find suitable employment, be free from personal harassment, and enjoy the liberties that the Constitution of this country guarantees. While we do not advocate doing away with these lists, society must be educated about why these offenders act the way they do and be able to discriminate the nuisance offender from the potentially violent one.

Just as important as understanding the context in which sexual offenders are placed in modern society is the plethora of offenses that may cause individuals to be labeled a sexual offender. Because these offenses are so varied, there is no one answer why individuals participate in any one of the offenses classified as sexual. There may be situational differences or nuisances within each offense that make them qualitatively different, or it may be that the offenses with which two individuals are convicted are the same, but the individuals or motivations behind the acts are different. In any event, it is clear that in order to begin to tap the base reasons or theoretical underpinnings why sex offenders, as an aggregate class, behave the way they do, we have to take a wide view of the issue of sexual offenders and their motivations.

This chapter will attempt to will be do that. We will examine the basic principles that psychiatrists, sociologists, and criminologists all accept as important in the development of children and adults and how developmental events may cause a individual to deviate from socially accepted norms of expressing themselves sexually. In doing so, we will present the reader with a brief yet thorough understanding of the four prevailing approaches that describe why and how sex offenders develop and mature differently from the rest of the population. These four approaches are the psychiatric and social learning models and the constitutional and sociobiological schools of thought.

❖ THE SOCIAL CONTEXT OF SEXUAL DEVELOPMENT

One of the most important of all anthropological, sociological, and physiological facts is that the human race is segregated into two sexes (Sumner, 1906). This segregation of sexes sets the stage for not only the reproduction of the species but for most of adult behavior (Freud, 1930;

Kinsey, 1947). Children learn very early in their lives the roles pre-scribed for their biological gender.

Boys learn to play ball, be aggressive in sporting activities, and engage in role-playing games that often involve simulated violence. Girls, on the other hand, often play with dolls and engage in nurturing behavior by dressing their toys, changing diapers, and feeding them. This is not to say that boys and girls do not engage in any games that cross roles; surely they do. But children learn from both their parents and society what roles to play and what is expected of them.

Just as children learn to play vari-ous games as youngsters, they also learn that society expects young girls to someday become mothers and young boys to become fathers. While today it

Both boys and girls are now "playing" more alike. This is much different from how they played in years past.

Boys still appears to be more aggressive and competitive. Is this nature or nurture?

is equally expected for both sexes to work outside the home, the role differences between and gender identities of the sexes are fairly well established by the child's fourth birthday (Rekers, 1988).

Along with the assimilation of a child's gender identity is the child's conceptualization of how the two sexes (female and male) com-municate and interact with one another. For instance, boys generally know that they should not punch or kick nor should they tackle girls with the same fervor that they may tackle other boys with. And girls have some idea that boys are just different from them. Boys generally do not like to skip rope, play rhyming-clapping games, or dance, espe-cially when in the company of other boys.

As a child's understanding of the distinction between the sexes grows, children learn how to interact with members of the opposite sex in socially desirable ways. With the onset of puberty, many boys and girls will commence predating behavior and will hold hands or share a kiss, often mimicking the sexual and social behavior exhibited by parents, older siblings, or celebrities they see on television. Around the age of 12 or 13 children, understand that sexuality (even it does not involve actual sexual contact) is an integral part of their lives. And that if they are to be a normal functioning member of society, some positive association with the opposite sex is required.

This progression continues into adulthood, with individuals accommodating their lives to be in line with normative definitions of appropriate development. These definitions and rules relate not only how the sexes socially relate to one another, but also the types of sexual or semisexual acts that they engage in. Some individuals may strive and fantasize only to be in a marital relationship with a normal sexual union, while others fantasize about something more. Why some people are satisfied with a sexual relationship with the opposite sex that involves little risk, while others need that extra bit of excitement for fulfillment, is a complicated question and one with no clear answer.

The extant literature suggests that the maturation process summarized in the preceding paragraphs is complex and depends on a number of intervening factors. For instance, what makes an individual sexually excited by being tied up and totally submissive to another? Or how does an individual learn to associate fire or urination with sexual excitement? We honestly have no idea, but we are sure that somewhere along the way, an intervening stimulus, whether it is internal to the individual or external in their environment, has been interjected in the psychosexual developmental process. This stimulus is a disturbance in many theorists' eyes, one that has left the individual in a state of incomplete socialization. Where something clearly went wrong, whether it be psychological, biological, or social, interceded to prevent the person from completely maturing. Each of these explanations will be covered in the following sections.

Consider the case of one violent sex offender who offered this reason for his sexual predations during an interview. He said that when he was 6 years old his father punished him for eating a banana that the father was saving for his morning breakfast. He said that he told his father that he did not eat the banana, but his father placed him in a corner for the entire day, refusing to allow his mother to permit the child even the opportunity to relieve himself in the bathroom. When the father came home, the young boy admitted to his father that he had eaten the banana. The parent spanked the child but let him out of the corner. The rapist said, "I learned the value of lying and of deceit. I found out that I could get my way. That whole incident changed my life forever" (authors' files).

❖ INDIVIDUAL-LEVEL EXPLANATION OF SEXUAL DEVIANCE

One of the most prominent explanations why sexual offenders, especially violent sexual offenders, commit the crimes they do is that there is something inherently wrong with the functioning of the offender's brain. In essence, both the psychological and the psychiatric model often posit that the cause of most deviant sexual crimes is inherent within the individual. Many students confuse the psychiatric and psychological criminological explanations, but there is a distinct difference.

Psychological Models of Deviance

Psychological models tend to emphasize both individual and environmental influences on criminality. The model also considers the mental processes that mediate the relationship between the individual and his or her environment. Most psychological models tend to denote various personality characteristics exhibited by offenders that if identified could predict future criminal behavior (Vito & Holmes, 1994). The emphasis for these theories is the identification of aberrant behavior or tendencies and how they are acquired, evoked, maintained, or modified (Bartol & Bartol, 1999). By searching for the root causes of antisocial motivation, theorists

Psychological Models

Emphasize the individual and environmental influences on the personality, both criminal and social

belonging to this school of thought focus on an individual's personality and identity. They believe that once these personality traits can be identified, it is then possible that others sharing these same characteristics may be prone to engage in similar acts given the right social circumstances (Mischel, 1973). One of the psychological models that most students in criminal justice and sociology are familiar with is the profile developed by the FBI to classify offenders into organized and disorganized killers. This profile was designed to help law enforcement officials and criminal profilers not only look into the personality of the offender, but also help them understand why an offender committed a specific type of crime. Another assumption of the profile is that organized or disorganized offenders are likely to engage in similar types of crimes with similar "signatures," or unique patterns in their methods or the condition in which they leave the crime scene.

Psychiatric Models of Sexual Deviance

The other model that most students in the social and behavioral sciences are familiar with are *psychiatric* models. Psychiatric models follow the traditional psychoanalytic perspectives established by the famous father of this school, Sigmund Freud (1856–1939). The crux of theories making up the psychiatric model derive their power by examining and exploring possible motivations and drives of offenders.

They begin with the assumption that all people are born with innate

The Psychiatric Model

Follows the traditional psychoanalytical perspectives advanced by its founder, Sigmund Freud

drives to fulfill their wishes and urges. These drives include the motivation to eat, sleep, and engage in sexual behavior to satisfy themselves and to populate the species. These drives are a natural part of mankind's evolution and have helped us adapt to and conquer our environment. According to Freud, there are three integral parts of the human psyche that control human behavior and compose the building blocks of an individual's personality. The first of these and the core of human behavior is the *id*. The id contains the unconscious and instinctual parts of the personality and contains the savage impulses of the individual that seeks instant gratification. Most of these impulses lie in the area of sex and aggression (Holmes, 1983; Redl & Toch, 1986).

The second part of the human psyche is the *ego*. The ego is best conceptualized as an insulating layer that attempts to protect the individual from the savage impulses of the id. While the ego still wants what it wants when it wants it, the ego-dominated person understands that there is a time and a place for everything. It is the conscious part of the personality that is able to delay gratification of the savage impulses of the id. In the ego's layer, however, there is no attempt to measure the social cost and benefit of engaging in any type of activity. This activity is left to the third layer, the *superego.*

The superego is the third and final building block of the personality in Freud's psychoanalytic theory. The superego is the mediator between the unconscious self and its external environment. This is the

Figure 2.1   Freud's Elements of the Human Psyche

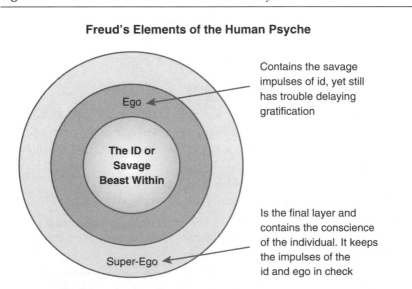

Freud's Elements of the Human Psyche

Ego

The ID or Savage Beast Within

Super-Ego

Contains the savage impulses of id, yet still has trouble delaying gratification

Is the final layer and contains the conscience of the individual. It keeps the impulses of the id and ego in check

level of the individual's psyche that tells the person what types of behavior are appropriate and which are not. While the superego is influenced by the outside world, most lessons about the consequences of behavior stem from experience and not perceptions of how the self would look relative to its environment.

Since Freud professed this personality theory, researchers have had 50 years to explore and test his theories. We still do not have definitive proof that any of these three layers does indeed exist, but our understanding of the human psyche is premised on their existence. Indeed, even our treatment methods and mechanisms are based on these three.

With psychoanalytic treatment, the psychiatrist or other qualified mental health professional tries to reach deep into the individual and uncover the base reason for a person's behavior. Hypnotherapy is one type of treatment that focuses not on the conscious mind, but rather the unconscious one. If Freud was right, then the target of traditional psychotherapy is the ego or even the id. The idea is that if psychiatrists can delve into these levels, well below what the conscious mind is able to do by itself, they will be able to uncover the root causes of antisocial behavior and correct it from the outside in.

Other types of psychiatric treatment, like that received by the majority of inmates in prison facilities across the country, rely on appealing to the superego and attempting to redefine for the individual what behaviors are acceptable and which are not. These traditional forms of treatment do little to remove hedonistic drives brought about by some type of pain or emotional scar, but rather try to apply a temporary fix or a Band-Aid to a gushing wound. For these reasons, it is easy to see that if we are indeed able to delve into the unconscious mind and discover the root causes of behavior, psychiatric treatment offers a lot more promise than the Band-Aid treatments that the criminal justice system has become so famous for. That is, however, dependent on the actual presence of the id, ego, and superego. But even after 50 years, there still is no proof that these three levels do exist.

What many people falsely believe psychiatrists ignore in their approach to and interpretation of criminal and violent behavior is the environment. While the psychiatric model relinquishes the importance of the environment, it does not ignore it. Most theorists sharing the psychiatric perspective believe that the source of most personality disorders is held within the individual and it is the individual that needs treatment—although the environment may trigger responses in an already wounded individual.

In summary, psychiatric theories posit that sex offenders at some point in life have experienced a fissure their individual personality and psychosocial development and that the offender does not truly understand why he or she desires or engages in these socially and often legally prohibited acts (Abrahamsen, 1952; Roche, 1958).

❖ THE SOCIAL LEARNING MODEL

A second prominent theoretical model that seeks to explain why individuals engage in sex offenses is the commonly known as the *social learning model*. This model is not only the most popular but also is the model most thoroughly researched of all the explanations of criminal behavior.

The social learning model proposes that individuals learn criminal acts and deeds and acquire motivations to commit crime from those things and people around them. The social learning model acknowledges that there may be differences in individuals and their cognitive skills and recognize that some people are just "wired" differently from others. However, they suggest that individuals themselves make choices to engage in illicit activities and are able to calculate both the costs and benefits of their earthly deeds (Samuel, 1981).

While this perspective seems to be simple, the process by which one learns and forms associations that lead to his or her participation in illicit deeds and how he or she weighs the costs and benefits of their participation is not. For example, one does not wake up one day and decide to molest children. Often, over the course of time, the individual becomes aware of an attraction to children. The individual may seek out others with a similar interest and subscribe to publications (or visit websites) with a focus on the sexual exploitation of children. During this intricate socialization experience, pedophiles learn that they themselves are not that different from others. Their observations, past experience, and subjective determination of the act itself lead them to begin to weigh the cost and benefit of approaching a child for sexual experimentation.

The Social Learning Theory

Crime is learned by experiences and people around them. But people make choices.

While this approach is similar to other cognitively based models, it is different in that the environment is not applying a direct stimulus to the individual. In other words, unlike rodents in laboratory experiments, the potential pedophile is not receiving an electric shock every time he or she has an irrational thought or deviant fantasy. It is the perception of the individual that shapes behavior and the likelihood for increased participation or interest. For that reason, a person who engages in a sex crime does it because of an express interest in gaining something (power, control, sexual pleasure, etc.) rather than some innate desire gone haywire (Rotter, 1972).

One of the most preeminent theorists of the social learning approach is Albert Bandura. In his research with aggressive children, he found that "people are not born with preformed repertoires of aggressive behavior. They must learn them" (Bandura, 1986, p. 200). What he essentially states is that while it is true that some people may have a problem with controlling their violent and aggressive tendencies, where, when, and how much violence they choose to use is based on learned patterns of behavior.

According to the social learning model, violent and antisocial behavior is learned in interaction with an individual's environment. This learning phase is divided into 3 separate and distinct phases. The first phase is what Bandura labels the *acquisition phase* (Bandura, 1986).

The Acquisition Phase

In the *acquisition phase*, the individual begins to assimilate into his or her personality characteristics of others by the process of observational learning. That is, individuals learn who they are and how they should behave by checking their innate impulses and comparing them with others in their environment. According to Bandura (1986) the acquisition stage is a passive one in which the individual accumulates a wealth of information without actually participating in either social forbidden or socially acceptable acts.

Studying aggressive and violent youth, Bandura, Ross, and Ross (1963) and Ross and Fabino (1985) found that children emulate the aggressive behavior of adult models, especially when the child is rewarded rather than punished for violent outbreaks. Youth learn modal types of behavior in interaction with the family and adult role models as well as in interaction with their social network of peers and behavior portrayed in the mass media.

While youth and many adults learn patterns of deviant and aggressive behavior from and in interaction with others, it is one thing to learn and be aware of these tendencies and quite another to act on them. In this regard, the social learning model also takes into account *instigation mechanisms* that propel an individual into action. Factors that are believed to instigate violent or aggressive behavior include biological and cognitive motivators.

Instigation Mechanisms

By the time we have reached and gone through puberty, most of us have some idea of how to get the things we want. We understand what it is to desire an object and also understand that there are appropriate ways of acquiring that object. Whether the object we desire is a new toy or a bicycle, the process is all the same. Most of us will work extra jobs, take on a paper route, save babysitting money, or ask our parents for an increase in our allowance. When the object that we desire is not a tangible object, however, like respect or popularity, it is often difficult from some children to conceptualize just how they can acquire that object using legitimate mechanisms. It is even more difficult for those among us who are not adequately socialized.

Using popularity as an example, it is conceivable that many under-socialized children may want the respect and popularity that they feel is due to them. Often when they do not receive it and are the victims of harassment or ridicule, they feel pain, not just physical pain, but psychological pain as well. The pain manifests itself in a number of ways, but for many who lack the cognitive skills to process the pain into appropriate channels, the result is often an act of overt aggression. The aggression can be sparked by "insults, verbal challenges, status threats and unjust treatment" (Bandura, 1986, p. 208). In sum, the instigation mechanism for aggression is learned and comes not from a innate drive to inflict pain but rather from learned mechanisms of behavior through which the individual is seeking to medicate him- or herself after an internal or external traumatic experience.

The Maintaining Mechanisms

Perhaps just as important as the instigation mechanism are the *maintaining mechanisms.* Maintaining mechanisms form the process by which inappropriate or aggressive tendencies are kept in the personal repertoire of individuals. While not mentioned specifically as the most important element of the social learning model, the maintaining mechanisms are in some theoretical circles the defining elements of an individual's decision to engage in violent or criminal behavior.

Maintaining mechanisms allow individuals to scan their environment and mentally check and see what behaviors work not only for themselves but for others to achieve their desired ends. In the case of a child molester, he may recognize that he has an attraction to children, and he may also have experienced some pain as a result of this desire, and he may choose not to act on his impulses since he has seen the costs of participation of sexual behavior with minors. This process is different from that described by the ego and superego under the psychiatric models, since the self does not have to experience either the pleasure or pain of participation personally. Others in their environment can serve as models whereby the internal cognitive processes of the individual are affected. According to Shoham and Seis (1993), this self-reinforcement through maintaining mechanisms is a key factor in the perpetuation of violent and criminal acts (Bandura, 1986; Bartol, 1986; Shoham & Seis, 1993).

❖ THE CONSTITUTIONAL MODEL

In today's world, almost all would agree that a person's psyche and the environment the person is brought up in play an important role in the person's propensity to engage in a life of crime and an even more important role in the propensity to engage in a sex crime. We all have heard and have come to accept that the major correlates of criminal behavior are poverty, inadequate educational opportunities, alcohol or drug dependency, and being a product of a broken home. There have, however, been criminological theorists who posited that one's decision to engage in a life of crime or serious sexual deviance is not a product of a lack of social bonding or a break or fissure in the personality of the individual, but rather a function of the genes that the individual received from a previous generation. In essence, most constitutional criminologists at the time believed that a large proportion of criminals were thrust into a life of crime not because of the social environment in which they were raised, but rather because of heredity.

While very few theorists at present believe that heredity is the sole cause of criminality, constitutional criminological theories still stand as plausible explanations why some individuals choose to live life on the fringe and others do not. While constitutional models may not be as strong predictors as some of the contemporary social-structural models, neither can researchers and students of the social sciences discount their importance. One does not have to look too far to see effects of heredity.

One of the most famous studies in the biological school of criminality is the study of the descendents of the Jukes. This study, conducted by Dugdale (1877) traced the descendants of Ada Jukes and found that most of her family members were either criminals, prostitutes, or welfare recipients (Dugdale, 1877). Other studies, such as the one conducted by Goddard (1912), reached similar conclusions.

Perhaps the best test of constitutional criminality lies in the research that that looked at the criminal propensity of biological twins raised since birth in separate homes. These studies have consistently found that twins sharing the same gene pool are more likely than fraternal twins raised in identical surroundings to subscribe to similar lifestyles than their counterparts (Christiansen, 1977; Lange, 1929; Rowe, 1985; Wilson & Hernstein, 1985).

Despite consistent findings over the years confirming that crime and aggressive propensities may indeed have a biological root, social scientists have continued to argue over how strong of a predictor biology is and what parts or our DNA makeup contributes to our innate violent and aggressive tendencies. While it is too much to address all the indicators that researchers have been able to discern that may predict a propensity to engage in violence, we will focus in this section on two. These are constitutional criminology and crime as biologically determined.

Constitutional Criminology

Perhaps the most famous constitutional criminologist was Cesare Lombroso (1836–1909). Lombroso was an Italian physician and amateur criminal anthropologist who proposed that crime and heredity were intricately related. In his book, *L'Uomo delinquente* (Criminal Man), published in 1876, he stated that some men were born with strong innate propensities to engage in a life of crime (Lombroso, 1876). Borrowing from the works of Charles Darwin, Lombroso felt that the criminal was a separate species of mankind who had not evolved as much as the rest of the population (Savitz, 1972). The traditions and ideas of Lombroso were solidified into what we currently call the *positive school* of criminology.

In the positivist tradition, many theorists, including Lombroso, believed that crime was a "natural phenomenon" for those individuals who were atavists, or biological throwbacks to an earlier time period (Goring, 1913; Lombroso, 1876). Lombroso professed that criminals could be identified by a series of distinguishing physical characteristics, such as their large appendages, insensibility toward pain, asymmetrical head, and many others.[1]

It is important to note that Lombroso retracted many earlier claims that these biological atavists were responsible for the majority of the crime problem. In his third revision of *L'Uomo delinquente,* he acknowledged that it was possible that this theory could help explain the criminality of only 35% to 40% of habitually violent criminals (Lombroso, 1917). Further, he even acknowledged that mental illness, psychological deficiencies, or even social-structural causes might better explain why the majority of individuals engage in violent crime.

Table 2.1   Characteristics of Lombroso's Born Criminal Type

Physical Attributes of the Born Criminal

1. Asymmetrical face

2. Unusually large or small ears

3. A low, receding forehead

4. Prominent eyebrows, jawbones, or cheekbones

Ancillary Attributes of the Born Criminal

5. Have more acute sense of touch on the left side of the body than on the right

6. Show a greater insensibility toward pain

7. Sharp vision, but more often than not colorblind

8. Less than average sense of hearing, smell, and taste

9. Are extremely agile, even at advanced ages

10. Recover quickly from wounds

11. Have little to no ability to distinguish between right and wrong

12. Complete lack of shame, remorse, honor, or pity

13. A passion for gambling and alcohol

SOURCE: From *Criminal Man, According to the Classification of Cesare Lombroso*, by G. Lombroso-Ferrero, 1911 (New York: G. P. Putnam's Sons).

Physical Characteristics and Crime

Other theorists claimed that certain biological factors determined the likelihood that an individual would engage in a life of crime. For instance, in the 1940s, William Sheldon introduced his theory linking physical attributes of a person's body and the person's personality (Sheldon & Stevens, 1940). This procedure he called *somatotyping*. After collecting and coding data on the physical measurements of 200 university men, Sheldon claimed to be able to delineate three main body types: the *endomorph, ectomorph*, and the *mesomorph*. He then took these body types and correlated them with three clusters of temperament that were displayed in his sample. These temperament classifications were, respectively, viscerotonia (a pleasure from eating and socializing), somatotonia (a tendency toward assertiveness and dominance, physical adventure, and exercise), and cerebrotonia (a tendency toward restraint in movement and emotional expression, and a love of privacy) (Sheldon & Stevens, 1942).

The endomorph is a person who is fat and soft. In his relationship with others, he is gregarious, jolly, and easy to get along with. According to Sheldon and Stevens (1942), the endomorph is the least likely to get into trouble with the law because his body type determines a personality and disposition disinclined to such behavior. The second body type was the ectomorph. The ectomorph is a thin and fragile individual. The ectomorph is easily excitable, afraid of people, and introverted. Sheldon postulated that the ectomorph is unlikely to engage in criminality because of a lack of self-confidence and an inability to sustain interpersonal relations with others (Sheldon, Hartl, & McDermott, 1949).

The final body type that Sheldon identified was the mesomorph. According to his theory, the mesomorph was the real problem. Mesomorphs he described as being athletic and muscular persons, and persons who craved adventure. Like Lombroso's biological atavist, the mesomorph, Sheldon claimed, were ruthless, psychopathic and indifferent to pain (Sheldon et al., 1949).

While Sheldon's theory was innovative at the time, he never developed a full or complete classification system that could precisely identify offenders. In Sheldon's study, respondents were scored on 3 items (attributes of each body type) using a 7-point scale. Thus, any individual would receive only 3 scores ranging from 1 to 7 denoting whether they scored high or low on the attributes of the that particular body type. While the meaning of the results were not exactly clearly stated, the inference was that a person who scored higher on one scale than on the other two should be categorized as belonging to that somatotype.

Sheldon's primitive study looking at personality and body type sparked a series of studies, each finding some link. For instance, Child (1950) found similar correlations between self-reported temperament and body type for a similar sample of 414 university students for mesomorphs and ectomorphs only (Child, 1950). And Cortes and Gatti (1965), studying adolescents, found significant correlations across all three somatotypes (Cortes & Gatti, 1965). A comparison of the correlations between the works of Sheldon and Stevens, Child, and Cortes and Gatti can be found in Table 2.2.

The results and findings of these somatotyping theories sparked interest in the study of body type as it relates to the development of personality, especially violent and aggressive personality types. So powerful was this influence that even the Gluecks alluded to their findings on delinquency and body types when they reported that delinquent boys were larger and stronger than nondelinquent youth (Glueck & Glueck, 1956). Even a follow-up study by Cortes and Gatti (1972) found that male delinquents in their sample were significantly more mesomorphic than their control sample of nondelinquents.

Table 2.2   Correlations Between Physique and Temperament

Study	N	Endomorphy and Viscerotonia	Mesomorphy and Somatotonia	Ectomorphy and Cerebrotonia
Sheldon & Stevens (1942)	200	.79**	.82**	.83**
Child (1950)	414	.13	.38**	.27*
Cortes and Gatti (1965)	73	.32*	.42**	.31*

*Significant at the .01 level

**Significant at the .001 level

SOURCE: From "Men and Their Bodies: The Relationship Between Body Types and Behavior," by R. Montemayor, 1978, *Journal of Social Issues, 34*: p. 1.

While Sheldon's somatotyping theory has recently fallen out of favor with mainstream criminological theory, it is clear that biology and heredity do appear to play some role in the display of violence and aggression.

❖ THE RISE OF SOCIOBIOLOGY

While most contemporary criminological theorist discount the relative importance of biological theories in understanding the nexus of crime causation, the publication of *Sociobiology* in 1975 by Edmund O. Wilson began to change many people's view of the role that biology plays in this nexus (Wilson, 1975). Wilson's view was that biology was not the *sole* determiner of an individual's decision to engage in a life of crime, but rather it played a role in that biological and genetic conditions affect how individuals perceive the way they fit into the social environment around them. In this view, biology, the environment, and social learning are all factors to be considered when examining why some people decide to engage in a life or crime and others do not. Sociobiologists therefore claim that these factors interact with each other and focusing on one factor alone is inadequate to explain the etiology of criminal offenders. For instance, a person's own genetic code may put that person at increased risk of engaging in violent or aggressive behavior, but it is often a condition in the environment that triggers the violent episode. It is then the perception of that act, whether it helped or hindered the individual in acquiring a goal, that serves as the maintenance mechanism allowing the aggression to remain a part of the personal repertoire of behavior for getting what the individual wants, when he or she wants it. Thus, there is a rational and determinate choice made by the criminal to commit the antisocial act. Today, criminologists interested in identifying these individual-level biological traits that predispose one to violence or aggression are commonly called trait theorists (Siegel, 1998).

Basic Propositions of Sociobiological Trait Theory

There are several core principles that separate biological trait theories from other, more popular sociological theories of crime causation (Ellis, 1990). These principles include the belief that not all human beings are born equal or with a blank slate. Hence, the combination of our biological differences and the environment we are all brought up in all predispose individuals to making rational choices or preclude them from making rational choices about engaging in a life of crime or participating in illicit activities. Included in these innate differences, in this model, is the proposition that not all people are born with same potential for learning. Learning includes academic achievement in the education system and the ability to process indicators in the environment that tell people which behaviors are acceptable and which are not. In this way, learning is controlled by and dependent on not only how much our parents and teachers push us in school, but also by our own brain and central nervous system's ability to process information quickly and efficiently (Herbert & Cohen, 1993).

The Sociobiological School

The elements of biology and environment interact to form the personality.

Another of the basic propositions of the biological-biomedical school is that a significant amount of crime is caused by instinctual drives. This is similar to the beliefs and followers of Freud who felt that crime was a result of the savage impulses of the id, however it differs in that members of the socio-biology believe that if the mind has not learned to suppress these urges, then it is natural state for many. Some theorists such as Ellis (1989) have gone as far as to claim that rape and other sex crimes may be caused linked to the male's instinctual drive to possess and control females (Ellis, 1989).

Chemical Imbalances and Hormonal Influences

Some interesting theories have arisen from the sociobiological school in the current literature. Some researchers have found that children who do not ingest the proper balance of vitamins and minerals have problems with their intellectual development, which then in turn affects their choice to engage in later aggressive, violent, and abnormal sexual activity (Krassner, 1986; Neisser, 1996). Other studies have shown links between crime and insufficient ingestion of vitamins C and B_3 & B_6 (Hippchen, 1978, 1981).

Exploring the relationship between food and aggressive behavior, Fishbein and Pease (1988) summarize numerous studies over the last 50 years that suggest causal influences from the ingestion of some foods and irritability, hyperactivity, seizures, and agitation. Further, Schoenthaler (1982) conducted a controlled experiment in a juvenile detention facility where he limited the sugar intake of offenders and kept track of the number of disciplinary actions. He found that the number of assaults, thefts, fights, and disorderly incidents decreased 45%.

There are still other biomedical explanations of criminal behavior. Wilson (1993) in his book *The Moral Sense* states that hormones or other body enzymes may hold the key to unraveling the question of why some people resort to violence and engage in criminal activity while others do not. Nowhere is this trend more evident than in the research using testosterone as an indicator of aggressiveness. For example, Beeman (1947) found that aggressive male mice injected with female hormones stop fighting. Similarly, others have found that that high levels of androgens in males contribute to aggressive and violent behavior (Booth & Osgood, 1993). And, further, one study found that the testosterone levels of incarcerated inmates convicted of violent crime was higher than that of similar males incarcerated for lesser offenses (Kreuz & Rose, 1972). Obviously, these findings have important policy ramifications.

Other research looking at female criminality have concluded that female hormones may play also a role in violent or aggressive behavior. In one study, Dalton examined the 156 female inmates admitted to prison and found that 49% of the offenses for which they were convicted were committed in the premenstruation period or during the cycle itself (Dalton, 1971). While Dalton's study does have methodological problems, and it is impossible to determine whether the premenstruation period caused the offender to be hostile and aggressive or other anxieties caused the menstrual cycle to begin, there does at least appear a correlation between the two (Horney, 1978). And until further research is conducted, this connection offers to be as plausible as many of the other biological, psychological, and sociological explanations for why individuals engage in violent and aggressive acts.

❖ CONCLUSION

From an examination of these three models of the etiology of behavior, specifically criminal behavior, it can easily be seen that each of the three has a different focus and different implications for treatment. The role of the unconscious is paramount in the psychology and psychiatric models. The social learning models views delinquency and deviance as a learned set of behavioral adaptation, with special attention being directed to significant others and the importance of symbols in the interaction with others. The change from criminal to noncriminal does not lie in many hours of psychotherapy, probing the unconscious or receiving injections or operations, but rather through a process of resocialization, relearning the predominant prosocial societal attitudes for positive functioning within the society. And finally, the constitutional or positive model certainly views criminality in a different perspective, and treatment is more predicated on pharmacological medical therapy, since criminals are thought to possess constitutional factors that predestine them to be violators.

Neither the models presented here, nor others not covered, are complete and satisfactorily predictive There are theoretical gaps in all the models. Volumes upon volumes could be written on theories of sexual deviance. It is not the purpose of this book to offer the definitive model on sex crime causation. The etiology must be considered to consist in multiple causes, and cures for behaviors that have been termed criminal must lie somewhere in the social world. What follows in this book is a general listing of sex crimes and a plan for societal action in the area dealing with the offender and the issue of respective responsibilities of the individual and society.

❖ DISCUSSION QUESTIONS

1. Should the psychoanalytic model of sexual development be given the same credence as it once held? Why or why not?

2. Which theory discussed in this chapter appears to be most valid? Explain your position.

3. What is your position on the merits of the biosociology and constitutional criminality models of the causation of criminal behavior?

4. Formulate your own theory of the violent sexual offender. Share your theory with others in the class.

❖ REFERENCES

Abrahamsen, D. (1952). *Who are the guilty?* Westport, CT: Greenwood Press.

Bandura, A. (1986). The social learning perspective: Mechanisms of aggression. In H. Toch (Ed.), *Psychology of crime and criminal justice.* Prospect Heights, IL: Waveland.

Bandura, A., Ross, D., & Ross, S. (1963). Transmission of aggression Through imitation of aggressive models. *Journal of abnormal social psychology, 66,* 3–11.

Bartol, C. (1986). *Criminal behavior.* New York: Simon and Schuster.

Bartol, C. R., & Bartol, A. M. (1999). *Criminal behavior: A psychosocial approach, 5th Ed.* Englewood Cliffs, NJ: Prentice-Hall.

Beeman, E. (1947). The effect of male hormones on aggressive behavior in mice. *Physiological zoology, 20,* 373–405.

Booth, A., & Osgood, W. (1993). The influence of testosterone on deviance in adulthood: Assessing and explaining the relationship. *Criminology, 31,* 93–118.

Child, I. (1950). The relation of somatotype to self ratings on Sheldon's temperamental traits. *Journal of personality, 18,* 440–453.

Christiansen, K. (1977). A preliminary study of criminality among twins. In S. Mednick & K. Christiansen (Eds.), *Biosocial bases of criminal behavior.* New York: Gardiner.

Cortes, J., & Gatti, F. (1965). Physique and self description of temperament. *Journal of consulting psychology, 29,* 432–439.

Cortes, J., & Gatti, F. (1972). *Delinquency and crime: A biopsychosocial approach.* New York: Seminar Press.

Dalton, K. (1971). *The premenstrual syndrome.* Springfield, IL: Charles C. Thomas.

Dugdale, R. (1877). *The Jukes: A study in crime, pauperism, disease, and heredity.* New York: Putnam.

Ellis, L. (1989). *Theories of rape.* New York: Hemisphere.

Ellis, L. (1990). Introduction to L. Ellis & H. Hoffman (Eds.), *Crime in biological, social and moral contexts* (pp. 3–18). New York: Praeger.

Fishbein, D., & Pease, S. (1988). The effects of diet on behavior: Implications for criminology and corrections. *Research on corrections, 1,* 1–45.

Freud, S. (1930). *Three contributions to the theory of sex* (Monograph Series 7). Washington, DC: Nervous and Mental Health Disease.

Glueck, S., & Glueck, E. (1956). *Physique and delinquency.* New York: Harper and Row.

Goddard, H. H. (1912). *The Kallikak family: A study in the heredity of feeblemindedness.* New York: Macmillan.

Goring, C. (1913). *The English convict: A statistical study.* London: His Majesty's Stationery Office.

Herbert, T., & Cohen, S. (1993). Depression and immunity: A meta-analytic review. *Psychological bulletin, 113,* 472–486.

Hippchen, L. (1981). Some possible biochemical aspects of criminal behavior. *Journal of behavioral ecology, 2,* 1–6.

Hippchen, L. (Ed.). (1978). *Ecologic-biochemical approaches to treatment of delinquents and criminals.* New York: Von Nostrand Reinhold.

Holmes, R. M. (1983). *The sex offender and the criminal justice system.* Springfield, IL: Charles C. Thomas.

Horney, J. (1978). Menstrual cycles and criminal responsibility. *Law and human nature, 2,* 25–36.

Kinsey, A. (1947). *Sex behavior in the human animal.* New York: Academic Sciences.

Krassner, M. (1986). Diet and brain function. *Nutrition reviews, 44,* 12–15.

Kreuz, L., & Rose, R. (1972). Assessment of aggressive behavior and plasma testosterone in a young criminal population. *Psychosomatic medicine, 34,* 321–332.

Lange, J. (1929). *Crime as destiny.* New York: Boni.

Lombroso, C. (1876). *L'Uomo delinquente.* Milan, Italy: Turin.

Lombroso, C. (1917). *Crime, its causes and remedies.* Boston: Little.

Mischel, W. (1973). Toward a cognitive social learning reconceptualization of personality. *Psychological review, 80,* 252–283.

Neisser, U. (1996). Intelligence: Knowns and unknowns. *Americans psychologist, 51,* 77–101.

Redl, F., & Toch, H. (1986). The Psychoanalytic Perspective. In H. Toch (Ed.), *Psychology of Crime and Criminal Justice.* Prospect Heights, IL: Waveland.

Rekers, G. A. (1988). Psychosexual assessment of gender identity disorders. In R. J. Prinz (Ed.), *Advances in the behavioral assessment of children and families.* Greenwich, CN: JAI Press.

Roche, P. (1958). *The criminal mind: The study of communication between criminal law and psychiatry.* New York: Gove Press.

Ross, R., & Fabino, E. (1985). *Time to think: A cognitive model of delinquency prevention and rehabilitation programs.* Johnson City, TN: Institute of Social Science and Arts.

Rotter, J. (1972). Some implications of a social learning theory for the practice of psychotherapy. In J. Rotter, J. Chance & E. Phares (Eds.), *Applications of social learning theory of personality.* New York: Holt, Rinehart and Winston.

Rowe, D. (1985). Sibling interaction and self-reported delinquency behavior: A Study of 265 twin pairs. *Criminology, 23,* 223–240.

Samuel, W. (1981). *Personality: Searching for the source of human behavior.* New York: McGraw-Hill.

Savitz, L. D. (1972). Introduction to G. Lombroso-Ferrero (Ed.), *Criminal man.* Montclair, NJ: Patterson-Smith.

Schoenthaler, S. (1982). Diet and crime: An empirical examination of the value of nutrition in the control and treatment of incarcerated juvenile offenders. *International journal of biosocial research, 4,* 25–39.

Sheldon, W., Hartl, E., & McDermott, E. (1949). *Varieties of delinquent youth: An introduction to constitutional psychiatry.* New York: Harper.

Sheldon, W., & Stevens, S. (1940). *The varieties of human physique.* New York: Harper.

Sheldon, W., & Stevens, S. (1942). *The varieties of temperament.* New York: Harper.

Shoham, S., & Seis, M. (1993). *A primer in the psychology of crime.* Albany, NY: Harrow & Heston.

Siegel, L. (1998). *Criminology* (6th ed.). Belmont, CA: West/Wadsworth.

Sumner, W. G. (1906). *Folkways.* Boston.

Vito, G. F., & Holmes, R. M. (1994). *Criminology: Theory, research, and policy.* Belmont, CA: Wadsworth.

Wilson, E. (1975). *Sociobiology.* Cambridge, MA: Harvard University Press.

Wilson, J. (1993). *The moral sense.* New York: Free Press.

Wilson, J., & Hernstein, R. (1985). *Crime and human nature: The definitive study of the causes of crime.* New York: Simon & Schuster.

❖ NOTE

1. For a complete list of these characteristics see Table 2.1.

3

Sex in History

❖ ❖ ❖

To understand the role and practice of sexual behavior, it is necessary to view it in historical perspective. One way to do so is to analyze certain family types, as they existed throughout the ages, and their modal viewpoints on sex and sexuality. This is the approach that will be taken in this chapter. Several types of families—ancient Jewish, Greek, Roman, and Christian—will be examined, along with their historical periods, to provide some perspective on today's views on sexual activity, both "normal" sex and socially judged criminal sex offenses. These particular cultures were chosen for a reason. It is hoped that the reader will be able to understand the evolution of sexual expression, freedom of behavior, and philosophy through time. The general pattern that should emerge at the end of the chapter is that as society progressed and humans began to conquer their environment, the philosophical support for repressing human sexuality (both male and female) began to relax. This pattern changed when the early Christian Church began to dominate the common culture of Europe and the rest of the enlightened world. This dominance continues in the world today, as traditional repressive asceticism continues to dominate our view of sex and its place in our lives.

❖ FAMILY TYPES

The Hebrew Family

Several centuries before the time of Christ, the ancient Jewish family had characteristics that grew out of necessity, because of the Jews' social status as well as the harsh environment that they lived in. The early Hebrew tribes were a small group of nomadic people who roamed around in desolate locations for centuries. Because of their circumstance and core religious values, they were persecuted by other cultures over the course of history. The harsh physical, social, and political environment they lived in prompted them to develop a strong sense of community and family to keep them together as a people. Overall, the early Hebrew families had four distinguishing characteristics. They were patriarchal, patrilineal, patrilocal, and polygynous.

In a patriarchy like that of the ancient Hebrew family, the father was the supreme commander. His word was law; he was the rabbi, the judge, the jury, and—in perhaps more than a few cases—the executioner. As a patrilineal society, Hebrews traced bloodlines through the father's side of the family.

Males, both adults and children, were granted higher status because of their gender. Male children were the desired offspring because they had specific inherent physical traits that were judged to be of higher value than those of their female counter parts. Male children were seen to the ones that could provide for the family as well as capable of doing heavier work and acting as warriors in battle. All wealth and property typically were passed down from the father to the eldest legitimate son (if there was one). The eldest married son also lived close to the father's home as in all patrilocal cultures). This son, the heir, would inherit his father's privileges, wealth, and property, as well as his father's responsibilities.

Of course, in some cases, wives were unable to beget children. Consider the case of Sarah and Abraham in the Old Testament. In that story, Sarah was barren and had not been able to bear Abraham the son he desperately desired. She encouraged him to seek a concubine who would bear him a son. Sarah chose Hagar for Abraham and from this union came a son, Ishmael. Later, Sarah herself bore Abraham his second son, Isaac. Although Ishmael had held the preferred position of firstborn, Isaac was legitimate, and so Ishmael was forced to relinquish his status to Isaac.

Of course, divorce was not granted to women in the early Jewish culture. Only the male was granted divorce and was also permitted to have multiple wives. This practice, polygyny (one husband with two or more wives), is suited for a family system where there are not enough men for all the women or when a drastic increase in the population is desirable. As stated earlier, the early Hebrew tribes lived in a very harsh environment and were often persecuted for their beliefs. Thus, it was wise to allow the men to take on multiple wives so that they could ensure their survival. In Old Testament tradition, it is clear that their God had no commandment condemning the practice of polygyny. Indeed, it was thought that everyone should marry, especially men. But one had to be careful not to commit adultery or fornication.

Sex in the Hebrew family was primarily reserved for procreation and for the pleasure of the male. Women were not to enjoy sex; instead it was their "pleasure" to raise the children and take care of the home.

The Greek Family

Before the time of Christ, the ancient Greek family took a pragmatic view of sexuality and how sex was to be practiced both inside and outside the family. Like the early Hebrew tribes, the purposes of heterosexual sex was seen to be procreation and, of course, marital enrichment. One of the unique factors of how sex was viewed in Greek society stemmed from the strong public and communal encouragement of homosexuality. For many in Greek society, the highest form of love affair was considered to be that between two males, one an adult and the other a young boy before puberty. In other words, homosexuality and pedophilia was institutionalized in Greek society and was part of their common culture.

The status of the woman was low in the Greek family. The married woman had principally only two roles: wife and mother. Her education was restricted to that which was required for her to run a household and fulfill the needs of motherhood. Indeed, married women were seldom seen in the public company of their husbands. If a man wanted to have an adult conversation with a woman about civics, astronomy, government, or philosophy, it was difficult, for there were only a few women educated in these areas. One educated group of women was the *hetaerae*. The hetaerae were prostitutes who were educated not only academically but also in ways to please their male customers.

The Greek male was allowed to obtain a divorce, something that was extremely difficult, and in most cases impossible, for the ordinary woman. The Greek family type was also male-dominated; sons were needed to carry on the family name, inherit family wealth, and act as warriors.

Sex in ancient Greece was not only for procreational but also recreational purposes. Homosexuality, lesbianism, hedonism, polytheism, and a warlike and monogamous family structure were all traits that typified the ancient Greek family.

The Roman Family

Like the Greek family, the Roman family was patriarchal, patrilineal, patrilocal, and monogamous. Nevertheless, the Roman family type was very important in the sexual history of the family, because the Roman family was the first family type that allowed equality for males and females. Belief in equality of the sexes led to the concept of bi-humanity—what was good for one sex was equally good for the other. Thus, the world of the private life, the home and family, was just as important as the world of the public sphere. Just because one was different from the other did not make one more important than the other.

The belief of bi-humanity was a concept pioneered by classical Rome that held that what was good for one sex was equally good for the other.

There were other important differences in this family. It was true, for example, that males were desired as children. They would act as warriors, inherit the family wealth, and carry on the family name. But daughters were also desired. They could accumulate property and even serve as elected officials in government and, under Roman law, could sue for divorce. The concept of hedonism became firmly implanted in the societal fabric—live for today because one does not know what tomorrow brings.

Many of the rituals found in wedding ceremonies today come from the Roman family. The parade through town, the wedding ring, and the carrying of the spouse across the threshold all date back to the Roman family before the time of Christ. It is true that the father was still in control of the family, but the mother was now treated as an equal.

The sexual values of the family included not only sex as procreation but also sex as recreation. Sex was something that was viewed as a normal part of a personality and was to be enjoyed. There was nothing wrong with sex. Neither homosexual nor heterosexual sex

Table 3.1   Family Types and Traits

Early Hebrew Family	Early Greek Family	Early Roman Family	Early Christian Family
Patriarchal	Patriarchal	Patriarchal	Patriarchal
Patrilocal	Patrilocal	Patrilocal	Patrilocal
Patrilineal	Patrilineal	Patrilineal	Patrilineal
Polygynous	Monogamous	Monogamous	Monogamous
Permitted divorced for the male	Permitted divorce for the male and for some females	Permitted divorce for either gender	Disallowed divorce for either gender
Desired male children	Desired male children	Desired male children	Desired female children
Monotheistic	Polytheistic	Polytheistic	Monotheistic
Prohibited homosexuality	Institutionalized homosexuality	Permitted homosexuality	Homosexuality was a major sin
Heterosexual sex was mainly for the male enjoyment; another role was procreation.	Heterosexual sex was mainly for the male in his enjoyment. Some females could enjoy sexual activity.	Heterosexual sex was to be enjoyed by both genders.	Sex was sinful. It was only to be used for procreation. So one could copulate only to populate, not recreate.
Women had extremely low status.	Generally, women had low status.	Romans instituted the concept of bi-humanity.	Women lost status here as the "source of all sin."

was sinful. Roman religion was predicated upon a plurality of gods, and these gods did not only deal with vengeance and war. There were gods of emotion and pleasure as well. Even when an individual became intoxicated, it was sometimes viewed as though he or she had received special visitation from the gods.

From all the special traits of the Roman family, the Christian family arose. But because early Christians were a small group of people, persecuted and reviled, it was only natural that they would overturn and replace many of the social and sexual values that the Romans held dear.

The Christian Family

After years of persecution, the Christian family gained power and recognition in Rome through an edict issued by Emperor Constantine in 313 AD. It is said that when Constantine was marching with his army across northern Italy preparing for battle with Maxentius, who also had laid claim to the empire of Rome. The legend states that when he looked up into the sky, the saw an image of a cross with two Greek letters chi and rho. These two letters were the first two letters of the Greek word for Christ. Along with these letters inscribed in the cross was an omen telling him that "with this sign, thou shalt conquer." Constantine took this to mean that the Christian god was speaking to him and that, if he bore the cross in battle, he would be victorious and consolidate his claim to the Roman empire. Constantine then carried the sign into battle and was victorious at the Battle of Milvian Bridge in 312. Having won the battle, Constantine issued the Edict of Milan in 313, which removed the penalties for professing and practicing the Christian faith.

While some scholars have questioned whether Constantine actually saw the cross or simply saw an opportunity to engage the Christians as followers, there is probably truth in both propositions. It is undeniably true that if someone looks into the sun, they are sure to squint their eyes. And many people viewing a bright light through the reflection of their eyebrows will see a cross. That fact, even the most adamant nonbeliever can understand. It was also true that the Christians at the time had a very strong moral code and that the religious often controlled their believers using crude but very effective informal methods. Thus it might have been the case that Constantine saw an opportunity to consolidate his power by allowing the Christians to operate freely in Rome and understood that if this religion was allowed to grow, it would be easier to control the population than if the society remained the hedonistic pagan one that Rome had been. That is, it would be easier for an emperor to control the people because he could rely not only on his own rule of law, but also the rule of religion. This principle has served many civilizations well and even today, in some areas on the Middle East, the radical religious groups are able to more readily control people than the state can.

Whether Constantine actually saw the image of the cross is actually irrelevant to this discussion. What is relevant is that with the ability to operate in the open, the Christian faith took off and its faith, teachings, and strict moral principles on sex and sexuality soon began to dominate western civilization. Prescribing values that were foreign to the traditional Roman family, the Christians went about overturning the values that were indigenous to the Romans.

Unlike the other three family types that have been discussed, the Christians believed that it was better to remain single, but if you could not contain yourself, it was better to marry than to burn (in hell) (I Corinthians 7:9). As St. Paul stated, "It is better that you remain as I" (that is, single). Of course, Jesus never uttered such words as these, but he may have set an example of his erotic-phobic posture (if the scriptures are factually accurate) when he doctrinally refused to be born of a natural sexual union between a husband and a wife and also when he refused to marry. Many theologians, and even the popular book the *Da Vinci Code* by Dan Brown, proposed that Jesus may have indeed married Mary Magdalene—if for no other reason than that there was a severe Roman tax placed upon single males once they reached a certain age. This tax almost ensured that every man would marry, because the average man at that time would have found it very difficult to pay the tax.

The Christian family incorporated many of the same traits as the earlier family types. It insisted, for example, on monogamy (if a man could not control himself, he therefore had to marry) but did not allow for divorce. The purest men did not marry at all, but instead dedicated all their efforts to the work of preparing for the next world.

Sex was considered utilitarian; it was not to be used for recreation, as was the practice of the Romans. Sex was for procreation and not for pleasure. After all, Mary, the mother of Jesus, was a virgin and did not involve herself in a conjugal fashion with her husband, Joseph. The Holy Spirit mystically impregnated her, and Joseph had nothing to do with the pregnancy. Moreover, Mary was free from the stain of original sin, a Christian dogma that was not made an integral part of the belief of the Church until several hundred years later.

It does not appear that Jesus was as firmly opposed to the joys of sex, as were many of his followers. After his death, however, the institution of the Church soon began to take a firm stand against the evils of sex and sexuality. This is best seen in many of the early Christian saints and martyrs.

Take, for example, St. Simon the Stylite. A hermit, he lived in a cave in the desert for years without bathing. He wore a rope around his waist, which became infected with maggots, and as the maggots fell from his festering wounds upon the floor of the cave, his famous prayer was, "Eat little children what God has given unto you." St. Perpetua, an early Christian martyr, made a vow of virginity when she was 7 years old. At 12 she married, and on the wedding night, her husband "demanded the marriage debt" (sexual intercourse). She refused, citing her vow of years past. Her husband gave her time to reconsider her vow, with the admonition that unless she relented, he would have four horses pull her body apart the next morning. She remained adamant, as did her husband, and she indeed was killed the next morning. Other examples are not as dramatic. St. Silvia, a virgin, refused to bathe. She washed only her fingertips for more than 60 years. It is not difficult to understand why there were so many virgins at this time. Jerome advised women, especially virgins, never to bathe because to see oneself nude would be an occasion of sin. In his letter to Laeta, he advised this mother of a 14-year-old daughter not to allow her daughter to bathe for this very reason.

The status of women fell drastically during this time. Women, after all, were considered to be the source of evil. If not for Eve, Adam would not have sinned. She led him to the devil's temptation and enticed him into sin. The concept of women as evil took deep root at this time; some early Church fathers became so entrenched in their belief in the inferior position of women that one theologian even stated that he believed that women were nothing but phlegm and bad blood. But women were needed despite all their supposed bad characteristics, for women begat the Church's most prized possessions, future followers and believers.

In spite of negative attitudes toward women, and in contrast to the desire of the other early family types for male children, the Christians wanted daughters because they stood a better chance of remaining virginal. It is easy to see with these early teachings how the sexual philosophy of traditional repressive asceticism began and permeated the sexual value structure of the early Christians. These feelings, with all the positive and negative values and attitudes attached, have certainly stayed with us to the present time. Sex is something to be done with someone with whom one has a positive emotional relationship. In some conservative Christian religions, procreation must still be a possibility. The violations that occur during daily transactions in our sexual lives are violations only because somewhere someone somehow designed arbitrary norms to establish normalcy and deviancy. The feelings of violations must somehow be negated. It is no wonder that a person feels somewhat helpless because of "normal" transgression of standards devised by statistics, culture, and religion.

❖ THE FAMILY IN THE MIDDLE AGES

As the family moved into the Middle Ages, the Church seized control and still exercises control to a great extent over attitudes and values on sex. The Church ecclesiastically mandated a list of sins that proscribed certain sexual acts that the Church believed were against natural and Church law. For example, masturbation was considered to be a sin punishable by a year of penance. Subsequent acts of masturbation resulted in longer periods of penance outside the church, including confessing this sin to passersby and collecting alms for the Church. Women were considered to be sinners if they loitered around the church building after midnight. There were sanctions against having sex with one's spouse on holy days and for 40 days before and after

Easter, and against acts of homosexuality. Obviously, birth control and abortion were viewed as abominations, because neither would lead to population increase, thus violating the primary purpose of marriage.

Sex during this time became intimately connected with procreation. And the status of women fell dramatically. The wife, a carnal creature, satisfied the carnal nature of man. Under the Church's view, the pure love relationship should never be consummated or tainted by sex unless one could not control oneself. True love at this time was an idealized, platonic arrangement, a love that was often never consummated.

Under the ever-watchful eye of the Church, sex was utilitarian—its sole purpose was procreation. This position was so firm that the Church went so far as to consider it sinful for a husband and wife to have sexual intercourse once the wife passed childbearing age.

The writings of the early Church fathers provided reinforcement for the position. Murstein (1974), for example, found that married persons who had coital relationships were believed by the Church to have committed only a venial sin as compared to the grave sins of those involved in fornication and adultery. Women were made for the man, and thus should occupy a position inferior to that of the man. Tertullian further added that women were the gateway to the devil, and because of their sin in the Garden of Eden, the Son of God had to die (Murstein, 1974, p. 94). Such attitudes were slow to change.

The Church laity received mixed messages. Paul, St. Augustine, and Thomas Aquinas were spokesmen for the married. St. Paul viewed sexuality within marriage positively when he reluctantly endorsed marriage if for no other reason that the Church needed new members. And many marriages of the time were arranged and devoid of true love or even attraction. One marriage involved a girl of 5 who had to be carried into the church in the arms of the priest.

But sex still had a degrading connotation attached. For example, newlywed couples were encouraged to refrain from sex on their wedding night. If they could not restrain themselves, they could pay the Church a moderate fee, which would allow the act to occur. In addition, a man who had intercourse with his wife could not go to church until after he bathed. A newlywed couple could not attend church until 30 days had passed after their wedding. Upon their return to church, they were to bring a gift as a form of penance. After childbirth, the woman had to wait 40 days before she could return to church.

There were proscribed days when sex was taboo. At one time, husbands and wives could have intercourse only on Tuesdays and Wednesdays. The other days were taken up with the duty of being a good Christian.

The Middle Ages was truly a time of intense struggle for power between the Church and the State. One manner in which the Church was able to gain such control was to gain authority over marriage and the family. This they did and did well. There were Church laws passed that allowed sexual intercourse only on certain days of the week (as mentioned earlier) and demanded that coitus terminate when procreation was not a biological possibility. It refused to allow divorce, allowing separation "from bed and board." Members of the Church were now bound to the arbitrary rules and Church laws passed by a professed celibate clergy.

As time passed into the early 20th century, especially in the United States, sex was being viewed more as a right of both sexes. Women demanded and won equal rights in all stages of their lives. While the women's movement has not been completely successful, as men generally are compensated more than women in the workplace, women have won the right to exercise their freedom in the area of sex and sexuality. The development of the birth control pill and other methods changed the course of women's sex lives at least to the extent that they were now biologically free to engage in recreational sex without the worry of an unwanted pregnancy. Finally, technology caught up with emerging values.

❖ CURRENT SEXUAL STANDARDS

Attitudes toward sex and sexuality have changed drastically since the time of the early Jewish family. In the early history of the United States, sex was still viewed as a method of propagation of the species. At the beginning of the 20th century, the status of women was still low. Women were beginning to elevate their own status, fighting for their own rights—the right to vote, for example—and as the society moved into the mid-20th century, women were demanding equal rights in all spheres of their lives, including their sexual lives and identity.

The old double standard began to crumble in the 20th century, but there is no doubt that remnants of the standard are still with us today. There are still many who believe that it is permissible for men to "sow wild oats" but not for women. Where did we get this idea and value? Such values and attitudes have been passed down from one generation to the next, with each generation accepting, changing, and adding to it in various ways. What is needed at a particular time by one generation influences what is deemed important and vital to the existence of the society.

Consider the current relatively liberal attitudes toward homosexuality, birth control, and abortion. All three of these practices represent some form of population control. If, because of some natural or human-made catastrophe, society suddenly needed a great increase in the number of children born, it is reasonable to expect that there would be a change in society's values and attitudes toward these practices.

The sexual standards that are apparent in today's society reflect the current needs of society. The philosophy of traditional repressive asceticism of early family forms is no longer a mainstream sexual standard. Sex only for the male and solely for procreation is not a viable standard for members of today's society. We have also moved away, as a society, from restricting sexual expression to those persons who are married.

The modal sexual expression appears to be sex with love or strong affection. This is coupled also with a sense of strong commitment and maybe even a plan for marriage. Of course, there are some who believe that love or strong affection is really not needed for sex to occur; swingers (mate swappers), for instance, hold to a sexual fun philosophy in which sex is viewed as recreational or even athletic. In the chapter on nuisance sex offenses, we will speak to swinging as a functional alternative to prostitution. Swinging, as an example of fun morality, is making a comeback on the American sexual scene. With the aid of the Internet, people can e-mail one another and exchange formatted pictures across the nation sharing not only their most intimate thoughts but also their own fantasies. Many will disagree with the practice of swinging, but the swingers we have talked with appear to love their partners and have compartmentalized their sexual practices, one having to do with love and the other with recreation and athleticism.

Some people feel that sex is too restricted, even among those who are in love and share some form of personal and relational commitment. This hedonistic philosophy includes the view that virginity, chastity, and monogamy are outdated and to a degree nonsensical. Those who hold this philosophy—a true "playboy" philosophy of sexual anarchy—may believe it a "waste" to restrict oneself to one partner or to be virginal. In this philosophy, virginity and faithfulness in monogamy are viewed as less than desirable. One should exchange sexual favors, and to restrict these favors is to circumvent one's own pleasure as well as those of the various partners one may come into contact with. Needless to say, not everyone agrees with either of the sexual philosophies.

❖ SEX IN THE 21st CENTURY

The sexual standards of today are a modification of the sexual standards and practices of yesterday. It would be nonsensical to believe that, just because we live in the 21st century, we are beyond the molding and shaping of sexual folkways and mores of years and generations past. We are products of that time and of those people. The emphasis that St. Paul placed on the celibate and nonsexual life of the early Christian has been passed down to this present generation. It is somewhat modified, and we do not all live in the traditional repressive ascetic tradition. Some may say that is unfortunate while others would argue that sex is something to be enjoyed. True, for many, love or strong affection must still accompany sexual acts between consenting adults. Others will argue that sex is a behavior not unlike tennis to be shared among consenting adults, none forced, and none clandestine.

So, what are the current standards that we live by in this new millennium? There are several, and let us examine each in this section.

The days of the old double standard is fading. The double standard holds that sex is something to be enjoyed for males only. Sex for enjoyment is the purview of the male, and he will practice sex with those females under his control. Women are not to enjoy sex, and they are to be sexually active only when procreation is a possibility. The sole purpose of sex for the female is to continue the survival of the species. The purpose of sex for the male is a combination of enjoyment and procreation. Needless to say, the main purpose for him is enjoyment and relationship enrichment. The content of this chapter makes it easy to see where the origins of the sexual philosophy arose. The sexual proscriptions of the early Church leaders demanded sexual behaviors that were in line with the teachings of the Church and its insistence upon morality in all aspects of life, including the sexual part.

There is a reverse double standard also. This sexual standard allows complete sexual freedom for the female while restricting the sexual activities for the males. This has never been a general sexual standard for any society. In most societies, the culture allows males more freedom in their sexual lives than females. In this philosophy, however, the males are not allowed any more sexual behaviors than the females in the single standard philosophy. Obviously, since historically societies have been controlled by males, the men would not allow this type of sexual standard to become the norm. Women are to be kept in a subservient position. Women were seen as chattel. They were to be under the control of the men, as fathers, husbands, and slave owners. Men, then, would not permit a sexual standard that would allow women to receive more pleasure than the male counterpart.

There is a third standard, the one and a half standard. In this standard, the old double standard is kept for the male. The man may have as many sexual partners as he may have without the necessity of love or strong affection. For the female, she may be sexual with a male with whom she feels love or strong affection. What this does in effect is to allow the woman sexual experiences before marriage as long as there is love or strong affection.

But perhaps the most common of sexual standards in today's society is the single standard. In this standard, both the male and the female are allowed sexual behaviors regardless of love or strong affection. In other words, what is good for one gender is equally as good and desirable for the other gender.

In our classes we have determined that most of our students subscribe to this single standard. Also, we have found that most of the students are also of the humanistic liberalism philosophy that allows sexual activities when love and strong affection is present and also when a strong sense of commitment is present that suggests a committed relationship in the present with some envisioning of marriage in the future. The marriage may be some time in the future, but it is an envisioned goal for both.

What we have determined then from our students—hardly a random sample we will agree—is that the young people of today are not as sexually active outside committed relationships as we may have once believed. Their relationships are with few others and especially with those whom they believe they share a future as a committed dyad.

❖ CONCLUSION

Sexual behavior has changed drastically through the ages, both in purpose and in character, from a strictly utilitarian purpose with procreation as a goal to goals of recreation and enrichment. But even with these different approaches to sex, and from a position that many would consider to be behavior within the normal range, there are many who operate outside what are now considered acceptable parameters of sex and violate the law in the process—individuals whose sexual behavioral patterns society has judged to be not only out of the normal but criminal as well.

❖ DISCUSSION QUESTIONS

1. Explain how each family type has influenced our modern families' sexual behavior and attitudes.

2. Trace the evolution of the status of women as the family changed through the centuries.

3. Which sexual standard is the most prevalent in American society today?

4. Are there cultural differences in sexual standards? subcultural differences? gender differences?

5. What do you consider the major benefits or liabilities of a single standard of sexual behavior? Give your reasons.

❖ REFERENCE

Murstein, P. (1974). *History of the Family.* New York: Praeger.

4

Nuisance Sex Behaviors

❖　❖　❖

There are many sexual behaviors that are completely abhorrent to the senses of most Americans. These practices become more visible as scores of sex offenders are placed in correctional institutions throughout the United States. Sex offenders in prisons currently number more than 234,000 *(Bureau of Justice Statistics, 2004)*. The preponderance of those offenders are involved in rape and other violent sex crimes.

However, there is a growing amount of serious literature that suggests that many rapists, lust murderers, and sexually motivated serial murderers have histories of sexual behavior that reflect patterns that in the past have been considered only nuisances—not behaviors to become seriously concerned about

Erotolalia

Deriving major sexual satisfaction from talking about or listening to talk about sex

Erotomania

A compulsive interest in sexual matters

(Holmes & Holmes, 2001; Masters & Robertson, 1990; McCarthy, 1984). Rosenfield (1985), for example, found that 62% of sex offenders in a prison sample revealed deviant sexual acts other than those for which they were sent to prison. This position will be reinforced by other studies we will cite later in this chapter. They admitted to sex acts such as incest, frottage, voyeurism, and bestiality. Sexual acts that cause no obvious physical harm to the practitioner or the victim we term *nuisance sex behaviors*. This chapter is devoted to discussion of these activities.

Nuisance sex behaviors are often viewed in a less serious fashion than sex crimes that cause serious trauma *and* death. But there may be great benefit in analyzing those who commit such nuisance sex acts; such analysis may indeed hold the key to understanding those who move into more serious sex offenses. While it may be true that Ted Bundy was a serial killer and a serial rapist who practiced anthropophagy and voyeurism in addition to being a necrosadistic sex offender, he admitted he started off his sex crimes as a voyeur when he was 9 years old (authors' files). Rule (2005) reports that Randy Woodfield, an incarcerated killer, exposed himself as a juvenile. Another sadistic killer admitted during an interview in prison that he also started peeping into the windows of women in his neighborhood when he was 9 years old. Neither of these three started their sexual crimes with rape or murder. They "progressed into degeneracy" (Holmes & Holmes, 2001).

❖   FETISHES AND PARTIALISMS

Scoptophilia (Voyeurism)

Scoptophiliacs (generally male), also known as voyeurs, receive sexual arousal by looking at private or intimate scenes. Money (1984) states that voyeurism is an allurement paraphilia. A *paraphilia* is an erotosexual condition of being recurrently responsive to, and obsessively dependant on, an unusual or unacceptable stimulus, whether perceptual or in fantasy, in order to have a state of erotic arousal initiated or maintained and in order to achieve or facilitate orgasm, since it involves a segment of the preparatory phase of an erotic and sexual encounter (Money & Werlas, 1982).The *Diagnostic and Statistical Manual of Mental Disorders* (DSM-III-R) attaches to this definition a time frame of "over a period of at least 6 months"(American Psychiatric Association, 1987). Kafka (1995) defines paraphilias as sexual impulse disorders characterized by intensely arousing, recurrent sexual fantasies, urges, and activities that are considered deviant with respect to current cultural norms. A paraphilia may be coupled with a compulsive force as well (Abouesh & Clayton, 1999).

Forsyth (1996, p. 279) believes voyeurism must contain a sexual component, "watching persons who are undressing, undressed, or in

---

Pictophilia

The deriving of one's principal sexual satisfaction from erotic pictures of nude paintings, drawings, or the like

---

the act of sexual intercourse." We believe that this paraphilia is broader than Forsyth's definition. Obviously, there are varying degrees of scoptophilia. Viewing X-rated videos or movies or reading hard-core pornography can be viewed as one form of voyeurism. Spying on people who are involved in sexual intercourse is quite another. Even watching popular television shows, like *Court TV*, may be a form of voyeurism (Valkenburg & Patiwael, 1998), although not the type of voyeurism that we are currently inspecting, but one that is more congruent with our definition. While our definition suggests that voyeurism must be construed on a continuum, there are certain elements that set it apart from the normal act of viewing a beautiful body or a nude painting. Many men would secretly peek into a window or through a keyhole in hopes of catching sight of a woman undressing, bathing, or interacting with a sexual partner if they knew there was no risk of detection. It would be a rare male who would not look at an attractive woman in a skimpy bathing suit at the beach (Haas & Haas, 1990, p. 552; Lahey, 1989, p. 527). Some voyeurs, though, will go to great pains to capture a look—one man reportedly attached mirrors to his shoes to catch reflected images from under women's skirts. We anticipate that the concept of voyeurism can be better understood if the invasion of a private scene becomes an integral part of the definition.

Erickson and Tewksbury (2000) developed a typology of voyeurs who frequent adult strip clubs. The clubs were visited using a "peripheral-member-researcher" technique. Each type had certain manners of behavior while viewing nude women in various acts in the club itself. The man experiences a gratifying sensation but it is actually the women, the dancers, who held the power in the club itself (Erickson & Tewksbury, 2000).

Acrophilia

Sexual arousal from heights or high altitudes

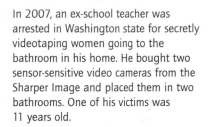

In 2007, an ex-school teacher was arrested in Washington state for secretly videotaping women going to the bathroom in his home. He bought two sensor-sensitive video cameras from the Sharper Image and placed them in two bathrooms. One of his victims was 11 years old.

SOURCE: *Seattle Times*, January 8, 2007

Types of Patrons in a Gentlemen's Strip Club

The lonely

The socially impotent

The bold lookers

The detached lookers

The players

The sugar daddies

SOURCE: Erickson & Tewksbury (2000)

The Internet has emerged as a source of personal and sexual gratification for the voyeur. One study reports that hidden JPGs on several channels fulfills the need of some paraphiliacs to invade typically private sexual scenes. The study suggests that the hidden format provides a functional alternative to the typical and historical behavior of the voyeur. In this sense, the person can access a channel that presents pictures of persons who are not aware of the invasion of their privacy. Sometimes pictures are posted with the consent of the person or persons in the picture (Holmes, Tewksbury, & Holmes, 1998).

The categories offered with Holmes et al.'s typology of the hidden pictures are broad and general. The pictures, usually in JPG or GIF format, sometimes are sent to an f-Server for inclusion into the collection of pictures, which will be arranged into categories. Other times, pictures are traded by one person with another. Sometimes the pictures are said to be of a wife or significant other, and the traders are trusted to send pictures of their own. The viewer is a voyeur, and in some cases the person(s) within the picture may have some traits and characteristics of the exhibitionist.

At a university, a maintenance man was arrested by the police for voyeurism. The man had erected a video camera in a woman's restroom. The camera was mounted in the ceiling and the lens was barely visible through the ceiling tile.

He had the responsibility of cleaning the restrooms in this classroom building. He would close the room while cleaning it and remove one tape from the camera and inserting another.

At times he would climb into the ceiling and watch the coeds sitting on the commodes. On the occasion of his arrest, one female student was in a stall when the cleaning man fell through the ceiling and into the next stall. The police were called and the man was arrested.

Money (1984, 1985) states that the voyeur learns from experience and will look for scenes that he can easily visually invade. His erotic excitement is in the forbidden act of looking at off-limits scenes that are private. Rarely will the scoptophiliac attempt to meet the victim or communicate with her. Seto and Kuban (1996) label the voyeur as "courtship disordered," since this paraphilia often interferes with normal courtship functions. Typically, after the act occurs, the scoptophiliac will move to a place where he can masturbate.

Voyeurs typically are not exhibitionists, but Abel, Abraham, Sullivan, and Harris (1988) report that in fewer than 2% of the cases they studied did voyeurs admit to only one paraphilia. The average number of paraphilias, including exhibitionism and frottage, was 4.8 per person. These authors also point out that in their study of 561 sex offenders, when multiple paraphilias existed in a single offender, one paraphilia initially was dominant. A second paraphilia then developed and overtook the first in dominance while the first continued for a number of months or even years, but at a greatly reduced intensity. Freund & Seto (1998) stated that voyeurism is less prevalent than exhibitionism as the etiology escalates into rape. The dynamics of the etiology of the voyeur does not seem to be severe enough to result in a violent sex offender, such as the rapist.

Categories of JPGs

Bathroom

Beach

Innocents

Cartoon

True crime

Oddities

Sexual activities

Bondage/discipline

Hidden

Exhibitionism

SOURCE: Holmes, Tewksbury, & Holmes, 1998

Nonetheless, though the practice is characterized as a nuisance sex practice, it still is objectionable.

In each scoptophiliac's mental state, there is a fantasy that provides a script for behavior. Sometimes the fantasies are violent and sadistic in content (Seto & Kuban, 1996). In addition, as with many other sexual paraphilias, voyeurism contains an overwhelming desire *(compulsion)* to spy upon a complete or virtual stranger who is in some stage of undress, having sexual intercourse, or in some other intimate situation (Freund & Blanchard, 1986). Many will

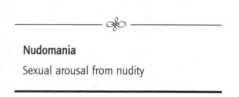

Nudomania

Sexual arousal from nudity

take extreme steps to satisfy this compulsion to invade the privacy of others.

But what kind of person is a voyeur? As suggested above, it may be true that there is a little bit of voyeur in each of us. But in those whose fantasy and compulsive psychological constructs override their better judgment, there appear to be some common characteristics.

Characteristics of the Voyeur

Voyeurs appear to be both sexually immature and frustrated (Chesser, 1971). Dwyer (1988) reports that often voyeurs deny they are sex offenders, have poor relationships with their fathers, have had overprotective mothers, have experienced early sexual trauma (which makes it more comfortable for them to see sex from afar), invoke religious justifications, lack sexual and social skills, have low self-esteem and high self-criticism, and do not take personal responsibility for their behavior. Other characteristics of voyeurs include great feelings of inadequacy and inferiority; also, many are quite young, often in their early 20s (Crooks & Baur, 1983, p. 595).

Table 4.1   Traits of Scoptophiliacs

- Sexually immature
- Sexually frustrated
- Poor relationship with the father
- Overprotective mother
- Childhood sexual trauma
- Poor social and sexual skills
- Low self-esteem and high self-criticism
- Young and chronic masturbator

Most voyeurs do not have serious criminal records, and, as a rule, they do not molest their victims (Katchadourian & Lunde, 1975). Still, as mentioned above, some serious sex offenders reportedly began their careers as sex criminals as voyeurs. Ressler (1986b) found that 71% of the sex-related murderers he studied reported early interests in voyeurism.

The etiology of the voyeur is not clearly understood; the cause is probably multifaceted, with biological, social, and cultural determinants (Holmes & DeBurger, 1988; Weiner & Rosen, 1999). The condition of the voyeur seems to have no particular treatment prescription. Lindsay, Marshall, Nelson, Quinn, and Smith (1998) studied two groups of offenders. One was treated in group therapy sessions and the other was treated individually. The group sample appeared to have adjusted better and the individual therapy group was not as successful. It may nevertheless be that the background of this offender is more a predictor of successful rehabilitation than the type of treatment offered (Furnham & Haraldsen, 1998). Or it may be for some voyeurs it is simply a matter of willpower (Twohig & Furnham, 1998). The method of treatment certainly deserves more study.

Prostitution

Prostitution is the exchange of sexual favors for economic or monetary gain. Prostitution takes many forms, and it is necessary to look at its various forms and the extent of its practice to get some idea of its dynamics.

Perhaps the most visible type of prostitution is the streetwalker. This sort of prostitute selects clients from the people who encounter the person on curbs and street corners. We both witnessed the practice firsthand when we were at Times Square recently. In barely a two-block walk we were approached three times for sex. Unfortunately, many will judge all prostitutes as streetwalkers. The streetwalker probably has the most dangerous of jobs in prostitution. A streetwalker does little screening of clients, which has led to many injuries and deaths among them. Many of the murders done by the Green River Killer in Seattle were streetwalkers hawking for customers (johns) along the fog line by the Sea-Tac Airport. Once the prostitute enters the vehicle of the client, the prostitute is now in the comfort zone of the client and is at their mercy. There are other dangers that all prostitutes face but perhaps are more common with the streetwalker: for example, disease, beatings, murder.

Other prostitutes work at clubs or strip bars. In addition to being an exotic dancer, the dancer may be coerced or physically forced to work as a prostitute. The johns then are typically the customers of the bar or club. Some bars have rooms reserved at the club for prostitution dates, so that the sexual encounters are done at the place of employment. The employer provides some safety for those in a dual career as an exotic dancer and prostitute.

The interview with Joyce took place over five years ago. She is still a prostitute, has been arrested several times for prostitution, still is on drugs, and is now a prostitute walking the streets in a high-crime area of the city. She looks much older than her years, and when we talked with her a month ago, she said that she has AIDS. Joyce is a model for the stereotypical bad things that happen to prostitutes in the downward spiral of their career development. At the time of her initiation into prostitution, she was very active during several of the city's conventions. She also was very busy during the week of the Kentucky Derby, when her contacts at the hotels secured customers for her on a split-fee basis. All these opportunities have faded along with her looks and health.

Excepts From an Interview With a Prostitute

The following is a taped interview with a 23-year-old prostitute. She has been a prostitute for five years. After graduating from an all-female private high school, she decided against college. Moving into several short-term menial jobs, she decided to turn to prostitution. This is a segment of her story.

Joyce—Out of all the girls I knew who are prostitutes, none of them came from the wrong side of the tracks. Only one came from less than a middle-class income, and one's parents were real wealthy. It was more rebellion that anything else.

Interviewer—How long have you been involved in this work?

Joyce—Since I was 18. That would be 5 years. It just happened. It was kind of, um, well, it was really funny, to be honest with you. We both had mutual girlfriends (motioning to the another prostitute in the room) whose father is kind of sick. In a lot of ways he was our good buddy. He would let us get away with things our parents wouldn't let us do. He introduced me to this lady. I had left home and was living with his daughter. She was really a neat lady. I thought that she was out of this world, and I really liked her. She fixed me up with this guy. Ginny was quite a bit older than me, and I still love her dearly. I said that I would go out with him, why not? I went out with him—and I hadn't slept with any more than three guys before in a period of a year because I was a virgin until the time I was 17—and we had a good time, too many drinks, and I went to bed with him. About four o'clock in the morning he got up to leave and gave me a hundred dollars. I had no conception of the idea that he expected to pay me. I didn't expect any money. The guy could have kept his money if he had any sense, I didn't know anything about it. So Ginny said that this was something that she did every once in a while. I said, "Well, that's great because that was about what I was making in a week at my job. So why not?" It just got to be a regular old habit. When I was too tired to go to work in the morning, I just wouldn't go. I quit my job. Then I was making more than two thousand dollars a week, all tax-free, and I had everything I wanted. Unfortunately, it all went up my nose and through a needle. In the past year, I made more than $100,000. You know how much I have in my bank? Nothing. Zero. (authors' files)

There are other forms of prostitutions. There are professional call girls who cater to a small but usually professional clientele. They often operate out of the nicer hotels and demand a higher fee for their services. Other prostitutes operate from massage parlors and small nude "encounter group" sessions. There are also male prostitutes, who usually involve themselves sexually for pay with other men.

Prostitution on the Internet

The proliferation of the Internet across the world has been a medium for not only the prostitute to advertise services but also for the exploitation of prostitutes (Hughes, 2003). Many prostitutes find nude pictures of themselves on the Internet after permitting their customers, for a charge, to take their pictures. Often stories accompany the pictures purported to be enacted fantasies, case histories, or the like.

Advertisements of sex for pay on the Internet take many forms. There are websites for massage parlors, independent prostitutes who do not work through an agency, escort agencies, and other sites. Although not found as yet in the United States, Sharp and Earle (2003) reports a site in England, "Punternet," that contains over 5,000 reviews of prostitutes in that country.

Issues in the Etiology of the Prostitute

What causes someone to become a prostitute is not clearly understood. Parsons, Bimbi, Koken, and Halkitis (2005) reports that child abuse, emotional, sexual, or physical, overwhelmingly plays an integral role in the etiology of a male prostitute. Fraad (1997) believes that many prostitutes come from homes where there is sexual abuse, particularly incest. In talking with several prostitutes we found that most of the women were disenfranchised from their own family, and most were also involved in drug use and alcohol abuse and maintained a relationship with a man who often served as an informal pimp. He was there for her protection and often took a great deal of her money. The women all had arrest records for prostitution. The beat police officers also knew the women and the strolls they walked. One officer stated that he mostly leaves the women alone unless there is some type of altercation between the prostitution and the john. He then arrests both. He added that he only worries about the women when he fails to see them after a day or two; he knows then that something has happened to them.

Percentage of Arrests for Prostitution by Race of Females in the U.S. 2004			
White	*Black*	*American Indian or Alaska Native*	*Asian or Pacific Islander*
57.2	40.3	0.8	1.0

SOURCE: www.infoplease.com, August 30, 2006

Consequences of involvement in prostitution are many and complex. On the one hand, some would believe there are no inequities in income between the genders. Weinberg, Shaver, and Williams (1999) report that women receive a higher pay than men in prostitution. Pyett and Warr (1999) and Stratford, Ellerbrock, Akins, and Hall (2000) report client violence and the risk of infection with sexually transmitted diseases from clients who refuse to wear condoms as unwanted consequences of being a prostitute. Many women who work in clubs where exotic dancing is the main drawing activity report that they were forced into prostitution (Kay, 1999). For many women who face the prospect of homelessness and extreme social isolation find the consequences of that prospect far outweighs the risks associated with prostitution (Sweet & Tewksbury, 2000).

Facts of Prostitution

- 70% of prostitutes have experienced multiple rapes by their customers, pimps, and strangers
- Some prostitutes are raped between 8 and 10 times a year
- Of those raped, fewer than 10% seek medical care
- Of those who are raped and are streetwalkers about 5% have been raped by police officers or those who produce badges and police identification
- More than 3 out of 4 prostitutes have considered suicide
- 85 to 90% of prostitutes who are arrested are streetwalkers
- At least 75% of prostitutes were sexually abused as children
- The average age of a woman who enters prostitution is 14
- It costs about $2,000 to arrest a prostitute
- Prostitution in the U.S. is a $14.5 billion industry.

SOURCE: Prostitutes Education Network, "Prostitution in the United States—The Statistics," http:www.bayswan.org/stats.htm; Promise for Women Escaping Prostitution, "Facts About Prostitution," http://www.sirius.com/~promise/facts.html

---

Triolism

One distinct form of scoptophilia is triolism. This paraphilia is a sexual pattern in which erotic stimulation is gained by watching oneself or oneself with others in sexual scenes. It appears from the literature that triolism may take several forms.

First, some triolists will gain sexual arousal and gratification from seeing themselves in some form of sexual scene. Some may photograph themselves in sexual acts. Jerry Brudos, a serial killer from Oregon, took pictures of himself in women's clothing, of his wife nude, and of at least three of his murdered victims. Ceiling mirrors, instant cameras, and video cameras may all be used by this type of paraphiliac in seeking sexual gratification (Ellis, 1986, pp. 26–28).

There are other triolists who seek pleasure by sharing a sexual partner with another person while the triolist looks on. An estimated 8 million couples have experienced this type of sexual behavior (Avery & Johannis, 1985, pp. 27–30). Triolism may also take the form of two couples having sexual relations at the same time in sight of each other. While there are single swingers, usually when one speaks of swingers in this context we are speaking of married or committed couples (Cargan, 1986). Swingers, or mate swappers, are often termed triolists, and at other times it is termed candaulism. In candaulism, a man exposes his partner, or pictures of her, to others. Sometimes women are coerced into the swinging scene to fulfill the desires of their husbands (Bowman, 1985, pp. 84–86; Jenks, 1998; McCary, 1978, p. 334).

Jenks (1985) reports that swingers are generally nondescript members of the community, but there are some characteristics that those in his study tended to have in common:

Candaulism

The practice of forcing one's partner to expose himself or herself or to become sexually involved with others (swinging)

- Had moved often in the past five years
- Were relatively new to the community
- Were members of the middle class
- Were conservative in their political views
- Identified little with religion
- Belonged to more community groups than nonswingers

There are two types of swingers, open and closed. Open swingers join national and local swinging clubs and have a wide range of sexual partners. Joining a club such as Select or Kindred Spirits, the swinging couple is exposed to a large number of persons who are potential partners (Holmes & Holmes, 2002). Closed swingers, on the other hand, have sexual experiences with only a few people, usually personal acquaintances.

Five Common Fears of the Swinger

- Fear that the children will discover their behavior
- Fear that family and relatives will discover they are swingers
- Fear that the employer will find out
- Fear of disease
- Fear of intimacy

Swinging cuts across socioeconomic lines—construction workers, physicians, nurses, professors, ministers, housewives, engineers, and others are represented in the triolist population. It is their preoccupation with sex that distinguishes them from the nonswinging population (Avery & Johannis, 1985, p. 30). The fun moralist, the swinger, sees sex for the sake of pleasure and can compartmentalize sex apart from love.

———————— ✀ ————————

Swinger Ad

C35-393—Married couple, 32 & 33, would like to hear from other married couples in the Louisville area for swinging & friendship. No B&D, husband is safe. We guarantee to be discreet and answer all ads with a photo and phone.

In the ad above, a married couple has placed an ad in a swinger's magazine. The couple is looking for other kindred spirits to have casual and impersonal sex with. Note the ad says no B&D (bondage and discipline). The ad also informs other couples that the husband is "safe," that is, has a vasectomy. Many couples will insist upon a photo when they receive a reply as well as an address and a phone number. One can see therefore that this sexual practice leaves one open to discovery. Many swingers will simply not answer ads that contain a post office box number.

Welcome to Our Web Page

We are Johnny and Kati, 26 and 27, respectively, living in Gastonia, NC. We have been together for three years and have experimented in the lifestyle for about one and a half years. And just recently joined Carolina Friends.

We enjoy watching TV, playing on the computer, going to movies and clubs, and cooking out. We also enjoy working out, aerobic exercise, running, and spending time with our children.

We are looking for couples, single men or single bisexual women, for friendship, fun, and games.

Interested? E-mail us and let's talk and perhaps get access to our secure and very racy webpage!

NOTE: The web page address has been deliberately omitted by the textbook authors.

There may also be a homosexual aspect to mate swapping. Sadock, Kaplan, and Freedman (1976) report that the practice allows the husband to see another male sexually active with his partner and in this way a small percentage of men can take the opportunity to explore various homosexual impulses. (See also Money & Musaph, 1977) Other research suggests that in most cases the husband forces the wife into swinging, but then it is the wife in most cases who wants to continue (D. Dixon, 1985; J. Dixon, 1985; Holmes, 1972).

J. Dixon (1985) reports that swinging couples appear to be sexually adjusted and that the swinging couples report better sexual experiences from these engagements than from traditional sexual liaisons with their current partner. They are just as likely to be accepting of premarital sex, homosexuality, prostitution, and drug use as nonswingers (Jenks, 1985). The emerging fear of AIDS may account for a perceived reduction in the number of couples who engage this sexual practice (Ramey, 1986). How real this decrease is seems to be unknown. We believe that the rate of

In 9 cases in 10, the husband talks the wife into swinging.

In 9 cases in 10, the husband wants to stop first.

swinging dropped for a while but has been increasing in the last few years as evidenced by the number of magazines, websites, and other methods of advertisement available.

Triolism seldom comes to the attention of those in law enforcement unless it affects family or personal functioning. Since so many are "in the closet," it is not known what the full impact of triolism is on sexual functioning. Obviously, a case such as Brudos is not at all typical of the many others who are involved in this paraphilia. Swinging, as a form of triolism, has been studied, but it does not appear to be a form of behavior that is, by itself, necessarily detrimental to the family (D. Dixon, 1985;

Polyamory

Literally means "loving more than one." More commonly means having a sexual relationship with more than one person.

J. Dixon, 1985; Holmes, 1972). The risk of AIDS and other venereal diseases certainly influences the decision of some triolists whether to become intimately involved with total strangers or even close friends in a swinging arrangement (Haas & Haas, 1990, pp. 321–322).

The etiology of voyeurism and its accompanying paraphilias are not clearly understood. Many believe, including these authors, that it may stem from an early exposure, by accident, to a nude body while dressing or undressing, without the consent of the naked person, in a private place such as one's bedroom. Since we do not understand the basic etiology, successful treatment must depend on the desires of the person to change. Behavioral counseling may be the best manner, while drug therapy does not hold any great promise.

Exhibitionism

Exhibitionism is the deliberate exposure of one's genitals under inappropriate circumstances. There are obviously appropriate places to expose oneself, for example, during sexual activities, a medical examination, and so forth. Typically, the exhibitionist (usually male) will expose himself to female strangers in public places, such as in parks, at bus stops, and in schoolyards. Exhibitionists are typically young, and many start their episodes when they are in their teens. While no one knows the exact number of such offenders in American society, it is estimated that many people every year are victims of the exhibitionist. There are some behaviors that involve deliberate exposure of the body parts—for example, "mooning"—that is not sexual in context even though a usually private part of the body has been exposed. At Mardi Gras, many visitors will disrobe and expose breasts, buttocks, and other body parts in exchange for ceremonial beads (Shrum & Kiolburn, 1996). This is not the type of practice we are concerned with here.

Exhibitionism

Over a period of at least 6 months, recurrent, intense, sexually arousing fantasies, sexual urges, or behaviors involving the exposure of one's genitals to an unsuspecting stranger.

The fantasies, sexual urges, or behaviors cause clinically significant distress or impairment in social, occupational, or other important areas of functioning.

SOURCE: Criteria summarized from American Psychiatric Association (1994). *Diagnostic and statistical manual of mental disorders* (4th ed.). Washington, DC: Author.

The exact reasons exhibitionists expose themselves are unclear. One theory is that the act of exposure, accompanied by masturbation, serves as a means of reducing stress. Of course, sexual excitement from the exposure itself should not be ruled out. Another theory is that a female has somehow damaged the exhibitionist and he is lashing out against all women in the hope that his psyche can be restored. Yet another theory is that the exhibitionist suffers from extreme feelings of personal inadequacy and a low sense of masculinity and needs affirmation to reinforce these feelings. Some theorize that the exhibitionist feels anger and resentment toward people in general and women in particular. The exhibitionist's intent, in directing the attention of others toward his genitals, is to shock and degrade the viewers.

Agoraphilia

Sexual arousal from open spaces or having sex in public

Agrexophilia

Sexual arousal from others knowing the person is having sex

For the exhibitionist, the sexual act is not intercourse, but exposure. By shocking the female victim, the exhibitionist reinforces the sense of power he needs for personal fulfillment. Having exposed himself to someone, the exhibitionist will often go to a private place in order to masturbate.

The reaction of the victim is important to the exhibitionist. If the victim is frightened, the exhibitionist experiences sexual excitement and may be impelled to masturbate. It is very rare for such a paraphiliac to have any type of direct physical relationship with a female to whom he has exposed himself. If a victim responds to an exhibitionist in a sexual manner, he will typically be bewildered, because the victim is not behaving in an appropriate way; thus, he is likely to run away but, in rare cases, some exhibitionists may later have a personal contact with his victims (Detroit Medical Center, 2007). Although no absolute relationship between exhibitionism and further sex crimes has been found, it is clear that some offenders do move from this type of crime to more serious ones (Detroit Medical Center, 2007).

The treatment of the exhibitionist is uncertain at best. There is disagreement even on the overall strategy. For example, one group may be in favor of aversion therapy and another group not (Ball, 1999). Psychotherapy with others seems to hold promise, especially with the younger exhibitionist (Paul, Marx, & Orsillo, 1999). Others recommend that true rehabilitation can only occur with long-term incarceration and treatment using a cognitive-behavioral treatment plan (Horley, 1995). In this therapeutic scenario, the long-term treatment is the recommendation of Lindsay et al. (1998), who admits that recidivism is extremely high among these types of sex offenders if for no other reason that the exhibitionist often believes that the victim shares some responsibility for the offense. Regardless, the therapist must be aware that the exhibitionist has personal issues of trust, shame, and the need for immediate gratification that must be addressed and resolved (Miner & Dwyer, 1997).

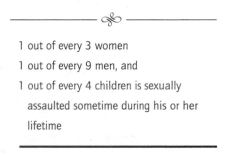

1 out of every 3 women

1 out of every 9 men, and

1 out of every 4 children is sexually assaulted sometime during his or her lifetime

SOURCE: The Women's Center, Louisville, KY, anonymous personal communication, January 2007

Transvestitism

The transvestite is typically a heterosexual male, often married, who dresses in the clothes of the other sex initially because of sexual reasons. Later, the transvestite will cross-dress to reduce stress. The transvestite may believe that the world of the female is a less stressful one. The perception may be that women are not faced with the same set of societal pressures. Thus, for a short period of time, the transvestite will enter that world and become part of a mental world where stress is reduced and the individual can live, if only temporarily, with some sense of mental peace.

This use of cross-dressing for stress reduction comes later, some time after the initial decision to cross-dress for sexual reasons. One transvestite said

> When I first started to cross-dress I was 5 years old. I was a little guy and found these large panties of my grandmother's. I tried them on, and they wrapped around me. But there was something magical about the panties. I even had some type of feelings in my genitals even at that age. I didn't know what it was at the time but it felt good.
>
> Later, when I married, I told my wife. She was not very understanding of my situation. She honestly tried to understand me, but she had too many prejudices and our married failed.
>
> Since my divorce I started go to some gay bars in town and even some adult bookstores. You would be amazed at how many people like myself I have found. Now I associate with these guys all the time. We go to athletic events, movies, and some other places. We also go to gay bars in town sometimes, well, most of the time dressed in drag. It really isn't pure sex all the time. Sometimes it just feels good. (authors' files)

The exact etiology is unknown. It may be that they suffer from an extremely low self-esteem (Bordan & DeRicco, 1997). It may also be that for some reason the world of the female appears to hold pleasant memories or it may be a place where there are fewer pressures than men normally experience in their lives. Many transvestites start their cross-dressing at an early age and accompany it with masturbation. Some classify the transvestite as a fetishist. We do not concur with this classification for the transvestite. We view the transvestite as a person with an inordinate desire for cross-dressing and note that the practice is not tied to one particular fetish object.

Many transvestites have learned to deal with their sexual proclivity and seldom come into contact with the criminal justice system. A social worker in an emergency room at the University of Louisville Hospital related that more than a few times she has attended male auto accident victims who, when their outer clothes were removed, were revealed to be wearing panties, bras, garter belts, and other items of women's apparel.

As stated above, the transvestite typically commences cross-dressing at an early age, and the cross-dressing becomes intimately attached to sexual feelings. The TRI-S (Society for the Second Self), a national self-help group for transvestites, states that after a few years, the transvestite recognizes that there is another dimension to cross-dressing. For a short period of time, while dressed in women's clothing, the cross-dresser retreats to the world of the female, a world in which he perceives there is little stress. In that time, he is in a world where there are few demands made on him, unlike the demands he faces in his male world.

Jerry Brudos was a transvestite. He had a fetish for women's high-heeled shoes and wore many pairs he stole from his victims (Stack, 1983). He also insisted that his wife wear a pair of his stolen shoes and even made at least one of his murdered victims wear the shoes immediately before he killed her. After killing four women, Brudos was arrested, charged, and convicted of three murders. He was sent to the Oregon State Penitentiary in 1968. One author (Ronald M. Holmes) has seen Brudos several times at the Oregon State Prison. He refused to be interviewed because his case was still under appeal! Brudos died in prison in March 2006.

It would be a mistake, however, to assume that all transvestites are sex offenders and come into contact with the criminal justice system as Jerry Brudos did. It is unlikely that anyone can accurately estimate the number of men who are transvestites. It is for most a hidden sexual behavior.

The transvestite should not be confused with the transsexual. The transsexual is a person has gender personal identity problems. The transsexual is biologically one gender and psychological the other. To rectify this situation, many transsexuals will undergo the pain and the expense of matching the body with the mind. The preoperative transsexual must determine whether the pain and the expense of surgery is sufficient to discourage going through with the operation. The decision is not easy to make, despite the lifelong pain and

---

Note from a transvestite

I am a 50 year old miner, of slight build and with 30 years of toil underground behind me. But I, Fiona, have a lifetime of clandestine experience, very mixed experience, to reflect on. It took me 45 years finally to come to terms with what I am and always have been. Oh! the relief. To come, at last, to understand, accept, develop, and enjoy, and cast off the cloak of guilt and self-imposed stigma.

SOURCE: http://www.beaumontsociety.org.uk/ March 17, 2001

mental suffering the transsexual endures because of being "trapped" inside an alien body. It may be exciting for someone to fantasize about inhabiting the body of the other gender, but to actually have to live within that body with no hope of realigning the mind with the body is another question.

The postoperative transsexual is one who has completed the sex reassignment surgery. While historically more males than females have sought the surgery, it now appears that the percentage is now almost equal (HBO Special, "What Sex Am I?" aired January 2007).

Frequently Asked Questioned on Transsexuals or Transgendered

What does transgendered *mean?*

A transgendered person is someone whose gender identity differs from conventional expectations of masculinity or femininity. Their gender identity differs from their physical sex as assigned at birth.

Who are transgendered people?

Transgendered persons include preoperative and postoperative transsexuals; transgenderists (persons living full-time in a gender opposite their birth sex with no desire to pursue surgery); transvestites (preferred term: cross-dressers, those whose gender expression occasionally differs from their birth sex); "mannish" or "passing" women, whose gender expression is masculine and who are often assumed to be lesbians, though this is not necessarily the case. Transsexual and transgenderist persons can be female-to-male (transsexual or transgendered men) as well as male-to-female (transsexual or transgendered women).

Are transgendered people gay?

Most transgendered persons identify themselves as heterosexual. Their intrinsic difference is their gender identity, not their sexual orientation: these are two different things altogether. However, transgendered people are perceived by most people as homosexuals, and thus are discriminated against in similar ways.

While cross-dressing is in itself often not a crime, there are some jurisdictions that dressing in another sex's clothing is against the law and the person is liable for arrest. This the law is worded to apply only to the male. Some jurisdictions make it illegal to be partially cross-dressed, for example, in bra and panties although not completely in drag.

The motivation to cross-dress often varies. As we have observed, the initial reason to cross-dress may be sexual, but later motivation arises the motivation is to enter into the world of the female where stress is viewed as lower. One may argue about the accuracy of the perception of the world of the female; but from the transvestite's perception of stress is less.

Infantilism

Some adults are interested in a sexual play activity in which they pretend to be helpless infants. Sometimes the persons participating in this dress play will wear diapers (diaperism) and drink milk from a baby bottle capped with a nipple. Sometimes the willing female partner will permit the partner to suckle at the breast while pouring milk onto the breast to simulate lactation.

The practitioner will also wear diapers and baby clothes during a sexual encounter. With some, the person will urinate and defecate into the diaper and wants the partner to change the diapers.

There is a national organization of practitioners of this paraphilia, the Diaper Pail Friends (www.dpf.com/aboutdpf.html). It claims a membership of more than 15,000. Practitioners are called adult babies (Abs), diaper lovers (DLs), and consenting partners. This form of paraphilia should not be confused with any form of sexual child abuse, pedophilia, incest, or other forms of child molestation.

Why does one choose to practice infantilism? There is no simple answer to this question. At first blush, one would think it is totally sexual. But there does appear to be an element of stress reduction for the practitioner of this form of sexual activity. This is similar to an element that is present in the practice of transvestitism.

Scatophilia

There appears to be some disagreement over the similarities between exhibitionists and those who make obscene telephone calls (scatophiliacs). In scatophilia, however, the acts are more aggressive and yet more distant than in exhibitionism (Nadler, 1968). The erotic gratification is gained from the narrations that transpire between the caller and the victim rather than from any form of genital sex.

In both cases, offenders typically are male, feel inadequate, have problems in developing relationships, experience feelings of isolation, perceive their fathers as supermen, and feel that their mothers never loved them (Oliver, 1974). Also in both cases, the act of either deliberately exposing himself or making an obscene telephone call is the only manner in which the paraphiliac can express himself sexually. Matek (1988) reports that imagery plays an important role for obscene phone callers. Some scatophiliacs may cross-dress to increase the sexual excitement (Dalby, 1988). Fantasy plays a large role; the caller hears the victim but does not see her. The telephone connection itself provides a pseudointimate scenario (Greenberg, Bruess, Mullen, & Sands, 1989; Matek, 1988).

Like the exhibitionist, the scatophiliac wants his victim, the person on the other end of the phone line, to be shocked, disgusted, or horrified by his demeanor or words. The scatophiliac depends on this reaction for erotic arousal and to facilitate orgasm through masturbation (Crooks & Baur, 1983; Money, 1980).

Of course, not all obscene phone callers are alike. Murray and Beran (1968) report five types of callers: obscene, anonymous, humorous, witty, and miscellaneous. Leising (1985) identifies three other types of callers: the chronic caller who is open about his reasons for calling (sexual), the caller who begins with a believable sexual problem but then becomes graphic or vulgar, and the sexually abusive caller who describes in a cold, detached manner how he raped or assaulted a female victim.

The obscene telephone caller typically makes his calls by dialing random phone numbers. Fortunately, obscene callers seldom make personal contact with persons they have called. Ressler (1986a), however, reports that in his sample of murderers who rape and mutilate, 22% reported interest in obscene phone calls; he does not mention what percentage of his sample followed up after making such calls. It appears, in any case, that the danger from the obscene phone caller is minimal. Of course, this maybe of little comfort to his victims (Dannenmeyer, 1988; Mano, 1985).

Narratophilia

Receiving sexual gratification or stimulation from listening to sexual stories (The term may apply to the passive partner in obscene telephone calls.)

If a person is victimized by an obscene caller and Caller Id is blocked, the telephone company can provide a pen register, which records the number where a call originated to a party's phone, or a polarity trap, which locks in the two numbers until the telephone company chooses to release the phones.

Technology has made it easier for the obscene phone caller. Professional narrators are employed by such companies as the Erotic Telephone Network and Dad Giils. These dial-a-porn services are a multimillion-dollar industry (Weir, 1987). In New York, for example, one such service paid the phone company $25,000 a day for subscriber service. The New York Telephone Company earns about $15 million a year from such payments. The service companies themselves also spend millions of dollars in advertising (Mano, 1985). Dannenmeyer (1988) found that the average cost to the consumer of live sex phone calls is $6; and the average cost for a recorded obscene message is $3.85. (Parents are often concerned about their children making calls to commercial dial-a-porn services; they may now have their phone companies block any calls from their phones to 900 or 976 numbers.

There are also obscene letter writers. These paraphiliacs will send letters to persons or organizations in the hope of eliciting the same reactions sought from the victims of obscene phone calls. Recently one author (RMH) was asked to offer a psychological profile of someone leaving obscene phone messages at the local airport. The man left messages two to three times a week at the airport and on at least one occasion mailed a note through the U.S. mail. The notes complained of the condition of the airport, but most of the content of the letter discussed his own interest in anal sex, acts of coprolagnia, and other such sexual paraphilias. The author met with the airport security and offered a profile detailing such items as age, race, sex, and education. The chief of the police unit at the airport stopped the discussion of the profile, reporting that the man had been arrested only a short time before. It happened that the psychological profile was fairly accurate. The man was educated, a Ph.D., married, from the local area, a professional educator, and a professional acquaintance of the authors. The man was arrested and in court entered a plea agreement that kept him out of jail and also out of federal prison, since sending obscene material through the U.S. mail is a federal offense.

Frottage

A frotteur is a paraphiliac who realizes sexual gratification from rubbing against certain body parts of another person. Often, this occurs when the victim, typically a stranger, is in a crowded but public place, such as a shopping center, elevator, or subway (Campbell, 1989, p. 294). Frotteurs experience fantasies that are accompanied by strong, irresistible urges to touch others. The fantasies often center on imagining that the victim wishes to have a caring, affectionate relationship with the frotteur (American Psychiatric Association, 1987, p. 283). The fantasies are often fueled by pornography that depicts acts of frottage (Templeton & Stinnett, 1991). Such depictions can be found on the Internet in addresses that deal with this form of paraphilia. For example, the Frottage Men's Club (mindspring.com/~frottage/page2.html) is such a location. On this website, which is predominately for male homosexuals, one can post instant messages, access a bulletin board, and place a personal ad.

The process of toucherism (another name for frottage) includes the fantasy, the urge to touch, the selection of a victim, the touching itself, and a preferred place where masturbation usually occurs. The process of

———————— ✄ ————————

Frottage

Derivation of sexual satisfaction by rubbing one's genitals or hands, even when fully clothed, against the body part of another, usually a stranger

offending includes an escape plan. The victim selected fits the frotteur's ideal victim type. The victim is viewed as sexually attractive, usually wearing tight-fitting clothes. The frotteur rubs his genitals against the victim's thighs or buttocks or fondles her genitalia or breasts (Encyclopedia of Mental Disorders, 2005). Victims often are amazed that this could be happening in public. In more than a few cases, victims may in fact reciprocate (Money, 1984).

The frotteur typically starts his behavior by adolescence, and most of the acts occur when the offender is between the ages of 15 and 25. This type of sexual disorder is found in a pronounced degree only in males; frotteurs are often intelligent, and most belong to the middle and upper classes. As is the case with many other paraphiliacs, frotteurs often have other types of paraphilias. Abel et al. (1988) report that the "average" frotteur has at most four other sexual "perversions."

It does not appear that the frotteur is a great danger to society. At the same time, the treatment of such offenders does not offer a *great* deal of optimism for change. It may be a reasonable concern that frotteurs may move into other types of sexual behaviors that offer more danger to others.

Klismaphilia

Klismaphilia is sexual arousal linked with receiving an enema, either in fantasy or in actuality (Bartol & Bartol, 1999; Cooper & Sacks, 1986). The klismaphiliac has become erotically fixated on the eliminatory function. How an individual becomes involved in klismaphilia is unknown. Lesee (1984) reports that it is often possible to pin down an early history of too much ado about enemas in the infancy of those who as adults practice this erotic behavior (also see Money, 1984).

———————— ✄ ————————

Catheterophilia

Sexual arousal from the use of catheters

Males especially are excited by klismaphilia and experience erections when they are administered enemas as youths (Haas & Haas, 1990; Knox, 1984, p. 403). But there are also women who practice this sexual behavior and who use it as a masturbatory device. Some consider it a substitute for genital intercourse.

The klismaphiliac can lead a normal life, with no one suspecting this sexual interest (Denko, 1973). Klismaphiliacs often indulge in their taste privately and secretly; at most, they may try to get others (usually males seeking females) to administer an occasional enema under the guise of constipation and attempt to conceal their pleasure from the administrator (Stoller, 1986, p. 6). But there are other devotees who practice klismaphilia in a variety of homosexual, transvestite, sado-masochistic, and other settings. Those in this latter group do not want to change, nor do they feel any form of shame because of their behavior (unlike those in the first group) (Denko, 1976).

There is no waning of interest in this sexual behavior. In fact, with the current focus on variant sexual practices, klismaphilia will probably become more widely discussed and perhaps more widely practiced. There is an abundance of websites that cater to the klismaphiliac. They offer goods for sale and also chat channels for those who wish to "talk" with others about their activities. These websites also attempt to legitimize and make the practice sound normal by stating that Marilyn Monroe and Mae West were both klismaphiliacs (www.nndb.com/lists/396/000086138/).

Bestiality

A common sexual theme found in pornography is bestiality, or sex with animals. Early history shows that bestiality has been chronicled from a long time. In ancient Greece a moral creature was one who obeyed his impulses. If sex was desired and no human being with a suitable orifice was available, a horse, mule, or deer was considered suitable (Dover, 1986). In 1300 A.D., an English law made sex with animals a capital offense. The penalty was later changed to life imprisonment, and then amended to 10 years in prison (Crew, 1986, pp. 70–71; Parker, 1987, p. 663). In early colonial America, Thomas Grange was burned to death for alleged crimes against a mare, a cow, two goats, five sheep, two calves, and a turkey. Recent reports from Los Angeles tell of a man who, after fights with his girlfriend, sought revenge by raping her pet chicken. After the second incident, the chicken died (Bullough, 1988).

Bestiality occurs in either sex. A male might, for example, induce or force an animal to perform oral sex upon him or may perform manual manipulation upon the animal. A female might induce an

In Waterloo, Iowa, a 46-year-old man was arrested by the police in the act of having sex with a sheep. Students at a local community college found the man naked and hiding in a hayloft at the college farm. A blue nightgown was found next to the sheep, and a halter rope was tied around the ewe's neck and its legs were positioned in such a way that its hindquarters were raised.

The man was charged with animal abuse because Iowa does not have a law prohibiting sex with animals.

SOURCE: APBNews.com, October 28, 2000

animal to perform sexual intercourse, cunnilingus, or other forms of sexual stimulation.

Another form of bestiality is termed *formicophilia*. In this paraphilia, sexual arousal comes from small creatures—ants, snails, and the like—crawling on a person's nipples or genitals (Dewaraja, 1987). Zoophilia is different from bestiality in that it includes no actual sexual contact with the animal. Contact with the animal takes the form of stroking or fondling only (Campbell, 1989, p. 810). Zoophiliacs should not be confused with those who have a pet and show affection for the family pet. Zoophilia is an unnatural fondness for animals, and, while short of sexual contact with an animal, does involve some distancing from human contacts (and in some instances from sexual contacts) to form physical but noncoital or otherwise sexual contacts with animals.

Arachnophilia

Sexual arousal from spiders

There is a darker side to bestiality. In the work that we have done with serial killers, we have noted that several had a history of cruelty to animals. Jeffrey Dahmer is such an example (Holmes & Holmes, 2001). He was thought to not only perform surgery on animals already dead but there are strong rumors that he tortured animals until they were dead. This was also true in the case of Henry Lucas (Egger, 1998; Norris, 1988), and other serial killers mentioned by (Hickey, 1997) and (Holmes & Holmes, 2001). This particular form of bestiality is coupled with an element of sadism, which is called zoosadism. This form of sexual paraphilia is an indicator of possible later sexual problems for violent sex offenders.

Zooeroticism

Deriving or seeking sexual satisfaction from relationships with animals

---

Outside Seattle, the authorities were notified a man had died while recording of video of having sex with a farm animal. Washington state is one of 17 states that do not have laws against bestiality.

The *Seattle Times* reports that a man died of acute peritonitis from perforation of the colon. He was 45 years old. In most cases the farm animal is a female. In this case the horse was a male. The police stated they are not investigating the case, since no law has been broken.

The farm is well known in the area as a place where people can visit and pay to have sex with an animal and have the act videotaped.

SOURCE: Seattle Times, "Videotapes show bestiality Ecumclaw police say," July 16, 2005.

How prevalent is bestiality? It has been reported that 17% of rural males have at some time experienced orgasm with an animal (Ammons & Ammons, 1987). The most common animals involved have been calves, sheep, dogs, cats, geese, and hens. Bestiality is perhaps best viewed as an act committed by many people, but typically when there is no suitable human partner. Although it does not involve a significant number of people, it continues to be an outlet for some.

Saliromania

Sexual gratification received from the destruction of defilement of nude statutes or paintings of females

---

Pygmalionism

The name of this sexual paraphilia comes from the classic story of Pygmalion, who fell in love with a statue he had himself made. Pygmalionism (sometimes called agalmatophilia), is a sexual attraction to a statue, doll, or mannequin. The inflatable doll, the collapsible doll, and other such items are very popular in adult bookstores. Pygmalionists may be persons who are, for one reason or another, unable to relate personally and sexually to other human beings. They have power and control over the inanimate object, and, moreover, the object can never reject their advances.

Technology has made many advances that can aid persons who have atypical sexual interests. In the case of the pygmalionist, for example, some of the more expensive dolls available have cassette players located within their "bodies" that can be used to play types that utter obscene words or phrases (coprolalia).

Gerontophilia

Gerontophilia is the use of an elderly person as a sexual object. This paraphilia is not easy to detect because of cultural influences on mate selection. For example, it is not uncommon for a woman to marry a much older man. It may indeed be that there is sometimes a financial element to this choice of partner.

When a young man assaults elderly women, it falls into the category of sadistic gerontosexuality (Ellis & Abarbanel, 1961). Typically, this type of offender manifests the following traits: obsessive personality, a history of enuresis until about the age of 25, a lack of interest in younger women, an inability to contain impulses, and a tendency to be violent and aggressive sexually (Oules, Boscredon, & Bataille, 1977). Additional characteristics include a need for power or a sadistic intent to do physical damage.

Rapes of elderly women are rare; only about 3% of all rapes involve victims over the age of 50. But when an elderly woman is raped, there is a stronger threat to life, and this attack often results in the murder of the victim (Bopp, 1987). The psychopathology of those who molest and murder older victims is more pronounced than that of those who assault younger women (Pollack, 1988). The incidence of this paraphilia is quite rare, but when it does occur in men, it often becomes dangerous. In women, the motivations behind gerontophilia are usually quite different; the gains are more often material than psychological.

Mysophilia

Mysophilia is an erotic interest in filth. While some professionals believe mysophilia is a form of masochism—it is difficult to imagine that someone can be amused or aroused by what many persons consider to be repugnant—it is indeed true that dirt, feces, and so on are erotically arousing to some. Some men, for example, are aroused by women's soiled underwear (McCary, 1978). Even erotic vomiting has been reported (Stoller, 1982). Hazelwood, Dietz, and Burgess (1983) tell of a young man who inserted a corncob into his rectum and then walked outside, dug a hole, and made mud using a garden hose. He then covered himself with mud and engaged in autoerotic asphyxia (for a discussion of autoeroticism, see chapter 10).

Automysophilia

Sexual arousal from being dirty or filthy

In Columbus, Indiana, police arrested an 11-year-old boy who had broken into a home to steal the woman's underwear.

The police stated that the boy was seen entering the house and was arrested as he was ransacking the dresser in the woman's bedroom

The police said they believe that the boy had broken into other homes to steal bras and panties.

The police remarked, "He (the boy) has some issues."

SOURCE: APBnews.com, December 19, 2000

Coprolagnia and Coprophilia

Mysophilia is also found in the forms of coprolagnia and urolagnia, in which erotic gratification is associated with feces and urine, respectively. The practice of urolagnia can take place by one person urinating into the mouth or onto the body of another person. Prevalent in the homosexual community, the practitioners are called golden shower devotees. In some major cities there are urolagnia *clubs,* where members hold meetings to engage in various "water sports," including urinating on each other and drinking urine (Shelp, 1987). Haas and Haas (1990, p. 557); report that about 4% of men and women have experienced "golden showers." One reported case involved a 17-year-old boy who consumed snow contaminated by horse and cow urine, and, while working as a part-time janitor in a school, drank from unflushed toilets (Dense, 1982, pp. 336–338).

Coprolagnia has been reported for years. Chesser (1971) tells of a Russian nobleman who insisted that his mistress defecate upon his chest. Another man had prostitutes relieve their bowels in a golden saucer, and he would eat the feces with a golden spoon. Recently a nurse died after being admitted to a hospital for the third time for a serious illness. After a thorough police investigation, it was ascertained that she had been injecting into her arm a mixture of water and the feces of her pet parrot.

Undinism
Sexual attraction to urine

Coprolagnia is not only a perverse form of sexual behavior, at least in the view of most people, but it can also be quite dangerous to the health of the practitioner because of the bacteria in feces and other potential health problems. Urolagnia, in contrast, poses no great health hazard. Urine from an otherwise healthy person is sterile and poses no great health risk. In the military, for example, the drinking of one's own urine is taught as a survival technique to prevent dehydration.

❖ CONCLUSION

There are many kinds of sexual expression, some of which members of a society approve and some of which they condemn. This chapter has dealt with behaviors that are probably considered by most to be either matters of personal preference or at least not vital societal concerns. In the next chapter, far more extreme forms of sexual expression will be discussed: incest and pedophilia. These two sexual behaviors directed against children must be viewed in a most serious fashion. In every case, the child is viewed as a victim.

❖ DISCUSSION QUESTIONS

1. Are there other nuisance sex crimes that are not included in this chapter? What are they? Explain them to the class.

2. Of the sex crimes and behaviors listed in this chapter, which do you consider to be most serious or dangerous? Why?

3. Bestiality is considered by many to be a victimless crime. Do you agree? Disagree? Give reasons for your position.

4. Have you even been victimized by an exhibitionist? What were the circumstances? How did you react? How did the exhibitionist react?

5. Connect to a website that concerns itself with one of the sex behaviors discussed in this chapter. What is the website address? What was the focus of the website? Was there a particular forum or policy discussed?

❖ REFERENCES

Abel, G., Abraham, T., Sullivan, T., & Harris, R. (1988). Multiple paraphiliac diagnoses among sex offenders. *Bulletin of the American Academy of Psychiatry and the Law, 2*(2), 153–168.

Abouesh, A., & Clayton, A. (1999). Compulsive voyeurism and exhibitionism: A clinical response to paroxetine. *Archives of Sexual Behavior, 28*(1), 23–30.

American Psychiatric Association. (1987). *Desk reference to the criteria from DSM-III-R.* Washington, DC: Author.

American Psychiatric Association (1994) *Diagnostic and Statistical Manual of Mental Disorders. Fourth Edition* (DSM-IV). American Psychiatric Association, Washington, D.C.

Ammons, C., & Ammons, R. (1987). Research Note. *Psychological Reports, 60,* 153–159.

Avery, C., & Johannis, T. (1985). *Love and marriage.* New York: Harcourt Brace Jovanovich.

Ball, C. (1999). Treatment of exhibitionism: Comment on R.H. et al. *Behavior Therapy, 30*(4), 725–726.

Bartol, C., & Bartol, A. (1999). *Criminal behavior: A psychosocial approach* (5th ed.) Englewood Cliffs, NJ: Prentice-Hall.

Bopp. W. (1987). *Crimes against women.* Springfield, IL: Charles C Thomas.

Bordan, T., & DeRicco, M. (1997). Identity formation and self-esteem in the male transvestite: A humanistic perspective. *Journal of Humanistic Education and Development, 35*(3), 156–162.

Bowman, H. (1985). *Marriage for moderns* (7th ed.). New York: McGraw-Hill.

Bullough, V. (1988). Historical perspective. *Journal of Social Work and Human Sexuality, 7*(1), 15–24.

Bureau of Justice Statistics (2004). *Criminal Offender Statistics*. Washington, DC: Retrieved October 17, 2007 from http://www.ojp.usdoj.gov/bjs/crimoff.htm#sex

Campbell, R. (1989). *Psychiatric dictionary.* New York: Oxford University Press.

Cargan, L. (1986). Stereotypes of singles: A cross-cultural comparison. *Archives of Sexual Behavior, 27*(3-4), 200–208.

Chesser, E. (1971). *Strange loves: The human aspects of sexual deviation.* New York: William Morrow.

Cooper, A., & Sacks, F. (1986). *The personality of disorders and neurosis.* New York: Basic Books.

Crew, L. (1986). *The gay academic.* New York: ETC.

Crooks, R., & Baur, K. (1983). *Our sexuality.* Menlo Park, CA: Benjamin/Cummings.

Dalby, J. (1988). Is telephone scatologia a variant of exhibitionism? *International Journal of Offender Therapy and Comparative Criminology, 32*(1), 45–49.

Dannenmeyer, W. (1988). Our house (banning dial-a-porn). *National Review, 409,* 32.

Denko, J. (1973). Klismaphilia: Enema as a sexual preference. *American Journal of psychotherapy, 27,* 232–250.

Denko, J. (1976). Klismaphilia: Application of the erotic enema device. *American Journal of Psychotherapy, 30,* 236–255.

Dense, R. (1982). Undinism: The fetishization of urine. *Canadian Journal of Psychiatry, 27,* 336–338.

Detroit Medical Center. (2007). *Special report.* Detroit. Michigan.

Dewaraja, R. (1987). Formicophilia, an unusual paraphilia, treated with counseling and behavioral therapy. *American Journal of Psychotherapy, 41,* 593–597.

Dixon, D. (1985). Perceived sexual satisfaction and marital happiness of bisexual and heterosexual swinging husbands. *Journal of Homosexuality, 11,* 209–222.

Dixon, J. (1985). The commencement of bisexual activity in swinging women over age 30. *Journal of Sex Research, 11,* 115–124.

Dover, K. (1986). *Greek homosexuality.* Cambridge, MA: Harvard University Press.

Dwyer, M. (1988). Exhibitionism/voyeurism. *Journal of Social Work and Human Sexuality, 7,* 102–112.

Egger, S. (1998). *Serial murder: An elusive phenomenon.* Englewood Cliffs, NJ: Prentice-Hall.

Ellis, A. (1986). *Time encyclopedia of sexual behavior.* New York: Hawthorne.

Ellis, A., & Abarbanel, A. (1961). *The encyclopedia of sexual behavior.* New York: Hawthorne.

Encyclopedia of Mental Disorders. (2005). Frotteurism. Retrieved March 14, 2008, from http://www.minddisorders.com/Flu-Inv/Frotteurism.html

Erickson, D., & Tewksbury, R. (2000). The "gentlemen" in the club: A typology of strip clubs. *Deviant Behavior: An Interdisciplinary Journal, 21*(3), 271–293.

Forsyth, C. (1996). The structuring of vicarious sex. *Deviant Behavior, 17*(3), 279–295.

Fraad, H. (1997). At home with incest. *Rethinking Marxism, 9*(4), 16–39.

Freund, K., & Blanchard, R. (1986). The concept of courtship disorder. *Journal of Sex and Marital Therapy, 12*(2), 79–92.

Freund, K., & Seto, M. (1998). Preferential rape in the theory of courtship disorder. *Archives of Sexual Behavior, 27*(5), 433–443.

Furnham, A., & Haraldsen, E. (1998). Lay theories of etiology and "cure" for four types of paraphilias: Fetishism; pedophilia; sexual sadism; and voyeurism. *Journal of Clinical Psychology, 54*(5), 689–701.

Greenberg, J., Bruess, C., Mullen, K., & Sands, D. (1989). Obscene phone callers. *Journal of Social Work and Human Sexuality, 11*(1), 15–25.

Haas, L., & Haas, J. (1990). *Understanding sexuality.* Boston: Mosby.

Hazelwood, R., Dietz, P., & Burgess, A. (1983). *Autoerotic fatalities.* Lexington: D.C. Heath.

Hickey, E. (1997). *Serial murderers and their victims.* (2nd ed.). Pacific Grove, CA: Brooks/Cole.

Holmes, R. (1972). *Sexual behavior: Homosexuality, prostitution, and swinging.* Beverly Hills, CA: McCutcheon.

Holmes, R., & DeBurger, J. (1988). *Serial murder.* Newbury Park: Sage.

Holmes, R., & Holmes, S. (2001). *Murder in America* (2nd ed.). Thousand Oaks, CA: Sage.

Holmes R., & S. Holmes. (2002). Swinging: A Functional Alternative to Prostitution. In R. Holmes and S. Holmes (Eds). *Current Perspectives on Sex Crimes,* pp. 13–23. Thousand Oaks, CA: Sage.

Holmes, R., Tewksbury, R., & Holmes, S. (1998). Hidden jpgs: A functional alternative to voyeurism. *Journal of Popular Culture, 32*(3), 17–29.

Horley, J. (1995). Cognitive behavioral therapy with an incarcerated exhibitionist. *International Journal of Offender Therapy and Comparative Criminology, 39,* 335–339.

Hughes, D. (2003). Prostitution online. *Journal of Trauma Practice, 3*(3–4), 115–131.

Jenks, R. (1985). Swinging: A test of two theories and a proposed new model. *Archives of Sexual Behavior, 14,* 517–527.

Jenks, R. (1998). Swinging: A review of the literature. *Archives of Sexual Behavior, 14,* 507–521.

Kafka, M. (1995). Current concepts in the drug treatment of paraphilias and paraphilia-related disorders. *CNS Drugs, 3*(1), 9–21.

Katchadourian, H., & Lunde, D. (1975). *Fundamentals of human sexuality.* New York: Holt, Rinehart, & Winston.

Kay, K. (1999). Naked but unseen: Sex and labor conflict in San Francisco's adult entertainment theaters. *Sex and Culture, 3*(1), 39–67.

Knox, D. (1984). *Human sexuality: The search for understanding.* St. Paul: West.

Lahey, B. (1989). *Psychology: An introduction* (3rd ed.). Dubuque, IA: William C. Brown.

Leising, P. (1985). The negative effects of the obscene phone caller upon crisis intervention services. *Crisis Intervention, 14,* 84–92.

Lesee, S. (1984). Klismaphilia. *American Journal of Psychotherapy, 51*(5), 175–183.

Lindsay, W., Marshall, I., Neilson, C., Quinn, K., & Smith, A. (1998). The treatment of men with a learning disability convicted of exhibitionism. *Disability, 19*(4), 295–316.

Mano, K. (1985, February). The phone sex industry: Part 2. *National Review, 37,* 59–60.

Masters, R., & Robertson, C. (1990). *Inside criminology.* Englewood Cliffs, NJ: Prentice-Hall.

Matek, O. (1988). Obscene phone callers. *Journal of Social Work and Human Sexuality, 11*(1), 15–25.

McCary, J. (1978). *McCary's human sexuality.* New York: Van Nostrand.

McCarthy, K. (1984, June 10). Serial killers: Their deadly bent may be set in cradle [interview with h. Morrison]. *Lost Angeles Times,* sec. 2, p. 6.

Miner, M., & Dwyer, S. (1997). The psychosocial development of sex offenders: Differences between exhibitionists, child molesters, and incest offenders. *International Journal of Offender Therapy and Comparative Criminology, 41,* 36–44.

Money, J. (1980). *Love and sickness.* Baltimore: Johns Hopkins University Press.

Money, J. (1984). Paraphilias: Phenomenology and classification. *American Journal of Orthopsychiatry, 38,* 164–179.

Money, J. (1985). *The destroying angel.* Buffalo, NY: Prometheus.

Money, J., & Musaph, H. (1977). *Handbook of sexology.* Amsterdam, Neth.: Elsevier/North Holland.

Money, J., & Werlas, J. (1982). Paraphilic sexuality and child abuse: The parents. *Journal of Sex and Marital Therapy, 8,* 57–64.

Murray, F., & Beran, L. (1968). A survey of nuisance telephone calls received by males and females. *Psychological Record, 18*(1), 107–109.

Nadler, R.(1968). Approach to psychodynamics of obscene telephone calls. *New York State Journal of Medicine, 68,* 521–526.

Norris, J. (1988). *Serial killers: The growing menace.* New York: Kensington.

Oliver, J. (1974). *Clinical sexuality.* Philadelphia: J.B. Lippincott.

Oules, J., Boscredon, J., & Bataille, J. (1977). A case of gerontophilia. *Evolution Psychiatrique, 42,* 243–257.

Parker, G. (1987). An exploration of bestiality as a crime. *Criminal Justice Abstracts, 19,* 663–671.

Parsons, J. T., Bimbi, D. S., Koken, J. A., & Halkitis, P. N. (2005). Factors related to child-hood sexual abuse among gay/bisexual male Internet escorts. *Journal of Child Sexual Abuse, 14*(2), 22–25.

Paul, R., Marx, B., & Orsillo, S. (1999) Acceptance-based psychotherapy in the treatment of adjudicated exhibitionists: A case example. *Behavior Therapy, 39*(1), 149–162.

Pollack, N. (1988). Sexual assault of older women. *Annals of Sex Research, 1*, 523–532.

Pyett, P., & Warr, D. (1999). Women at risk in sex work: Strategies for survival. *Journal of Sociology and Social Welfare, 35*(2), 183–197.

Ramey, J. (1986), Fear of AIDS in alternative life styles. *Society for the Study of Social Problems, 16*, 223–241.

Ressler, R. (1986a). Murderers who rape and mutilate. *Journal of Interpersonal Violence, 1*, 273–287.

Ressler, R. (1986b). Sexual killers and their victims: Identifying patterns through crime scene analysis. *Journal of Interpersonal Violence, 1*, 288–308.

Rosenfield, A. (1985, April). Sex offenders: Men who molest, treating the deviant. *Psychology Today*, 8–10.

Rule, A. (2005). *The I-5 killer.* New York: Signet.

Sadock, B., Kaplan, H., & Freedman, A. (1976). *The sexual experience.* Baltimore: Williams & Wilkins.

Seto, M., & Kuban, M. (1996). Criterion-related validity of a phallometric tests for para-philic rape and sadism. *Behavior Research and Therapy, 34*(2), 175–183.

Sharp, E., & Earle, S. (2003). Paying the price, UK network of sex work projects. from www.uknsw.org/uknsw/_Paying_the_Price_response.pdf.

Shelp, E. (1987). *Sexuality and medicine* (Vol. 2). Dordrecht, Neth.: Reidell.

Shrum, W., & Kiolburn, J. (1996). Ritual disrobement at Mardi Gras: Ceremonial exchange and moral order. *Social Forces, 75*, 324–358.

Stoller, R. (1982). Erotic vomiting. *Archives of Sexual Behavior, 11*, 361–365.

Stoller, R. (1986). *Sexual excirement: Dynamics of erotic life.* New York: American Psychiatric Press.

Stack, A. (1983). The lust killer. New York: Signet.

Stratford, D., Ellerbrock, T., Akins, J., & Hall, H. (2000). Highway cowboys, old hands, and Christian truckers: Risk behavior for human immunodeficiency virus infection among long-haul truckers in Florida. *Social Science and Medicine, 50*(5), 737–749.

Sweet, N., & Tewksbury, R. (2000). Entry, maintenance, and departure from a career in the sex industry: Strippers' experiences of occupational costs and rewards. *Humanity and Society, 2*(1), 136–161.

Templeton, T., & Stinnett, R. (1991). Patterns of sexual arousal and history in a "normal" sample of young men. *Archives of Sexual Behavior, 20*(2), 137–150.

Twohig, F., & Furnham, A. (1998). Lay beliefs about overcoming four sexual paraphilias: Fetishism, paedophilia, sexual sadism, and voyeurism. *Personality and Individual Differences, 24*(2), 267–278.

Valkenburg, P., & Patiwael, M. (1998). Does watching court TV "cultivate" people's per-ceptions of crime? *Gazette, 60*(3), 227–238.

Weinberg, M., Shaver, F., & Williams, C. (1999). Gendered sex work in the San Francisco Tenderloin. *Archives of Sexual Behavior, 25*(6), 503–521.

Weiner, D., & Rosen, R. (1999). Sexual dysfunctions and disorders. In T. Millon & P. Piney (Eds.). *Oxford textbook of psychotherapy* (pp. 410–433). New York: Oxford University Press.

Weir, S. (1987). Thrills on the line. *New Society, 81*, 17–18.

5

Incest

❖   ❖   ❖

It is important to remember that incest is not all physical contacts between an adult and a child that are expressions of love. Physical contacts between a father and a daughter, or a mother and her son, may run a gamut of acts that should not be arbitrarily termed incestuous. Sexual child abuse is the exploitation of the child by an adult. Incest is sexual involvement with a relative of the child with whom law prohibits marriage. It is easy to see, then, that incest and pedophilia are not synonymous. In cases of incest, the abuser may be the biological father, the stepfather, the mother, the stepmother, or a sibling. In addition, the repercussions, regardless of the perpetrator, are equally serious (Rudd & Herzberger, 1999).

❖ PHYSICAL AND
    NONPHYSICAL TYPES

Not all sexual contacts between the adult and the child involve physical contact. There may also be contacts that don't involve touching. Touching offenses are those that are normally thought of when one thinks of

—————— ⚮ ——————

What is incest?

Any use of a minor child to meet the sexual or sexual/emotional needs of one or more persons whose authority is derived through ongoing emotional bonding with that child.

SOURCE: Blume, S. (1987). Post-incest syndrome in women: The incest survivor's after effects checklist. Siecus Report, *15*(1), 1.

sexual activity: kissing, fondling, touching of the genitals, rape, and so forth. Nontouching sexual activity includes acts such as saying things

95

that arouse the interest of the child, exhibitionism, voyeurism, and patterns of sex play where the child is a viewer of the sex act.

Selected Statistics on Incest

- Research indicates that 46 percent (46%) of children who are raped are victims of family members (Langan & Harlow, 1994).
- The majority of American rape victims (61%) are raped before the age of 18; furthermore, an astounding 29% of all forcible rapes occurred with a victim who was less than 11 years old. Eleven percent of rape victims are raped by their fathers or stepfathers, and another 16% are raped by a relative (National Center for Victims of Crime and Crime Victims Research and Treatment Center, 1992).
- A nationally representative sample of state prisoners serving time for violent crime in 1991 showed that, of those prisoners convicted of rape or sexual assault, two-thirds victimized children and almost one-third of the victims were the children or stepchildren of the assailant (Greenfeld, 1997).
- In a study of male survivors of child sexual abuse, more than 80% had a history of substance abuse, 50% had suicidal thoughts, 23% attempted suicide, and almost 70% received psychological treatment. Thirty-one percent had violently victimized others. (Lisak, 1994)

❖ THE MALE PERPETRATOR

The most frequent incestuous relationship is between the father and a daughter. There are other offenders, such as grandfathers, cousins, and brothers. It is important to bear in mind that the victim can be either male or female. It is a myth that only little girls are involved in incest with the fathers. This is simply not true. Small sons may also be used for anal and oral sex. One prisoner interviewed said his biological father raped him until he was old enough to physically reject the attacks of his father. This man is presently in prison for rape and sodomy committed against his own family members, including his wife, sons, and three daughters. After participating in a prison rehabilitation program for sex offenders, he discovered personality faults within himself that included low self-esteem and low self-confidence. Despite this self-discovery, the parole board has not seen fit to release him from his long prison sentence.

There is some evidence to suggest that the younger the offender at the time of his abuse within the family, the more apt the offender is to use violence on the victim. Evidence suggests that, in the majority of the cases, the violence does not turn fatal (Holmes, 1983). The incestuous father, for example, is often found to be immature and have little self-esteem, with high expectations for the child he has selected for sexual abuse. It may be that males with conflicting and misunderstood sexual needs may seek their children as sexual partners. Or it may be a form of punishment, viewing the child as an extension of his own self. Of it may be that this is a manner of punishing the female partner. Regardless, the end product is that the child is punished, degraded, defiled, and humiliated by a powerful adult in a family setting.

❖ THE FEMALE OFFENDER

Mother and son or mother and daughter incest is thought to be quite rare. But it may be less rare than some believe.

Mother-child incest is rarely reported. On the other hand, this form of abuse may go underreported because of the unwillingness of society to accept that this form of illegal sexual activity occurs.

A Poem from Beth—An incest survivor

Silence is my agony.

I dare not speak.

I close my eyes tightly.

I dare not flinch.

I calm my breathing.

I mustn't give away that I am awake.

You touch me under my blankets, and groan.

I feel vomit rise to my throat.

Now you take away my blanket and spread my legs.

My heart pounds wildly.

I cannot jump and run.

I feel your tongue on me and I feel faint.

I see stars.

Misconceptions of the female incest offender:

Mother-son incest occurs only when intercourse occurs.

Boys cannot be victims of sexual abuse.

Sexual abuse is perpetrated only by males.

Motherly love is free of sexual intentions.

Mother-son incest is caused by mental illness. (Miletski, 1995)

I am going to DIE.

You are sucking the life out of me.

When you sucking the life out of me.

When you leave I can breathe again.

I get up and look into the mirror.

I see a monster.

It is me!

I want to DIE!

I can't live with the silence.

Why didn't I scream?

I strain to see the reason that I have caused all of this.

What is it about me that makes you act like this?

I am evil and I need to be destroyed.

Reprinted with permission of the Louisville chapter of Parents United.

❖ FAMILY RELATIONSHIPS AND INCEST

Families in which a child is victimized by an adult male contain relationships between the adult partners that are not equal. The male and the female do not see themselves as equal partners in the relationship. In some cases, the marriage is in trouble. For example, one partner may judge himself or herself to be superior in intelligence, earning power, or sexual prowess, and the inequality in the partnership is expressed in the sexual aggression against the child victim.

It may be that when one parent provides the primary financial support for the family, the other parent is unable to provide the nurturing needs of the family members. In some cases, the male relates to the adult female in the family as another child within the family, not as an equal. Sometimes the female may yield to such a secondary role within the family unit. Other times, she may leave the family or simply refuse to accept this social definition of inferiority. In this latter scenario, the child selected to be abused may have to accept the duties and responsibilities that were at one time provided by the physically or psychologically absent parent: cooking, cleaning, ironing, washing, taking care of the other children in the family. This often includes sexual duties.

❖ THE ETIOLOGY OF THE INCESTUOUS OFFENDER

Incest, like pedophilia, has many causes. One common motivational factor is retaliation against the female by the male partner for actual or imagined unfaithfulness. There also is, in many cases, a feeling of "entitlement" to one's own children, that they are the father's "sexual property." Among other parents who perpetrate incest, two general characteristics are a general lack of impulse control and a confusion of roles in which the child is seen as an object to fulfill the needs of the adult despite the child's inability to meet those needs. These two characteristics are common not only to instances of sexual abuse but also to child abuse cases in general. The practice of incest may cross from one generation to another. This point is well documented in many rural areas where incest has become a common practice among many families.

> **Sleep–a poem by DJ**
>
> Thunder raged across my bed,
>
> Screams emitted from my head.
>
> Daddy, please come and tell me it's okay.
>
> Dreams of bunnies
>
> Instead of snakes today.
>
> Boxes, boxes capturing me,
>
> Let me out was my plea.
>
> Here comes mother instead.
>
> I wish I lay here dead.

Reprinted with permission of the Louisville chapter of Parents United.

If there is more than one female child in the home, the male caretaker many times may abuse all these children, sometimes concurrently, but more often consecutively. Often the incest becomes public when the older abused daughter wishes to protect her siblings from similar abuse by reporting her own abuse. Other times, when the daughter determines that all the daughters in the family are victimized, after being told by her male parent that she was the "special" daughter, the "chosen" one, her sense of protectiveness for the others is lost and the trauma of her situation drives her to report the pattern of incest. In some other cases, a daughter reports the incest because the male caretaker refuses to allow the daughters to have friends outside the home. The male perpetrator of incest often has a rigid, uncompromising attitude when his daughter starts to show an interest in boys.

Incestuous relationships usually last from 1 to 6 years and start at various ages. Once many thought that teenagers were more often the victims than younger children. This may not be the case, but apparently in at least some families, the incest activity starts early in the children's lives. Girls are more often the victims, but the number of boy victims is beginning to increase (Holmes, 1983).

Father Raped His Daughter to Teach Her About Sex

A father in Charleston, West Virginia, was sentenced to prison for raping his 13-year-old daughter. He admitted to the judge that he raped his daughter to teach her about sex and birth control.

James Duncan was sentenced to two consecutive prison terms of 10 to 20 years.

In court, the judge remarked that there were other ways for teaching one's child about sex than raping her. The daughter, however, stated that her father did not do this for pleasure, that there was a message in his rapes. The defendant stated that his only motive was to keep his daughter from becoming an unwed mother.

SOURCE: APBnews.com, April 9, 2001.

In families with incest, there appear to be a set of problems that in some fashion enable the incest to start and continue. Trepper, Niedner, Mika, and Barrett (1996) report that incest is a symptom of a multiple-problem family. Saunders, Lipovsky, and Hanson (1995) list the following items as indicators of a family in a sexual crisis that can result in incest:

- The family are social isolates.
- The male caretaker exercises a high degree of control within the family.
- The family places a strong emphasis on moral and religious issues.
- The family exhibits much relationship distress between the parents or caretakers.
- The nonoffending parent feels under great pressure for some behavioral change or changes.
- The parents experience substantial sexual discord between themselves.

The female caretaker usually has a reason to suspect that the male partner is involved in an incestuous relationship with one of the children. But when the law enforcement agency confronts the woman, she will sometimes blame the child victim, accusing the child of fabricating the incident. The message here is that the male caretaker is the preferred one in the family rather than the child who is abused. The mother, for example, may believe that if she presses the incident, she will be left alone to raise the children with all its financial burdens, including food, clothing, and shelter. From this perspective, the mother may believe that the daughter is left to the child's own resources and, if she feels it necessary, will sacrifice the child for sake of the financial and emotional support of the offending caretaker.

The mother's response (if she is the innocent person in the incestuous activity) at the reported incident(s) may be shock or horror. If the marriage is poor, she may be angry enough to commence separation activities. But if she does not view the marriage as bad, she may need some help to see the events in perspective. If she calls the police, the partner may be sent to jail, and then how is she to cope with the day-to-day living responsibilities? Moreover, she often fears that friends and neighbors will become aware of the alleged event. The mother then has really four considerations: (1) what her loyalty to the child calls for, (2) whether to threaten the partner without pressing charges, (3) to tell others whom she trusts whose points of view she trusts, and (4) whether to seek professional counseling. If she seeks counseling, one would hope that the offending partner becomes a partner in the counseling.

In some instances, the female partner of the incestuous offender may be emotionally dependent upon the partner, insecure in her dealings with others, and therefore may be reluctant to share with the criminal justice system.

The mother in a relationship with a man who is an offender has a precarious decision to make. At first glance, it may appear that the decision to report the incest is an easy one. Many believe that incest is the first taboo (Hendrix & Schneider, 1999), and for that reason believe that the decision to report is an easy one. But this is not the case. Mothers often receive great blame from the courts, the criminal justice system, and the society (Fong & Walsh-Bowers, 1998), for failing to report any abuse, sexual, physical, or emotional. But many are reluctant to do so. One reason suggested by Kreklewetz and Piotrowski (1998) is that mothers had often themselves been victims of sexual abuse within their family of origin. While the mothers are rarely perpetrators themselves, they at least passively permit the victimization of their own child. Some may argue that there is something psychologically disturbed in a woman who will not report incest within her own family. Such a question was addressed by Joyce (1997) in her research. She found that mothers of sexually abused children were not significantly more psychologically disturbed than mothers of children who were not sexually abused. Thus, there are other factors in the decision to report or not to report the incest. But what is disturbed are the findings of Candib (1999) and Fitzroy (1999), who report that mothers who participate in the sexual abuse of their child are in some fashion looking to attain or regain power within the family. The abuse takes many forms, including genital mutilation and other forms of violence.

❖   THE EFFECTS UPON CHILDREN

A child sexually abused by a relative is different from one abused by a stranger. The incest victim cannot run away and go home for help and comfort. The child may endure many of the following forms of abuse, and there is a feeling that there is no one she or he can go to for help: sexual contact that includes oral-genital or anal penetration, genital touching, sexual kissing, hugging, sexual glaring at the victim, disguised touching, verbal invitations for sexual play, verbal insults about body parts, reading pornographic material aloud to the child or making the child view it, and exposure to inappropriate sexual activity (Caruso, 1987).

Incest has both short-term and long-term effects on a child. Winderlich et al. (1996) report that eating disorders are an almost immediate effect. They report that 38 women in their study exhibited binge eating, vomiting, alcohol abuse, suicidal thoughts, self-mutilation, and cigarette smoking. Self-mutilation was also found by Turell and Armsworth (2000) in their study of almost 100 women who were survivors of incest.

As the child advances into adulthood, other effects arise. One effect is on sexual values and attitudes, For example, as the victim moves into adulthood, the victim often views sex negatively. This effect was found by Newman and Peterson (1996), along with a variety of other dysfunctions.

Many survivors of incest develop amnesia:

When a child is abused, her mind cannot handle what happens to her. It's too much. Even if the mind remembers some of the abuse, it will bury most of it. It may remember the events, for instance, but bury the emotions. What the mind does is take the memories, put them deep in the unconscious, and build a wall around them. The mind also pulls the memory apart. It stores the different parts of a memory—the event (the visual picture of what happened), the mention (like the terror or the sexual feelings), and the identity of the perpetrator(s), and put them in different parts of the mind. Some parts are easier to access than others are. There is a "layering effect, with the worst memories at the bottom." (A Few Facts About Incest, hand-out at the SIA conference, August 1, 1991, anonymous)

Another dysfunction found was an involvement in occultism. Robinson (1999) reports that many "dabblers" in satanism report that they have been victims of incest and are apt to report their victimization.

Some of the sexual dysfunctions are frigidity, participation in prostitution, sexual promiscuity, and other sexual aberrations. Accompanying these effects is a general sense of anger directed toward the caretakers. One victim currently in prison for a violent personal offense stated in an interview that she was angry with her father for his incestuous actions but angrier with her mother, who she believed had the power to stop the abuse and should not have permitted it to continue for more than ten years. This effect was also found by Voth and Tutty (1999), who reported that female victims felt apathy toward their mothers or even lacked affection entirely because they perceived that the mothers did not intercede in their behalf.

There are other deleterious effects of sexual abuse within the family. Herman and Hirschman (1981) report that 33% of their sample of sexually abused victims had run away during their teenage years; only 5% of their control group had done so. Benward and Densen-Gerber (1975), in an early study, reported that 23% of their incest group had run away from home, but only 11% of the nonincest group.

In an unpublished study completed with the local missing and exploited child unit, we found that there appears to be a "career development ladder" for juvenile runaways. The rungs are (1) victims of incest and other forms of sexual abuse, (2) juvenile prostitution, and (3) exposure to and involvement in child pornography.

Problems in relating to others, problems in the school setting and in the community, and delinquency all are unhealthy effects on children who are victims of sexual child abuse. But perhaps the greatest damage is the destruction of the children's self-concepts. Many incest victims blame themselves, as the last stanza of Beth's poem earlier in this chapter shows.

❖ TREATMENT

Treatment efforts have centered largely on the total family as the unit for treatment. The child is abused and therefore treatment must be offered. One of the problems in offering treatment is the lack of clear research distinguishing among the various types of abuse (Bernet & Chang, 1997). And, Hunt and Baird (1990) notes, it can be unclear whether the child has been abused by a single person or by a ring of offenders. No one treatment approach works significantly better than another. There are many treatment modalities offered the incestuous family: individual therapy, family therapy, psychoeducational skills training, chemical castration, and relapse therapy among them (Brown & Brown, 1997). In any treatment modality, the goal is to reintegrate the offender into the community (DiGiorgio-Miller, 1998).

The therapist should understand that male and female caretakers often view incest differently. Haig (1999) reports that females are more averse to incest than their male counterparts. One reason for this difference may be biological; but another may be that in this society women have more to lose than men because of their roles as nurturers, protectors, and the stable force around the child.

The incest offender is often found to have suffered abuse in their own lives as children (Crawford, Hueppelscheuser, & George, 1996). In such cases, the therapist must take this into consideration as an issue to be resolved in the therapy plan. This is not the only issue to be addressed. Bevc and Silverman (2000) found that the parents and the children in the abusive family report significantly more nudity in the home and that the parents had more physical contacts with children than in families who reported no sexual activity. This physical closeness with children makes sexual victimization all the easier for the incestuous offender. Also, this may cloud the issue of whether the offender is an incestuous offender or a pedophile (Studer, Clelland, & Aylwin, 2000; Vargas, 1999).

Whether force was used requires special attention. Wheeler (1996) studied 150 child molesters and 122 nonmolesting men who volunteer for his study. He reported that more than 9 of 10 incestuous offenders reported that they used pornography, and their fantasies of incest with their daughters were related to usage of sexual materials in which physical force was used to obtain sex. Stermac, Davidson, and Sheridan (1995) found in their study of incest offenders that more than half their sample demonstrated nonsexual forms of physical violence within the home, and this violence was directed toward both the spouse and the child. These acts of violence were perpetrated not only by relatively young offenders; Stevens (1995) found that the majority of the male perpetrators in her study were grandfathers, and they were "serious, violent" offenders. Their crimes against their grandchild included the most serious forms of sexual abuse. Fischer and McDonald (1998) stated that there is a relationship between the age of the victimized child and the use of physical or verbal force. The older the child, the greater the need for a controlling device, and the controlling device appears to take the form of violence for many perpetrators.

The treatment of an incest offender needs to examine the various layers that exist within the personality of the offender. The past experience of the perpetrator, the interest in pornography, the gender of the offender (Green, 1996), and a great many other issues and concerns. It must not be forgotten that the rate of recidivism is still low for those caught and brought to the attention of the justice system (Firestone, Bradford, McCoy, Greenberg, Larose, & Curry, 1999). Although success in treatment may be minimal, the incest offender is usually reintegrated into the community and, without some type of treatment, more children will remain at risk.

❖ CONCLUSION

The sexual abuse of one's own child is for most people the most despicable of all crimes. The question one asks is, typically, how could one do that to his or her child? Certainly the offender knows that this victimization is wrong, at least in an overwhelming number of cases. But we did see in one example that the father raped his daughter to teach her a lesson. The victimization of children has grown to such pandemic proportions in the United States that each citizen should be vitally concerned with the ramifications of the atrocious acts of incest. Children should not and must not be viewed as objects to be used, abused, and discarded like broken toys. They are the future of our society, and we, as concerned adults, must protect them from those who would do them harm.

❖ DISCUSSION QUESTIONS

1. Among all sex crimes, incest is viewed by most as the most horrible. Why do you think that is?

2. Doing a little research on your own, which form of relational incest do you believe is most prevalent? Why do you think this is so?

3. Studies in the chapter show that the age range of victimization is quite large. Additional studeies suggest that the gender of the child also vaires. What does this suggest as to the extent and character of the problem of incest in this country?

4. Does the age of the offender suggest the extent and character of the victimization?

5. What are some possible strategies for reducing the crime of incest in this country?

❖ REFERENCES

Benward, J., & Densen-Gerber, J. (1975). Incest as a causative factor in antisocial behavior. *Contemporary Drug Problems, 4,* 323–340.

Bernet, W., & Chang, D. (1997). The differential diagnosis of ritual abuse allegations. *Journal of Forensic Science, 42*(1), 32–38.

Blume, S. (1987) Post-incest syndrome in women: The incest survivor's after effects checklist. Siecus Report, *15*(1), 1.

Bevc, I., & Silverman, I. (2000). Early separation and sibling incest: A test of the revised Westermack theory. *Evolution and Human Behavior, 21*(3), 151–161.

Brown, J., & Brown, G. (1997). Characteristics and treatment of incest offenders: A review. *Journal of Aggression, Maltreatment, and Trauma, 1*(1), 335–354.

Candib, L. (1999). Incest and other harms to daughters across cultures: Maternal complicity and patriarchal power. *Women's Studies International Forum, 22*(2), 185–201.

Caruso, B. (1987). *The impact of incest.* Center City, MN: Hazelden Educational Materials.

Crawford, P., Hueppelscheuser, M., & George, D. (1996). Spouses of incest offenders: Coaddictive tendencies and dysfunctional etiologies. *Sexual Addiction and Compulsivity, 3*(4), 289–312.

DiGiorgio-Miller, J. (1998). Sibling incest: Treatment of the family and the offender. *Child Welfare, 77*(3), 335–346.

Firestone, P., Bradford, J., McCoy, M., Greenberg, D., Larose, M., & Curry, S. (1999). Predictions of recidivism in incest offenders. *Journal of Interpersonal Violence, 14*(5), 511–531.

Fischer, D., & McDonald, W. (1998). Characteristics of interfamilial child sexual abuse. *Child Abuse and Neglect, 22*(9), 915–929.

Fitzroy, L. (1999). Mother/daughter incest: Making sense of the unthinkable. *Feminism and Psychology, 9*(4), 402–405.

Fong, J., & Walsh-Bowers, R. (1998). Voices of the blamed: Mothers' responses to father-daughter incest. *Journal of Family Social Work, 3*(1), 25–41.

Green, J. (1996). Mothers in "incest families." *Violence Against Women, 2*(3), 322–348.

Greenberg, D., Bradford, J., Firestone, P., & Curry, S. (2000). Recidivism of child molesters: A study of victim relationship with the perpetrator. *Child Abuse and Neglect, 24*(11), 1485–1497.

Greenfeld, L. (1997). *Sex offenses and offenders: An analysis of data on rape and sexual assault.* Washington, DC: Bureau of Justice Statistics.

Haig, D. (1999). Asymmetric relations: Internal conflicts and the horror of incest. *Evolution and Human Behavior, 20*(2), 83–98.

Hendrix, L., & Schneider, M. (1999). Assumptions on sex and society in the biosocial theory of incest. *Cross-Cultural Research, 33*(2), 193–218.

Herman, J., & Hirschman, L. (1981). Families at risk for father-daughter incest. *American Journal of Psychiatry, 138,* 735–756.

Holmes, R. (1983). *The sex offender and the criminal justice system.* Springfield, IL: Charles C Thomas.

Hunt, P. and M Baird. (1990). Children of sex rings. *Child Welfare, 69*(3), 195–207.

Joyce, P. (1997). Mothers of sexually abused children and the concept of collusion: A literature review. *Journal of Child Sexual Abuse, 6*(2), 75–92.

Kreklewetz, C., & Piotrowski, C. (1998). Incest survivor mothers: Protecting the next generation. *Child Abuse and Neglect, 22*(12), 1305–1312.

Langan, P., & Harlow, C. (1994). *Child rape victims, 1992.* Washington, DC: U.S. Department of Justice, Bureau of Justice Statistics.

Lisak, D. (1994). The psychological impact of sexual abuse: Content analysis of interviews with male survivors. *Journal of Traumatic Stress, 7*(4), 525–548.

Miletski, H. (1995). *Mother-son incest: The unthinkable broken taboo.* Brandon, VT.: Safer Society Press.

National Center for Victims of Crime and Crime Victims Research and Treatment Center. (1992). *Rape in America: A report to the nation.* Arlington, VA: Author.

Newman, A., & Peterson, C. (1996). Anger of women incest survivors. *Sex Roles, 34*(7–8), 463–474.

Robinson, C. (1999). Profiling the satanic/occult dabblers in the correctional offender population: Preliminary findings for Project Gangmill. *Journal of Gang Research, 7*(1), 35–66.

Rude, J., & Herzberger, S. (1999). Brother-sister incest—father-daughter incest: A comparison of characteristics and consequences. *Child Abuse and Neglect, 23*(9), 915–928.

Saunders, B., Lipovsky, J., & Hanson, R. (1995). Couple and familial characteristics of father-child incest families. *Journal of Family Social Work, 1*(2), 5–25.

Stermac, L., Davidson, A., & Sheridan, P. (1995). Incidence of nonsexual violence in incest offenders. *International Journal of Offender Therapy and Comparative Criminology, 39*(2), 167–178.

Stevens, G. (1995). Grandfathers as incest perpetrators: Dirty old men or predatory offenders? *Journal of Crime and Justice, 18*(2), 127–141.

Studer, L., Clelland, S., & Aylwin, A. (2000). Rethinking risk assessment for incest offenders. *International Journal of Law and Psychiatry, 23*(1), 15–22.

Trepper, T., Niedner, D., Mika, L., & Barrett, M. (1996). Family characteristics of intact sexually abusing families: An exploratory study. *Journal of Child Sexual Abuse, 5*(1), 1–18.

Turell, S., & Armsworth, M. (2000). Differentiating incest survivors who self-mutilate. *Child Abuse and Neglect, 24*(2), 237–249.

Vargas, J. (1999). Relatives or strangers? The effects of the relationship between perpetrators and victims of rape on the processes of the criminal justice system. *Revista Brasileira de Ciencias, 14*(40), 63–82.

Voth, P., & Tutty, L. (1999). Daughter's perceptions of being mothered by an incest survivor: A phenomenological study. *Journal of Child Sexual Abuse, 8*(3), 25–43.

Wheeler, D. (1996). The relationship between pornography usage and child molesting. *Federal Probation, 15*(2), 34–48.

Winderlich, S., Donaldson, M., Carson, D., Staton, D., Gertz, L., Leach, L., et al. (1996). Eating disturbance and incest. *Journal of Interpersonal Violence, 11*(2), 195–207.

6

Pedophilia

❖ ❖ ❖

There are few human behaviors that society views as more obscene and despicable and that provoke more public outrage than sex crimes against children (Heck, 1999; Holmes & Holmes, 2001; Walsh, 1994). The pedophile is judged to be a human predator who targets and victimizes defenseless children and a sex offender of the most perverse kind. This same judgment is made of the incestuous perpetrator whom we covered in chapter 5. With the Internet sophistication at a point where pedophiles can solicit children in a relatively safe environment (Esposito, 1998), the incidences of police reports and arrests for child molestation and pedophilia have greatly increased (Sullivan, 1999). Certainly the incidences sexual abuse of children either inside or outside the family is something that no society in this millennium can tolerate (Parsons, 2000). Unfortunately some people believe that children are objects for sexual use and abuse. But what is the extent of child sexual abuse?

Approximately 24% of one study's female subjects had sexual contacts before adolescence (Ellis & Abarbanel, 1973). Another study found that almost 20% of all children, regardless of gender, experienced some form of sexual abuse before their 18th birthday (O'Brien & Goldstein, 1988). Wyatt (1985) found that almost 50% of young women between the ages of 18 and 36 had been sexually abused before their

18th birthday, a finding unsupported by Baker & Duncan (1985), who found the percentage much lower. Regardless of the number or percentage of children who are victimized, the problem must be considered a significant one. To equate numbers with the physical, sexual, and emotional well-being of children is a position that evades the seriousness of this social problem.

❖ THE PEDOPHILE

The word *pedophile* in its etymology means a "lover of children" (Holmes & Holmes, 2001), although this is not a popular way to view the behavior. Pedophiles are more often called child molesters. We will use the term *pedophile* here because there is often more to the behavioral pattern of this kind of offender than simply the molestation of the child. Thomas (1985) states that pedophilia is a fondness for children, an unnatural desire for sexual relations with children, a definition shared by Kear-Colwell and Boer (2000). If one accepts this definition, it is easy to see the overwhelming difficulty it implies for the treatment and rehabilitation of such offenders (Musk & Swetz, 1997).

Sexual interest in children is perhaps not as infrequent as we would like to believe. In Briere's (1989) sample of 193 male undergraduate students, 21% reported sexual attraction to children, 9% described sexual fantasies involving children, and 5% admitted to having masturbated to such fantasies. And 7% indicated some likelihood of having sex with a child if they could avoid detection and punishment.

Etiology of the Pedophile

The etiology of pedophilia is unknown. Salter (1989) suggests a number of predisposing factors that cause a person to become a child molester. Offenders sometimes have deviant arousal patterns that make them sexually attracted to children, but for others child molestation may be their way of acting out responses to nonsexual problems. Tingle, Bernard, Robbins, and Newman (1986) found that pedophiles most often come from homes with domineering mothers and passive or even absent fathers. Sexual orientation apparently is unrelated to pedophilia. Blanchard and Dickey (1998) sampled 721 convicted white male pedophile offenders and found no difference between the homosexual offenders and heterosexual offenders. Marshall, Cripps, and Anderson (1999) reported that the 30 incarcerated child abusers in their study suffered from low self-esteem and poor coping skills. Marshall and

Mazzucco (1995) reported similar findings. They also studied pedophiles' parental attachments, discovering that molesters were more likely to have been sexually abused and experienced a deep sense of maternal rejection.

Smallbone and Dadds (1998) found in their study that pedophiles had particularly difficult relationships with their mothers character-ized by a combination of anxious experiences and avoidance in their maternal experiences

Briggs and Hawkins (1996) also found abuse in the histories of their sample of 84 incarcerated child molesters. Ninety-three percent had been sexually, verbally, and physically abused as children. Hummel, Thomke, Oldenburger, and Specht (2000) found similar back-ground information with an additional element of absent parents.

Myths of Child Molestation

- The child molester is a "dirty old man."
- Truth—The majority of child abusers are under the age of 35.
- The offender is a stranger to the child.
- Truth—In almost three cases in four, the offender and the victim know each other.
- The child molester is retarded.
- Truth—There are no significant differences in intelligence between incarcerated child molesters and the general public.
- The child molester is an alcoholic or drug addict.
- Truth—Drug abuse is essentially not a concern; about one in three reported them-selves as having an alcohol problem.
- The child molester is a sexually frustrated person.
- Truth—Many child abusers are married, and others have additional sexual outlets with other persons.
- The child abuser is insane.
- Truth—Few child molesters are mentally ill or legally insane.
- Children are more at risk from gays.
- Truth—No studies show gays abuse children more than heterosexuals.

Blanchard and Dickey (1998) report that gay molesters reach puberty earlier than heterosexual molesters who molested physically mature victims. It may be that the onset of puberty in the early life of the molester plays an integral role in the victim selectivity process. This obviously needs further study. It may be that birth order plays an important role in the etiology of the pedophile; Bogaert, Bezeau, and Kuban (1997) reported that the homosexual-bisexual pedophile had a later birth order than the heterosexual pedophiles in their study in

Canada. Glasser (1988) suggests that as a result of their sexual deviation, pedophiles are unable to identify with others, may create a false self, and struggle with intense but unrecognized guilt. But as Sawle, Kear-Colwell, Gary, and Jon (2001) and Kear-Colwell and Boer (2000) found, pedophiles and child molesters suffer from early experiences that caused them psychic trauma. There are various types of pedophiles, for example, family offender, the "Pied Piper" (suburban good neighbor), a worker in an industry serving children, a person in an occupation with authority over children (such as a minister), and the street predator. It is important to try to understand the etiology of all types of offender and how personality change can occur.

❖ TRAITS OF PEDOPHILES

Special care must be taken to distinguish between the causes of pedophilia and the traits of pedophiles. In this section we will address the research findings of the traits of pedophiles.

Most Pedophiles Are Male

Pedophiles are typically male (Murray, 2000), but not all are. Condy, Templer, Brown, and Veaco (1987) suggest that women who molest children are a great deal more prevalent than once thought. Often when a woman is accused of sexually molesting a child, social values impede her arrest and prosecution. Recently a high school teacher arranged for several of her male students to come to her home for tutoring and sex. Soon the word was spread throughout the school about this teacher. The police arrested her and she was charged with rape and sexual abuse of four male students, all under the age of 15. In a jury trial, she was found innocent of all charges. Incredibly, one father remarked that his son should consider himself lucky to have had a sexual experience with an older woman. One wonders what his reactions would have been if the teacher were a male, or the victim were his daughter rather than his son.

Another female offender was Mary Kay Letourneau, who served a 7½-year sentence in a Washington State prison for her sexual involvement with a 13-year-old boy. The relationship commenced when the victim was a student in her elementary school class. Letourneau has given birth to two children fathered by the youth, one born in prison. While such cases of female offenders are rare, they do exist.

Low Self-Esteem and Other Psychological Traits

Various studies have shown that the child molester suffers from a low self-esteem. Fisher, Beech, and Browne (1999) found that their research group of 140 child molesters reported significant lower self-esteem than a group of nonoffenders. This finding was reinforced by Marshall, Champagne, Brown, and Miller (1997), who compared 32 child molesters with 32 nonoffenders and found the offenders suffered from low self-esteem, a finding further supported by Ward, McCormack, and Hudson (1997).

Lack of empathy and a fear of intimacy are also challenging psychological traits of the pedophile. Marshall et al. (1997) report that child abusers scored significantly lower on these traits than a control group of nonoffenders. (See also Cheit, Freeman-Longo, & Greenberg, 1997; Lotke, 1996; Weinrott, Riggan, & Frothingham, 1997).

Heightened Arousal by Children

Pedophiles are highly aroused by seeing children in playful situations and even by ads in the newspaper for children's swimsuits, underwear, and similar displays of children. Child pornography plays an integral part in the fantasy that pedophiles have for children. Westley Dodd admitted to looking at children in National Geographic as a means of becoming sexually aroused (authors' files). Wheeler (1996) reports that more than 9 of 10 pedophiles in his sample reported fantasies of victimizing children. The molesters in Wheeler's study were more likely to view soft-core pornography, a type that involved nudity or consenting sexual activities between adults. Contrary to this study, our own research, in the cases we have assisted with local police departments, found that every child molester, without exception, had some form of child pornography in his possession at the time of arrest (unpublished report). Pornography by itself does not cause someone to be a sex offender, be it a pedophile or a lust killer (Maddox, 1996). It may fuel the fantasy, but other life's experiences play a more important role.

Challenged in Social Skills

Molesters admit feelings of aloneness and unsatisfying social relationships (Fisher, Beech, & Browne, 1999; Ward et al., 1997). Gudjonsson and Sigurdsson (2000) found that child offenders were significantly introverted despite a readiness to establish relationships, a desire they found most difficult to fulfill. Most offenders appear to have great difficulty in relating to adults in normal day-to-day experiences. Some may feel intimidated by adults, especially women, and feel more comfortable with children.

Sexual Activity

Pedophiles engage in a wide range of sexual practices with children: holding, fondling, and kissing, sexual intercourse, various acts of sodomy, and murder. The range of such sexual activities will be explained further later in this chapter when we define certain categories of pedophiles. Hunter, Hazelwood, and Slesinger (2000) report that in general, the aggression of child molesters tended to intimidation rather than physical force. Contact with the molester is, unfortunately, in some cases fatal. This child sexual sadist often reduce the victim to an object level and use words that denigrate the victim (Eisenman, 1997).

Unless it is the mysoped, sexual penetration is unlikely with young children. The home of the victim is often the site where the victimization occurs, but, of course, this too will vary with the type of pedophile. When girls are victims, the home is the usual site for victimization. When boys are molested, the sexual abuse may take place outside the home and the perpetrators may be strangers (Murray, 2000) unless the molester himself is a homosexual (Hodge & Canter, 1989). In most cases of pedophiliac actions, the sexual act may be seen as a substitute for adult sex because the sexual act with a child is more controlling for the pedophile while with another adult that act may be intimidating, repulsive, or frightening (Holmes & Holmes, 1996).

Criminal Records

Pedophiles often have no or minor criminal records, and, for that reason, are not familiar names or faces to the criminal justice system. Pedophiles come to the attention of the criminal justice system because of their sexual interest in and illegal sexual acts with children. Many law enforcement agencies set up sting operations in their eagerness to detect and arrest child molesters. One detective in Arvada, Colorado, Walt Parsons, has been very active in his investigation of pedophiles. Posing as child, Parsons places ads on the Internet inviting queries from those who are interested in having sex with him. He placed one such ad and within the day received a reply from a man in New Mexico. The man was arrested once he arrived at an apartment in Arvada. In his possession were ropes, chains, other restraints, a whip, and a teddy bear!

Simon (1997) tested the assumption that child offenders are "offense specialists," that is, that they commit only one type of crime. In this case, it would be only child sexual abuse. In this study, 142 consecutive pedophiles were evaluated and compared to rapists and violent personal offenders. The findings reported that the past criminal records for all three groups contained a variety of offenses. But child abusers were significantly less versatile than the other groups. In other words, pedophiles are more likely to be offense specialists than the other two groups.

An interesting finding was reported by Horley, Quinsey, and Jones (1997). They reported that molesters generally have a positive view of the police, courts, and legal processes. The child molesters' reports of their contacts with the police characterized them as "kinder and less repulsive, deceitful, and unpleasant" than the control group of nonsexual offenders did. What accounts for these feelings is not clearly understood. Certainly the crime is distasteful to those both inside and outside the criminal justice enterprise. In some fashion, the relationship that develops between the molester and the agents of the criminal justice enterprise is viewed more positively by the child sexual offenders. This may have something to do with the interrogation strategies used by the police to solicit information or a confession. The helping professions within the criminal justice enterprise are less judgmental in their dealing with pedophiles; maybe it is the result of the feeling that the pedophile is ill and needs treatment.

Feelings of Remorse

Gudjonsson and Sigurdsson (2000) reported that feelings of remorse will vary with the type of pedophile. This too will be discussed when we deal with the types of pedophiles. But, as Geer, Estupinan, and Manguno-Mire (2000) report, remorse plus a feeling of empathy in the pedophile hold promise that he might be a successful candidate for treatment and rehabilitation. But we must add that in the cases we have found dealing with pedophiles, remorse is short-lived and denial rises within the pedophile (Nugent & Kroner, 1996).

As a group, clerics may have the highest rate of remorse for having perpetrated sexual violence against children. Langevin, Curnoe and Bain (2000) report that clerics

- Are highly educated
- Are older than other pedophiles
- Are predominately unmarried

- Have few antisocial personality types
- Enjoy a longer delay before criminal charges are filed
- Lack prior criminal charges
- Tend to use force more often in their offenses

Little in the above report is surprising except the last finding, the use of force. Haywood, Kravitz, and Grossman (1996) report the clerics in their study that compared clerics who molested children with non-cleric child offenders, the clerics

- Report fewer victims
- Choose older victims
- Choose male victims
- Are less likely to engage in multiple paraphilic behaviors
- May be less seriously psychologically disordered, possibly as an influence of their unique training and socialization process

Multiple Sexual Victims

Pedophiles arrested for their crimes of sex against children often report that they have molested before (Petrosino & Petrosino, 1999). Al Carlisle, a recently retired prison psychologist, estimates that a pedophile may molest as many as 100 children before he is caught (Carlisle, 2006). The numbers will vary, but the pedophiles we have interviewed in prison report numbers that range from 6 to more than 200. It is difficult to offer a firm number from self-reported data, for self-reported numbers are suspect at best. Even the low numbers may be an attempt to minimize the number of offenses and the high number may be an attempt to exaggerate the number of victims. But we believe it is safe to say that child molesters are serial offenders who, despite their feelings of shame, remorse, or sympathy, will not cease until interdiction is offered.

❖ SITUATIONAL CHARACTERISTICS OF PEDOPHILES

Contrary to the public perception, the pedophile rarely physically harms the child unless the molester is a mysoped (an aggressive and sadistic child abuser). Haas and Haas (1990) report few pedophiles use either physical or verbal force. This is a controversial statement, and many law enforcement personnel will disagree. What we mean here is that the reaction to the abuse by the significant others (particularly the parents or other principal caretakers) has a greater effect on the child's own perception of the abuse than the reaction of others who are less personally significant.

The majority of heterosexual pedophiles are neither senile nor mentally defective. They tend to be conservative and moralistic, and some even require alcohol before they commit their offenses. In Kentucky, there are more than 1,000 sex offenders free in the community and on some form of supervision (Massie, 2000). Some have criminal records, and others do not. One who does not is a well-respected physician, Dr. Fred Rainey, more than once elected president of the Kentucky Medical Association and a state Jaycee, pleaded guilty to abusing 7 teenagers. Rainey entered the Alford plea, was sent to prison, and was released within a few weeks on shock probation[1].

Seduction is typically the ploy used in gaining sexual entree with children. There is no clear evidence that a particular gender is overwhelmingly preferred.

Many pedophiles of all types have adult sexual outlets. Many are married. Some have known to marry women with children in order to have access to the children; this molestation is typically classified as incest, because of the victim's relationship with the child offender. But there may indeed be serial pedophiles who marry more than once to gain access to children. As Murray (2000) reported, the availability and vulnerability of the children are overarching elements in selecting the victim.

❖ TYPES OF PEDOPHILES

Pedophiles are not alike. For example, they differ in their sexual preferences in the age and gender of their victims. A typology of pedophiles can be formulated from victim characteristics, type of sexual activity, motivation, and the preferred age of the victim. Most pedophiles have a three- or four-year age span of preference. That is to say, pedophiles, like the overwhelming number of sex offenders, are age-specific. If the preferred victim is, for instance, 9 years of age, the child offender will typically select a child somewhere in the age range of 7 to 11.

Pedophiles are interested usually in children who have not as yet reached puberty. Child sexual offenders who are interested in victims who have reached puberty are termed hebephiles and would not think of having a sexual encounter with a child who has not reached puberty.

The gender of the child also plays an integral part in the selection of the victim. Typically, pedophiles select victims of a certain gender as well as a certain age. It is somewhat unlikely for a pedophile to molest both boys and girls. The case of Wayne Williams, the so-called Atlanta Child Killer, was convicted of the murders of two adults, a 21-year-old and a 27-year-old. He was suspected of the murders of children from the age of 7 to the age of Nathaniel Cater, the 27-year-old. Also, there were both males and females among the victims, all in all, an unusual circumstance (Dettinger & Prugh, 1984). Incidentally, Williams has never been charged with any of the killings of young children in Atlanta.

Professor Gets 105 Years for Importing Boy for Sex

Former Florida Atlantic University professor Marvin Hersh was sentenced to 105 years in federal prison for smuggling a Honduran boy into the United States for the purpose of sex.

The computer scientist and mathematician was arrested in 1996. The molester first contacted the boy and sent him toys, money, and clothing. He brought the boy to Boca Raton when the boy was 15 and also abused his younger brother and faked a birth certificate to try to show that the older boy was his natural son.

SOURCE: APBnews.com, May 26, 2000

Table 6.1   Typology of Pedophiles

Element	Naïve Offender	Regressed Offender	Sadistic Offender	Fixated Offender
Harmful to the Child	No	No	Yes	No
Aggressive Personality	No	No	Yes	No
Antisocial Personality	No	No	Yes	No
Child Sexual Preference	No	Yes	Yes	Yes
Knows the Child	Yes	No	No	Yes
Intercourse Occurs	No	Yes	Yes	Yes

It is important to note that the sexual preference of the pedophile does not necessarily reflect his adult sexual orientation. Many times, the police will arrest a pedophile who molests young males and then discover that the child offender is married with children of his own. Law enforcement professionals often become confused because they tend to believe that if a child molester abuses males he must be a homosexual. This is simply not the case.

October 1, 2000

Dear Dr. Holmes,

After you left, I started to think about what we had talked about, how did I select my sex partners.

Reflecting back, I think the reason was quite simple. I was able to. There is no deep, dark message in the depths of my brain. I was simple able to. The boys came to me the first of each month because they knew that was when I got paid. They wanted money and I wanted sex. I gave the boys other things besides money, tickets to concerts, lottery tickets, athletic shoes, and other things. After they got what they wanted, they let me have sex with them.

The boys were prostitutes. I would never molest a child. But these boys let me have my way with them strictly for the money or the gifts. It was just that simple.

Sorry to disappoint you. No Freud needed here. I don't consider myself to be a prostitute. Really, what is the difference between what I did and the female prostitute? I paid for it. Is there any difference? I don't think so.

It's dinnertime. See you in 2 weeks.

Sincerely,

John B.

SOURCE: A letter from a convicted child molester currently in prison

The Mysoped

Some pedophiles are intent on molesting children with the express desire of harming their victims physically. This type of pedophile, usually male, has made a vital connection between sexual arousal and fatal violence. Typically, the child is a stranger to this aggressive and sadistic child offender. It appears also that this offender will stalk his victim rather than use any form of seduction (the method typical of many pedophiles).

The mysoped will often abduct a child from places where children gather: playgrounds, school, shopping center game rooms, and other such places. He will usually not attempt to seduce or otherwise induce the child to go with him; he simply takes the child by force. There are some exceptions to this example. Westley Dodd, a mysoped, abducted one child, Lee Eisley, age 5, from a schoolyard. He encouraged the child to go with him and promised him to take him to McDonald's and buy him a toy at a toy store. He strangled the boy and hung him in his closet when he went to work. After coming home at the end of the day, Dodd committed sexual acts against the corpse and expressed a desire to perform "exploratory surgery" on the child. Dodd was executed for his crimes (authors' files).

Often the mysoped will mutilate the body of the child, commit acts of necrophilia (Dodd is an example), and sometimes will cut off the boy's penis and insert it into his mouth. Small girls are also victims of the mysoped. One serialist told us

> I got her (a 12-year-old) to my home. My brother was working the late shift so I knew I would have her all to myself. I ravished her for 12 hours and then strangled her. I inserted 7 pounds of rocks inside her vagina, up her rectum, and down her throat. That was gratifying. Only after all my fantasies were realized, I decided that I must dispose of her body before my brother gets home, he knew nothing of my desires. (authors' files)

The mysoped will often terrorize the child as a part of his fantasy; he lives to feed off the terror of his victim. Some times a weapon is used, and the crime is premeditated and ritualized. Sadism is an integral part of the mysoped's predation, with the death of the child being the desired end (Burgess, Holstrom, Sgroi, & Groth, 1978).

A Suspected Mysoped and Accused Cannibal

In Great Falls, Montana, Nathaniel Bar-Jonah is a suspect in a child murder case involving several young boys, including 8-year-old Zachary Ramsey. The police believe that a bone found buried beneath the floor of Bar-Jonah's garage belongs to Zachary or another child.

The investigators also believe that Bar-Jonah cooked a stew and made pies from the bodies of the young children he had slain, which he shared with his neighbors.

SOURCE: APBnews.com, December 26, 2000

Excepts from Westley Dodd's Diary

Incident 3 will die maybe this way: He'll be tied down as Lee was in Incident 2. Instead of placing a bag over his head as I had previously planned, I'll tape his mouth shut with duct tape. Then, when ready, I'll use a clothespin or something to plug his nose. That way I can sit back, take pictures and watch him die instead of concentrating on my hands or the rope tight around his neck—that would also eliminate the rope burns on the neck. . . . I can clearly see his face and eyes now. . . . Electrocution also a good means for *quick* death. If I can get *it* home, I'll have more time for various types of rape, rather than just one quickie before murder.

SOURCE: Dodd's diaries, obtained through the Open Records Law

What kind of personality does this violent personality possess? Lanning and Burgess (1995) report that the mysoped actually have little contact with children outside their offenses. They rank low in social competence, are less frequently married than other pedophiles, are more apt to fit the classification of sadist, and are more likely to use a weapon in their crimes against children. An antisocial personality is another trait of the mysoped (Firestone, Bradford, & Greenberg, 1998). Other Firestone et al. findings are that as children they were more likely than other molesters to be removed from their home, were more violence-prone in their relationships with others, had been charged or convicted of past violent and nonviolent nonsexual offenses, and a history of substance abuse.

The Regressed Child Offender

The regressed offender is one who has been involved with adults in "normal" sexual relationships. This type of child offender experiences the child as a pseudo-adult (Burgess et al., 1978). Typically married or in a longstanding relationship, this sex offender is often launched into a sexual act or series of sexual acts with children because of some precipitating event.

A Letter From a Regressed Child Offender

I had never thought of molesting children. I was a deacon in my church, a Cub Scout leader, and a youth minister. I had been around children all my life with no intent to harm them. One day I came home from work and my wife said that there was something she wanted to talk to me about. She said, "Tony, you physically disgust me and I never want you to touch me again!" This really affected me as you can imagine. In the next two weeks, I was coming up for a big promotion and I knew that if I did not get it I would never be promoted before I retired. I'm 60 years old and this would have been my last shot. It came down to me and a young fellow at work, 30 years old. He got the job.

I was crushed. That weekend I and the Cub Scout troop went on a scouting trip. As usual there were two people to a pup tent, and there was a young 9-year-old sharing a tent with me. It started raining and thundering and the boy got scared. He asked if he could come over to my side of the tent and climb into my sleeping bag. Well, one thing led to another and before long I was fondling him. This led to other young boys, which went on for over a year.

SOURCE: Interview with a Regressed Child Offender (authors' files)

Tony was finally discovered and arrested. This offender, like others in the regressed category, had a normal history, including adolescence with good peer relationship and experiences. Because of some situation or occurrence in his life—a poor job performance review, an unfaithful wife, some social maladjustment, or whatever—the regressed offender develops feelings of inadequacy that frequently result in alcoholism as well as child molestation.

The regressed offender prefers children he does not know. Usually the child is a female, but of course this is not always the case. Tony, for example, was different. He got the children who were available to him. His victims were victims of opportunity.

In prison, Tony joined a sex offender's treatment program and was successful in obtaining parole. He went back to his community but lost his job and his marriage. Despite having a graduate degree in mechanical engineering, he could obtain only menial work. He died recently of a heart attack.

Johnston and Johnston (1997) report that the regressed offender is likely to be well adjusted and come from an intact home. The regressed child offender has a better chance of not reoffending than other sexual child offenders,, especially if the precipitating situational event can be discovered and remedied.

The Fixated Offender

The fixated child offender has not really developed past the point where he, as a child, found children attractive and desirable. In other words, he has become "fixated" at an early stage of psychosexual development (Burgess et al., 1978). The fixated child molester's pedophiliac interest started in adolescence; unlike the cases of regressed child offenders, there is no precipitating cause in his child abuse. His interest in children is persistent, continual, and compulsive. Unlike the regressed offender, male victims are the preferred targets of abuse (Johnston & Johnston, 1997).

The fixated offender has little activity with age-mates, is single, and is considered to be immature and uncomfortable around adults (Burgess et al., 1978). This offender is like a child in his lifestyle and behaviors. Burg (1983) suggests that many pedophiles select children as sexual objects because youths are less critical of their partners' performance than are adults. But a more practical reason for some is that the child is simply available. John, whose letter appeared earlier in this chapter, was convicted of multiple counts of sexual child abuse. His victims of choice were young boys, 13 to 15 years old. John admitted his sex acts with willing victims (according to his statement), and he paid the boys for sex. He added in an interview that he would only have sex with inner-city boys because they were "more mature" than suburban boys. The letter was sent from prison, which he expects to be released from within the next five years.

The fixated child offender is not interested in physically harming the child. He loves children and does not desire to do anything that might harm them. He courts a child, buys the child gifts as a seduction ploy, and slowly becomes physically intimate with the child. Oral-genital sex is the norm, and actual intercourse develops only after a generous period of time has passed.

The Naïve Offender

Many child offenders are incorrectly diagnosed as having some type of brain dysfunction, such as senility. Obviously some pedophiles fall into this category, but most do not. Only a few are involved with children because they do not understand the true nature of their offenses or the societal rules prohibiting the involvement of adults with children in a sexual manner. Some do suffer from organic problems or senility and are unable to appreciate the impact of what they have done; for example, the elderly grandfather or the older gentleman who lives down the street may suffer from impaired intellectual functioning and not understand the ramifications of his actions. This offender likes to hug, fondle, kiss, lick, or stroke a child, with no intent to attempt sexual intercourse.

❖ PEDOPHILE ORGANIZATIONS

Child sex is a topic that immediately raises the ire of most Americans. Many are adamantly opposed to mercy for those who intentionally and with full mental capacities sexually abuse children. However, there are more than a few groups that not only favor child sex but also have joined forces with others who share their point of view. Perhaps the three most famous or infamous groups are the Rene Guyon Society, the North American Man/Boy Love Association (NAMBLA), and the Childhood Sensuality Circle (DeYoung, 1989). There are several others.

Status: Supervision

Robbie Barton

Alias: Barton, Robert Michael

Department of Corrections Inmate #: V02435   **Date of Birth:** 07–18–1972

Race: White   **Sex:** Male   **Height:** 6"01"

Hair: Brown   **Eyes:** Green   **Weight:** 180 lbs.

Last Reported Address: 1650 Bansi Street, Orlando, FL 32828

County: Orange   **Date Address Entered:** 11–18–99

Qualifying Offenses

Lewd, Lascivious Child, Under 16.

Victims: Gender: Unknown; **Minor?** Yes

Barton is a sex offender under Florida law. Positive identification cannot be established unless a fingerprint comparison is made.

The Rene Guyon Society

The Rene Guyon Society is a national association of persons who are vitally interested in promoting legislation that would permit adults to have sex with children. Indeed, the group's motto reflects its attitude: "Sex before age 8 or it's too late." The group's statements repeatedly assert that none of the members of the society has anything to do with breaking the sex laws on children. Children, however, should be allowed to involve themselves with older men, especially members of the society. Because children suffer from too much "body guilt," they should be encouraged to have sexual intercourse and other forms of sexual activities to rid themselves of this "body guilt." In addition, adult males suffer from body guilt and should be allowed to have sex with children but don't because of their guilt. The way to eliminate body guilt, both as a child and as an adult, is for children to have sex with adults, preferable those who are members of the Rene Guyon Society. At one time, the national spokesperson for the Rene Guyon Society was Tim O'Hara. O'Hara's real name is Jonathon Evan Edwards. The Rene Guyon Society was named for a former French judge in Thailand and author of several books and papers dealing with human sexuality, including the sexuality of children. It was formed in 1962 by seven couples during a lecture on human sexuality (Wallace, 1999). They push for the abolishment of laws prohibiting pedophilia. For example, they want adults to be able to perform anal sex on children as young as 4. They also say that children performing oral sex on adults will end thumb sucking. According to them, men should be able to have sex with girls as young as 10. They believe that if laws restricting child sexuality are not changed, there will be more youth involved in prostitution, contracting venereal diseases, and committing suicide. State rape laws should be changed to allow parents and guardians to give their consent for their children to have sex. Newsletters have contained slogans such as "Children keep family sex secrets."

They believe in bisexuality starting at age 4, 5, and 6 with an adult if protected with contraceptives. They maintain, however, that while they advocate legalizing sex with children, no member of their society has sex with children, since it is against the law in this country.

How many members does the Rene Guyon Society have in the world? The number is unknown. They allege that they have more than 5,000 members, but the actual number may be as low as 1, Jonathon Evan Edwards. The society may be headquartered in Beverly Hills, California (Wikipedia, January 2007).

The North American Man/Boy Love Association

NAMBLA is another organization that promotes child sex. This organization has several chapters in large cities and its mailing address is easily retrievable from the World Wide Web as well as its e-mail address. NAMBLA was founded, according to its publications, as a response to the oppression of men and boys involved in consensual sexual activity. Its has two national headquarters in San Francisco, CA and Midtown Station, New York.

NAMBLA is dedicated to making consensual sexual acts between adults and boys legal. NAMBLA was formed in 1978 in Boston. It held its first national conference in the same year. Members of NAMBLA argue that the men are motivated by love, not money. NAMBLA promotes pedophilia as a lifestyle. They help defend men accused of child sexual abuse, and they lobby against laws that prohibit child sexual abuse. They also wish to educate the public on the benevolent nature of man/boy relationships.

The Home Page Announcement of NAMBLA

WELCOME! The North American Man/Boy Love Association (NAMBLA) was formed in 1978. It was inspired by the success of a campaign based in Boston's gay community to defend against a local witchhunt.

NAMBLA's goal is to end the extreme oppression of men and boys in mutually consensual relationships by:

- building understanding and support for such relationships;
- educating the general public on the benevolent nature of man/boy love;
- cooperating with lesbian, gay, feminist, and other liberation movements;
- supporting the liberation of persons of all ages from sexual prejudice and oppression.

Our membership is open to everyone sympathetic to man/boy love and personal freedom.

NAMBLA calls for the empowerment of youth in all areas, not just the sexual. We support greater economic, political and social opportunities for young people and denounce the rampant _ageism_ that segregates and isolates them in fear and mistrust. We believe sexual feelings are a positive life force. We support the rights of youth as well as adults to choose the partners with whom they wish to share and enjoy their bodies.

We condemn sexual abuse and all forms of coercion. Freely-chosen relationships differ from unwanted sex. Present laws, which focus only on the age of the participants, ignore the quality of their relationships. We know that differences in age do not preclude mutual, loving interaction between persons. NAMBLA is strongly opposed to age-of-consent laws and all other restrictions which deny men and boys the full enjoyment of their bodies and control over their own lives.

NAMBLA does not provide encouragement, referrals or assistance for people seeking sexual contacts. NAMBLA does not engage in any activities that violate the law.

We call for fundamental reform of the laws regarding relations between youths and adults. Today, many thousands of men and boys are unjustly ground into the disfunctional [sic] criminal justice system. Blindly, this system condemns consensual, loving relationships between younger and older people. NAMBLA's Prisoner Program, with limited resources, works to provide a modicum of humanity to some of these people. _Click here_ to find out more.

NAMBLA is a political, civil rights, and educational organization. We provide factual information and help educate society about the positive and beneficial nature of man/boy love. _Become an active member! You can help in this historic struggle!_

SOURCE: http://www.nambla.org/welcome.htm. Retrieved October 17, 2007.

The Childhood Sensuality Circle

The Child Sensuality Circle (CSC) was formed in 1971 by retired social worker Valida Davila. The CSC have several pamphlets such as

"Porno for Children," and "A Child's Sexual Bill of Rights" that list what they believe to be children's rights:

- The right to experience sensual pleasures without shame or guilt
- The right to learn lovemaking as soon as he or she is able to understand
- The right to loving relationships, including sexual relationships, with parents, siblings, or other adults and children
- The right to a sex life based on natural desires without regard for tradition

Pedophile Information Exchange (PIE)

Originating in England in 1974, PIE maintains that society and its law on sex with children inflict damage on children. At its peak, PIE had only 250 members, but it was one of the better-known organizations in the 1970s. The organization wanted to build a sense of community for pedophiles, and to provide a public forum for debate. They claim that most pedophiles desire gentle and mutually stable relationships. Moreover, PIE said that pedophilia is a normal desire if only the rest of society would admit it. PIE had five aims:

1. To clear away, where possible, the myths connected with pedophilia by various means, including the making public of scientific, sociological, and similar information

2. To give advice and counsel to those isolated or lonely because of their pedophile orientation

3. To help those in legal difficulties over sexual acts with underage partners that took place with the latter's consent

4. To campaign, as members see fit, for the legal and social acceptance of pedophilia love

5. To provide a means whereby pedophiles might get in contact with each other

PIE wants the age of consent to be abolished. They would replace it with a stepwise approach

1. Children under 4 are unable to communicate their consent.

2. Children 4 to 9 can communicate consent; relationships can be stopped only by parents.

3. In children 10 to 17, only minimal interference is allowed.

Howard Nichols Society

David Sonenschein, a former consultant to the 1970 Presidential Committee on Obscenity and Pornography, ran this group. He is also a pedophile. The society was formed in 1981. The name was taken from a fictional character in the movie *Fallen Angel* who preyed upon young girls.

Sonenschein was arrested in 1983 after police found copies of his pamphlet, "How to Have Sex with Kids," in his apartment. He was found not guilty of the charges on child sexual abuse. In one publication, Sonenschein provided hints for child molesters in their selection of victims. "Friends are a good source. . . . It's also a good idea to get to know the parents . . . you can get babysitting tasks." He goes into further detail about the best way to sexually abuse children.

Despite what many believe, we must recognize there are people from many walks of life who believe that sexual predation upon children is desirable and should be legal in every jurisdiction. Fortunately, from our perspective, there is no effective movement to make this a possibility. We should realize that, while most child abusers do not physically harm children, there are exceptions; witness the case of Westley Dodd. But we should also not confuse this with the psychological damage that adults may do when they sexually abuse children. These people need to be identified and incapacitated for the protection of our children. While incapacitated, however, we should also realize the child abuser needs to be treated by mental health professionals and not released until the individual is certain not to molest and abuse children. This may be an impossible task. But it is better to keep a child abuser in a correctional setting for an indeterminate period of time than to release the person to abuse an innocent child.

❖ CONCLUSION

Those who sexually abuse our most treasured are committing acts that are viewed as heinous and despicable. As many as 27% of incarcerated pedophiles have committed other criminal acts that do not involve the sexual abuse of children (Petrosino & Petrosino, 1999). The crimes that involve children, as well as their other criminal acts, cannot be tolerated in U.S. society or any other culture. They must be treated for the protection of our children and for their own well-being. But it is our position that children must be protected from these predators, which usually means incarceration while undergoing treatment.

All states within the United States have some form of Megan's Law in operation. Megan Kanka was a 7-year-old girl living in New Jersey. She was brutally raped and murdered by a twice-convicted sex offender who lived across the street from her. From her death sprang a widely accepted plan. This plan was enacted into law that provides a community with the names of sex offenders who live in their neighborhood. Kentucky, for example, has a Megan's Law. Indiana has Zachary's Law, named after a young boy, Zachary Snider, who was killed by a neighbor, also a convicted sex offender. Each state has a website that someone can access, and by entering the name of the offender with the city and county (or parish in Louisiana), basic information can be obtained.

Kentucky State Police
  Sex/Criminal Offender Registry Website
  THE KENTUCKY STATE POLICE DOES NOT GUARANTEE THE ACCURACY OF THE INFORMATION PROVIDED
  "UNDER KRS 525.070 & 525.080, USE OF INFORMATION FROM THIS WEBSITE TO HARASS A SEX OFFENDER IS A CRIMINAL OFFENSE PUNISHABLE BY UP TO 90 DAYS IN THE COUNTY JAIL. MORE SEVERE CRIMINAL PENALTIES APPLY FOR MORE SEVERE CRIMES COMMITTED AGAINST A SEX OFFENDER."

NAME:	EDGAR B. LUCAS	
ALIASES:	DANNY LEE LUCAS	PHOTO UNAVAILABLE
ADDRESS:	10510 LAGRANGE ROAD	
CITY/STATE:	LOUISVILLE/KY	
ZIPCODE:	40223	
COUNTY:	JEFFERSON	

PHYSICAL CHARACTERISTICS

SEX:	MALE
RACE:	CAUCASIAN
DOB:	08/10/1944
HEIGHT:	5'10"
WEIGHT:	170
HAIR:	BROWN
EYES:	BLUE
DATE OF REGISTRATION:	03/28/1999
LENGTH OF REGISTRATION:	LIFETIME

OFFENSE(S) REQUIRING REGISTRATION:

510.060—RAPE 3RD DEGREE
510.040—RAPE 1ST DEGREE

REMARKS:	NONE

In the example from Kentucky, the name, address, a photo, and other pertinent information is given. Inserting the ZIP code produces the names of convicted sex offenders, and clicking on a name produces a page appears with the sort of information shown in the example. Each community can access this information and take steps to protect itself and its children (Risley, 1997). The state of Ohio has a similar program, and the case of Robbie Barton was viewed earlier. Zetitz and Farkas (2000) report that some communities now have initiated community meetings to alert neighbors about a released sex offender, thus not relying on individuals to secure this information on their own.

Despite protest over depriving the sex offender of his rights, Megan's Law is one means in alerting the public to a pedophile residing in their neighborhood. More efforts need to be directed toward the identification, apprehension, incarceration, and treatment of those who do terrible harm to our most precious asset, our children.

❖ NOTE

1. Shock probation refers to a condition of release that offenders may apply for to be released from state custody. Offenders must show that the release will not will not unduly depreciate the seriousness of their crime, that they are not a threat to the community and will follow through with intense physical or other rehabilitation efforts. Most jurisdictions require that an offender serve 6 months in jail or prison before they are eligible.

❖ DISCUSSION QUESTIONS

1. Not all pedophiles are alike. Discuss this statement.

2. There are national and international organizations that have a goal of legalizing sexual contact with children. Select one pedophile organization. Report this back to the class concerning its name, philosophy, goals, and objectives.

3. What could be some strategies to combat this serious social problem?

4. Should the names (possibly also including their pictures) be published on the Internet when pedophiles are released from correctional facilities? Defend your position.

❖ REFERENCES

Baker, A., & Duncan, S. (1985). Child sexual abuse: A study of prevalence in Great Britain. *Child Abuse and Neglect, 9,* 457–467.

Blanchard, R., & Dickey, R. (1998). Pubertal age in homosexual and heterosexual sexual offenders against children, pubescents, and adults. *Sexual Abuse, 10*(4), 273–282.

Bogaert, A., Bezeau, S., & Kuban, M. (1997). Pedophilia, sexual orientation, and birth order. *Journal of Abnormal Psychology, 106*(2), 331–335.

Briere, J. (1989). University males' sexual interest in children: Predicting potential indices of "pedophilia" in a nonforensic sample. *Child Abuse and Neglect, 13,* 65–75.

Briggs, F., & Hawkins, R. (1996). A comparison of the childhood experiences of convicted male child molesters and men who were sexually abused in childhood and claimed to be a nonoffender. *Child Abuse and Neglect, 20*(3), 221–233.

Burg, B. (1983). *Sodomy and the perception of evil.* New York: New York University Press.

Burgess, A., Holstrom, L., Sgroi, S., & Groth, S. (1978). *Sexual assault of children and adolescents.* Lexington, MA: D.C. Heath.

Carlisle, A. (2006, September 2). Personal communication.

Cheit, R., Freeman-Longo, R., & Greenberg, M. (1997). Symposium: The treatment of sex offenders. *New England Journal on Criminal and Civil Confinement, 23*(2), 267–462.

Condy, S., Templer, D., Brown, R., & Veaco, C. (1987). Parameters of sexual contact by boys with women. *Archives of Sexual Behavior, 16,* 379–394.

Dettinger, C., & Prugh, J. (1984). *The list.* Atlanta: Philmay.

DeYoung, M. (1989). The world according to NAMBLA: Accounting for deviance. *Journal of Sociology and Social Welfare, 16*(1), 111–126.

Eisenman, R. (1997). Denigration of a victim in individual psychotherapy by violent vs. Seductive child molesters. *Psychological Reports, 81*(3), 1276–1278.

Ellis, A., & Abarbanel, A. (1973). *The encyclopedia of sexual behavior.* New York: Jason Aronson.

Esposito, L. (1998). Regulating the Internet: The new battle against child pornography. *Journal of International Law, 39*(2–3), 541–565.

Firestone, P., Bradford, J., & Greenberg, D. (1998). Homicidal and nonhomicidal child molesters: Psychological, phallometric, and criminal features. *Sexual Abuse, 10,* 305–323.

Fisher, D., Beech, A., & Browne, K. (1999). Comparison of sex offenders to nonoffenders on selected psychological measures. *International Journal of Offender Therapy and Comparative Criminology, 43*(4), 473–491.

Geer, J., Estupinan, L., & Manguno-Mire, G. (2000). Empathy, social skills, and other relevant cognitive processes in rapists and child molesters. *Aggression and Violent Behavior, 5*(1), 99–126.

Glasser, M. (1988). Psychodynamic aspects of paedophilia. *Psychoanalytic Psychotherapy, 3*(2), 121–135.

Gudjonsson, G., & Sigurdsson, J. (2000). Difference and similarities between violent offenders and sex offenders. *Child Abuse and Neglect, 24*(3), 363–372.

Haas, L. and J. Haas. (1990), Understanding sexuality. Boston: Mosby.

Haywood, T., Kravitz, H., & Grossman, L. (1996). Psychological aspects of sexual functioning among cleric and non-cleric alleged sex offenders. *Child Abuse and Neglect, 20*(6), 527–536.

Heck, W. (1999). Basic investigative protocol of child sexual abuse. *FBI Law Enforcement Bulletin, 68*(10), 19–24.

Hodge, S., & Canter, D. (1989). Victims and perpetrators of male sexual assault. *Journal of Interpersonal Violence, 13*(2), 222–239.

Holmes, R., & Holmes, S. (1996). *Profiling violent crimes: An investigative tool* (2nd ed.). Newbury Park, CA: Sage.

Holmes, R., & Holmes, S. (2001). *Murder in America* (2nd ed.). Thousand Oaks, CA: Sage.

Horley, J., Quinsey, V., & Jones, S. (1997). Incarcerated child molesters' perceptions of themselves and others. *Sexual Abuse, 1*, 43–55.

Hummel, P., Thomke, V., Oldenburger, H., & Specht, F. (2000). Male adolescent sex offenders against children: Similarities and differences between those offenders with and those without a history of sexual abuse. *Journal of Adolescence, 22*(3), 305–317.

Hunt, P., & Baird, M. (1990). Children of sex rings. *Child Welfare, 69*(3), 195–207.

Hunter, J., Hazelwood, R., & Schlesinger, D. (2000). Juvenile perpetrated sex crimes: Patterns of offending and predicting violence. *Journal of Family Violence, 15*(1), 81–93.

Johnston, F., & Johnston, S. (1997). A cognitive approach to validation of the fixated-regressed typology of child molesters. *Journal of Clinical Psychology, 53*(4), 361–368.

Kear-Colwell, J., & Boer, D. P. (2000). The treatment of pedophiles: Clinical experience and the implications of recent research. *International Journal of Offender Therapy and Comparative Criminology, 44*(5), 593–605.

Langevin, R., Curnoe, S., & Bain, J. (2000). A study of clerics who commit sexual offenses: Are they different from other sex offenders? *Child Abuse and Neglect, 24*(4), 535–545.

Lanning, K., & Burgess, A. (Eds.). (1995). *Children molesters who abduct: Summary of the case in point series.* Washington, DC: Government Printing Office.

Lotke, E. (1996). Sex offenders: Does treatment work? *Corrections-Compendium, 21*(5), 1–3.

Maddox, B. (1996). Perverts won't get much out of *Lolita*. And to blame   films for child abuse misses the point. *New Statesman, 127*(4832), 40–41.

Marshall, W. L., Champagne, F., Brown, C., & Miller, S. (1997). Empathy, intimacy, loneliness, and self-esteem in nonfamilial child molesters: A brief report. *Journal of Child Sexual Abuse, 6*(3), 87.

Marshall, W., Cripps, E., & Anderson, D. (1999). Self-esteem and coping strategies in child molesters. *Journal of Interpersonal Violence, 14*(9), 955–962.

Marshall, W., & Mazzucco, A. (1995). Self-esteem and parental rejection. *Sexual Abuse, 7*(4), 279–285.

Massie, J. (2000, January 5). Personal communication.

Murray, J. (2000). Psychological profile of pedophiles and child molesters. *Journal of Psychology and Human Sexuality, 134*(2), 221–224.

Musk, H., & Swetz, A. (1997, May). Pedophilia in the correctional system. *Corrections Today, 59*(5), 24.

Nugent, P., & Kroner, D. (1996). Denial, response styles, and admittance of offenses among child molesters and rapists. Journal of Interpersonal Violence. *11*(December), 475–486.

O'Brien, S., & Goldstein, S. (1988). Why did they do it? Stories of eight convicted child molesters. *Journal of Law and Criminology, 34*, 35–48

Parsons, M. (2000). Protecting children on the electronic frontier. *FBI Law Enforcement Bulletin, 29*(10), 22–25.

Petrosino, A., & Petrosino, C. (1999). The public safety potential of Megan's Law in Massachusetts: An assessment from a sample of criminal sexual psychopaths. *Crime and Delinquency, 45*(1), 140–158.

Risley, H. (1997, August). Is your neighbor a sex offender? Community notification laws prompt examination of public disclosure policies. *Corrections Today, 59*(8), 86.

Salter, A. (1989). *Treating child sex offenders and their victims.* Newbury Park, CA: Sage.

Sawle, G. A., Kear-Colwell, J., Gary, A. S., & Jon, K.-C. (2001). Adult attachment style and pedophilia: A developmental perspective. *International Journal of Offender Therapy and Comparative Criminology, 45*(1), 32.

Simon, L. (1997). The myth of sex offender specialization: An empirical analysis. *New England Journal on Criminal and Civil Confinement, 23*(2), 387–403.

Smallbone, S., & Dadds, M. (1998). Childhood attachment and adult attachment in incarcerated adult male sex offenders. *Journal of Interpersonal Violence, 13*(5), 555–573.

Sullivan, S. (1999). Policing the internet. *FBI Law Enforcement Journal, 68*(6), 18–21.

Thomas, C. (1985). *Taber's cyclopedic medical dictionary.* Philadelphia: F.A. Davis.

Tingle, D., Bernard, G., Robbins, L., & Newman, G. (1986). Childhood and adolescent characteristics of pedophiles and rapists. *International Journal of Law and Psychiatry, 9*(1), 103–116.

Wallace, H. (1999). *Family violence: Legal, medical, and social perspectives.* Chicago: Allyn & Bacon.

Walsh, A. (1994, Winter). Homosexual and heterosexual child molestation: Case characteristics and sentencing differentials. *International Journal of Offender Therapy and Comparative Criminology, 38*(4), 339–353.

Ward, T., McCormack, J., & Hudson, S. (1997). Sexual offenders' perceptions of their intimate relationships. *Sexual Abuse, 9*(1), 57–74.

Weinrott, M., Riggan, M., & Frothingham, S. (1997). Reducing deviant arousal in juvenile sex offenders using vicarious sensitization. *Journal of Interpersonal Violence, 12*(5), 704–728.

Wheeler, D. (1996) The relationship between pornography usage and child molesting. Federal Probation. *15*(2), 34–48.

Wikipedia. (2008, February 26, 2008). Rene Guyon society. Retrieved March 15, 2008, from http://en.wikipedia.org/wiki/Ren%C3%A9_Guyon_Society

Wyatt, G. (1985). The sexual abuse of Afro-American and White-American women in childhood. *Child Abuse and Neglect, 9*, 507–519.

Zetitz, R., & M., F. (2000). Sex offenders community notification: Examining the importance of neighborhood meetings. *Behavioral Science and the Law, 18*(203), 393–406.

7

Child Pornography

❖ ❖ ❖

Perhaps nothing causes as much personal and more outrage as child pornography (Holmes & Holmes, 2001; Strange, Doyle, & Miller, 2000). Commonly called "kiddie porn" or "child porn," this type of pornography has been universally outlawed in the United States. But most of the child pornography that is confiscated by law enforcement officials in the United States has been imported from foreign countries. How widespread is this distribution of child pornography across the world? There is no easy answer to this question, and the answer will vary from one country to another. It may be more prevalent in some countries, while other countries deny any organized or commercial production of illegal child pornography. In other words, there is no clear agreement on the prevalence and cooperation among countries in the making and distribution of child pornography (Taylor & Clemetson, 2001).

Child Pornography

The use of underage children in various media for the purpose of sexual arousal for the viewer

Child pornography is produced, collected, purchased, and traded by those interested in making money in this illegal venture or those interested in sex with children. Doubtless, pedophiles and other types of child abusers collect child pornography, and those in law enforcement often find huge collections in their possession when arrested. In a case of a minister arrested only recently, the police found hundreds of pictures, movies, videos, drawings, and collages of hundreds of children in various sexual poses and scenarios. His pornography of choice was pictures, stories, and other materials of young boys prior to puberty. The people in that community were shocked to learn of his arrest. He was a "pillar of the community," active in his church as well on various public and civic groups, serving as chair on several community boards. Many adults have been arrested in sting operations advertising for children for sexual purposes. Many are teachers, and it appears that the genders are equally represented. Table 7.1 contains selected alleged perpetrators gleaned from such a site.

Table 7.1   Selected Examples of Alleged Child Sexual Offenders, 2006

Name	Age	Alleged Offense
Karri Hall	n/a	Baring her breasts to a 14-year-old male student
Cameo Patch	29	Sex with a 17-year-old student
Kyle Sabo	25	Sex with two students, one male and one female
Wendie Schweikert	36	Sex with an 11-year-old
Debbie Selmen	35	Encouraged a female student to bare her breasts
Dana Snyder	24	Sex with a 14-year-old student
Laura Spurlock	36	Sex with 18-year-old student

In a different state, a computer operator was questioned by the police when fellow workers notified law enforcement of their concern about him. He was always talking of the Polly Klaas case, and fortunately he made a critical error in judgment when he showed some of this drawings that depicted Polly bound, her breasts skewered with a sharp instrument, and finally deceased. No evidence was found showing that this man had carried out his fantasy about killing young females fueled by his own drawings, but his interests are on record with the local criminal justice system. Illustration 7.1 is one of his drawings.

❖ CHILD PORNOGRAPHY AND THE LAW

Many countries have passed laws and regulations on pornography in general and child pornography in particular. China has been leading

Illustration 7.1

the world in the enactment of laws regulating pornography. But no country has been successful in developing laws and the enforcement of such laws to combat adult, child, and Internet pornography. Before 1977, there were few laws on either the state or the federal level that regulated the production, distribution, or sale of child pornography. Today, however, every state and the federal government have laws that prescribe penalties against those who exploit children sexually. In addition, these jurisdictions have laws that make possession and distribution of child pornography a crime (Walsh & Wolak, 2005). The Protection of Children Against Sexual Exploitation Act extended the federal government's role to include prosecution of those involved in child pornography. This law has also made it illegal to transport children across state lines for immoral purposes.

All states have passed legislation against child pornography. More than a few states have merely amended their adult pornography laws to include acts that involve children. Other states, however, have devised new laws that deal specifically with children. Under these laws, penalties are prescribed for those who use children in a sexual performance, promote a sexual performance by a minor, or distribute and sell materials that depict children in sexual scenes. The fundamental question of defining pornography is not addressed and is only vaguely alluded to by the inclusion of a broad, three-pronged criterion of obscenity and an accompanying definition of "sexual performance" (Pope, 1978).

❖ TYPES OF CHILD PORNOGRAPHY

Many publications exist that cater to adults who are interested in seeing children posed in sexual situations. One study estimates there are as many as 264 magazines produced and sold in adult bookstores in the United States that deal with sexual acts between children or between children and adults (Densen-Gerber & Hutchinson, 1978). In our dealings with pedophiles we have never been involved with any who did not have some type of child porn in their possession. Some of this pornography was homemade and some was of the commercial variety.

There are several types of commercial child porn. First, there are magazines that are not unlike *Playboy* or *Penthouse*. These magazines contain pictorial essays of young boys or girls in sexually suggestive poses as well as letters from adults who desire to have sex with children or who describe their sexual activities with children. These magazines typically cater to pedophiles who are interested in having sex with either young males or young females. It is unusual, for example, for a child porn magazine to contains photos and stories about both sexes.

Magazines

Publications such as *Lollitots* and *Lolita* are aimed at pedophiles interested only in young girls. These magazines contain pictures of young females, often engaged in poses that are obviously designed to arouse erotic feelings. There are also editorials that reflect a philosophy that the real dangers to our society are the widely held negative attitudes regarding child nudity and sex with children. *Piccolo*, *Rare Boys*, and *Tommy* are examples of child porn that caters to the homosexual pedophile. The contents of these magazines are similar to those of the publications that feature young girls.

Federal Laws on Child Pornography

The Sexual Exploitation of Children Act

Prohibits the use of a minor in the making of pornography, the transport of a child across state lines, the taking of a pornographic picture of a child, and the production and circulation of materials advertising child pornography. Additionally it prohibits the transfer, sale, purchase, and receipt of a minor when the purpose is to use the child in the making of child pornography. It also prohibits the transportation, importation, shipment, and receipt of child pornography by interstate means.

The Child Protection Act of 1984

Defines anyone under the age of 18 as a minor. Thus, a sexually explicit photograph of anyone under the age of 18 is child pornography.

The Child Sexual Abuse and Pornography Act

This law banned the production and use of advertisements for child pornography with a provision of civil remedies for personal injuries suffered by a child victim. It also raised the minimum sentences for repeat offenders from imprisonment of not less than 2 years to imprisonment of not less than 5 years.

The Child Protection and Obscenity Enforcement Act

This act made it illegal to use a computer to transmit advertisements for or visual depictions of child pornography and it prohibited the buying, selling, or otherwise obtaining of temporary custody or control of children for the purpose of producing child pornography.

Telecommunications Act of 1996

This act makes it illegal for anyone using the mail or interstate or foreign commerce to persuade, induce, on entice a minor to engage in any sexual act for which the adult may be criminally prosecuted.

Child Pornography Prevention Act of 1996

States that child pornography includes anything that depicts the sexual conduct of real minors and that which appears to be a depiction of a minor engaging in sexual acts. People who alter pornographic images to look like children engaged in sexual congress can now be legally prosecuted.

Books

Another type of child porn takes the character of paperback novels. In these books, a child typically becomes the object of the sexual aggression of the reader. These paperback novels often contain graphic violence directed against a child, a powerful adult figure who victimizes a child, and a final scene in which the victimization becomes cyclical.

Internet, Pictures, Chat Channels

Photographs purchased through the mail and ads exchanged through computer bulletin boards are other methods of child porn exchange. Personal computers with high-speed Internet connections have opened the door for many pedophiles to use the Internet for a variety of purposes, which we will discuss later in this chapter. On the Internet, the pedophile can achieve sexual arousal by viewing pictures of children in sexual scenarios, by visiting websites that offer pornography and identify other websites of interest to pedophiles, and by "talking" on chat channels to others, including children. Today there are more than 1 million sites that deal with sex, pornography, and various aberrant interests (Quayle & Taylor, 2002). There are also more than 30,000 usernet newsgroups for child pornography (Quayle & Taylor, 2001).

Relational Pornography

Relational pornography, pornography created for the creator's own use, takes various forms. Poems, stories written by those interested in sex with children, and newspaper advertisements that feature children in swimwear or underwear all become items of sexual arousal for some pedophiles. These ads in themselves are not pornographic in nature—they are intended only as sales promotions. However, when they interact with the fantasy of the pedophile, they can become a form of child porn.

❖ WHO VIEWS CHILD PORN

There are several audiences for child pornography. Pedophiles compose the largest number of people who view child porn. Just as "normal" adults view pornography for various reasons, including sexual arousal, so do pedophiles. The curious form another group of persons who view child porn. Many wish to see such pornography because they have not seen it before; they are simply curious about the content. For most of these viewers, this is a one-time occurrence.

Yet another group is composed of those persons who are involved in the manufacture of child pornography. A great deal of child pornography comes from Scandinavian countries; it is also produced in Mexico, Spain, the United States, and other countries. The persons who produce such materials must view their own products as well as those of others, to see what topics are "hot" in child porn.

Lured into prostitution and then pornography, pimps are often involved. With promises of friendship, money, or drugs, pimps locate clients for child porn. Child porn materials are marketed through a subculture of black-market contacts who make them available to ready customers. They are often shipped through the mail, and recently, with the technological advancements made on the Internet, instant connections are made and photos are sent almost instantly from one predator's computer to another's. Mitchell, Finkelhor, and Wolak (2005) found that almost 80% of those arrested for child pornography charges have admitted to having sex with children and had had on average 30.5 child sex victims. It appears from such data that exposure to child pornography tends to support child sexual abuse. Further, it serves to lessen the personal and moral inhibitions of the child. The collections of relational child pornography often contain pictures of children the predator has sexually abused.

Child Pornography—From the Eyes of a Child Porn User

Sitting in a prison visiting room, we sat across from an elderly man, a former minister of the Episcopal faith. He had been sentenced to a multiyear prison term for the possession of child pornography.

The police had contacted one author (RMH) to offer an opinion on the content of the child pornography that was seized in his home and the meaning of such pornography. Most of the material was commercial child porn that he had purchased through the mail, at one of several adult bookstores in the area, and others he had traded with other pedophiles in his neighborhood and community. Such publications included *Lollitots, Lolita,* and others that depicted nude young girls not yet out of puberty.

There was another form of kiddie porn that we have termed relational pornography. This is the type that one makes for oneself or views otherwise innocent photos or advertisements but which the pedophile or child molester judges to be sexually arousing.

One such picture was an advertisement for Chee-tos. This ad showed a young girl, perhaps 12 years of age, holding a bag of Chee-tos in her left hand. Her right arm was bent at her hip, and the expression on her face was one of gentle annoyance at the adult male (presumably her father) who had just pulled a Chee-to out of the bag. His eyes were looking down toward the bag of treats that she held in front of her.

We questioned him about this advertisement in his collection. We asked him to explain it to us and why he would keep this advertisement in his collection.

"You don't get it, do you?" He said. "The man (he did not say father) has just reached inside the bag and while reaching he had the perfect chance of feeling her breast. His eyes are not looking into the bag but inside her shorts she is wearing. Also, look at the way her mouth is opened. Just right!"

We went back to the office and reexamined the ad. What looked like an innocent picture in the beginning was pornographic to the child abuser. Did the food company deliberately construct this advertisement to contain such sexual elements?

This same man explained to us how sexually aroused he became each spring when the department stores showed ads of young girls on the beach in their swimwear. Needless to say, these ads were a part of his collection.

In Wheeler's (1996) study of 150 child abusers, more than 90% reported having some fantasies about committing sexual offenses against children. Child molesters were far more likely to view child pornography than biological fathers who molest their children. While some molesters said that the child pornography served a cathartic effect, slightly more than one in three child abusers reporting using child pornographic materials shortly before committing a sexual offense. Holmes and Holmes (2001) report similar findings. Wolak et al. (2005) stated that the viewer of child pornography tended to be white, male, and above 25 years of age. Forty percent were dual offenders— viewed child pornography as well as sexually abused children.

There are legitimate reasons for viewing child pornography. Law enforcement and other social, political, or educational groups must sometimes view this material to gauge the content and to judge its legal status, or to formulate some type of psychological profile of the person who possesses such materials. We have consulted with several police departments on the content of child pornography to give the police an idea as to the personality of the owner.

❖ HOW DO CHILDREN BECOME INVOLVED IN PORNOGRAPHY?

It appears that children who become involved in child porn come from diverse sources (Holmes, 1984; Schultz, 1980). First, there are "sporting clubs" composed of parents who arrange for their children to appear in sexually oriented photographs. There are parents who swap photographs, videos, and films of their children with other parents and commercial enterprises for fun and profit (Bahlmann & Thomas, 1979; Holmes, 1983).

Burdiit (1978) states that often children who are involved in pornography are intimidated by adults who hold power over them. Schultz (1980) reports a case of one couple who took in children off the streets, who would then have to pay their "rent" by performing in child porn productions. In another case, a couple with a 6-month-old child were arrested by police when it became known that they were involving their infant in childhood prostitution with men. In addition to the prostitution case, the police discovered that the father was filming the sex between the child and the adults and selling the videos as child pornography. The couple was granted probation by the court, and the child was released to the couple's custody.

In a southern city, an elderly man posed as a researcher for a sex research institute in California (no such organization existed). He enticed young girls into his home under the pretense of gathering data. He administered them a "test" that consisted of fifty-six questions. Some of the questions were

- What is your age? (Item 1)
- Have you ever felt or played with a mans (sic) dick? (Item 26)
- Would you play with a mans (sic) dick if you had the chance? (Item 27)
- Do you know a mans (sic) you would play with? (Item 29)
- Do you know a man that you would let play with your pussy? (Item 32)
- Have you ever been fingerfucked by a man? (Item 37)

The man also had a scoring sheet. With each young girl who took this "test," he maintained a scoring sheet. If they answered the above items positively (with the exception of Item 1), he would demand sex from them. He would tell them that if they did not have sex with him he would tell the parents about the results of the test, including other questions about lesbianism and coitus.

This same abuser ran another ruse. He would invite some other young girls over for counseling sessions. A deacon in his church, he would hold sessions in his home for religious education. After he formed a judgment on the possibility of involving them in sex with him, he would invite a small group to his home for "special sessions." He had taped a "radio" question-and-answer program on the sexual play of young girls. The radio program was called "Mr. Sex Man." He placed the cassette player in the gutted frame of his radio in his living room. After a snack and small talk he would turn on the radio program at the top of the hour because "this was when the program would come on." Recall that this man was in his late 60s at the time of his arrest. His purpose was to show how normal it would be for young girls (10–12) to enter into a sexual relationship with an old man.

The questions included

- How old does girl have to be to do sex things with a (sic) old man?
- Is it better for a little girl to do sex things with an old man or a young boy?
- What kind of little girl does a (sic) old man like to do sex things with?

- Does an old man like a young girl to suck his dick?
- Does a (sic) old man like to suck a little girl's pussy?
- Have you, Mr. Sex Man, ever played with a little girl's pussy?

The narrative by the abuser would start with a question, and the question would be followed by an answer that was always positive and validated the sex play between the old man and the young girl. Mr. Sex Man was in effect giving permission for the young girl to have sex with this man. After all, as Mr. Sex Man had already informed the audience, the old men have more to offer the young girls in the areas of experience, technique, and a willingness to teach the young girl the proper way to perform sexually.

Mr. Sex Man was arrested by the police after the word got around the neighborhood about his activities. He was sentenced to a local prison, where he died of natural causes.

In Illinois, a summer camp was found to be a front for enticing children into child porn. Confidential film-developing services are yet another source of child pornography. There is a widespread belief that organized crime is involved in the child pornography industry, but this does not appear to be the case (Illinois Legislative Investigative Committee, 1980).

❖ WHO ARE THE CHILDREN IN CHILD PORNOGRAPHY?

There is a lack of empirical research on the extent and the characteristics of the children who are involved in child pornography. Baker (1978) states that there are more than 30,000 children annually involved in the child porn industry; more than 3,000 under the age of 14 are in Los Angeles alone. How accurate is that estimate? No one knows exactly, but we should not measure a social problem only by statistical data.

Some characteristics appear to be common to children involved in child pornography:

1. Involved in childhood prostitution

2. Ran away from home

3. Came from a broken home

4. Is between the ages of 8 and 17

5. Was an underachiever in school or home

6. Has no strong moral or religious affiliation

7. Shows poor social development

8. Has parents who are physically or psychologically absent

In an unpublished study conducted for the Exploited and Missing Child Unit in Louisville, Kentucky, we interviewed 34 juveniles who admitted being involved in child pornography. Their core social variables showed interesting similarities. For example, children involved in the child porn industry are frequently runaways. Some children flee their homes because of abuse, rigid discipline, or a variety of other reasons, such as pregnancy or emotional problems. Family disorganization and discord are associated with juvenile participation in child porn. The youths reported that few of their parents were married (14.6%), and only one in five admitted to having a close relationship with his or her parents. Only 20% reported close relationships with their brothers and sisters. The responses of this sample indicate a malaise in relationships within the family. Although the data obtained in this study suggest a high rate of divorce within such families, marital status may not be as important as the amount of conflict present in the family. Divorce, as a process, may be a problem-solving technique and may create a situation that is healthier than the one that might exist if the conflicting parents remain together.

An Interview with a Child Porn User

The following is an excerpt from an interview with John B., an incarcerated pedophile. The interview occurred in a medium-security prison. John had been sentenced to 600 years in prison for possession of child pornography, child abuse, sodomy charges, and a variety of other sex-related charges. He is 63 years old.

John:	I find pornography to be beneficial to me. It releases stress for me. When I look at it I find my blood pressure goes down, and I feel a certain amount of sexual pleasures flowing through my body as I think about the models in the pictures. It is, at least for me, one way that I can eliminate a desire to find a child. But it is never a complete substitute.
Question:	When did you first start looking at child pornography?
John:	You probably don't remember the old 8 pagers. As a kid, I was exposed to those by the older boys in the neighborhood. They showed me pictures of Popeye and some other comic characters involved in sex. I thought they were disgusting. But they showed me

one of young boys doing oral sex. It was an immediate turn on. So from that time on I was hooked.

Question: Where did you obtain your collection of child pornography?

John: For a long time I was fortunate to get some of it from friends. But it is everywhere. My favorite source was National Geographic magazines. People might not know it, but there are always pictures of naked people in the magazines. People get upset with the naked women, but often in the background are naked children hanging on to the legs of their mothers or walking in a pool of water. I looked at ads in the newspapers, especially in the spring or summer, for swimsuits, underwear, pajamas, and other things that had children wearing the clothes.

After I finished my term in the Navy, I came back home and got a job at a porn shop. We had no child pornography on the shelves. The manager kept a small amount under the counter for those customers that he knew, people he knew were not police or cops. He, and later I, would sell this to those people. I would take some home and look at it after I closed the store in the early morning. I would bring it back the next day when I went to work. I knew all about *Rare Boys, Piccolo*, and a lot of other magazines that I would look at.

Unfortunately, I have been in prison too long to have used the Internet. I talk to some of the new guys and they tell me what's on the Internet now.

Question: When was the last time you have seen any type of child pornography?

John: Last week. Yes, last week. One of my neighbors (a fellow prisoner) had some brought in by a visitor.

Question: Did it have an effect upon you?

John: Oh yes. I spent a long time looking at it. I had a glorious time masturbating. It's been a long time.

Without exception, the children admitted to the use of alcohol and drugs, especially marijuana and amphetamines. In more than four of five cases, the children said they had run away from home—another indication of family discord. Perhaps because of the problems in the home—with discord, aggression, hostility, and anomie—the runaway behavior may be viewed as another problem-solving technique. But in most cases this behavior results only in the child's moving from one bad situation to another. Involvement in child pornography may be a matter of survival for many children, as is involvement in prostitution.

The general findings of this study present a psychological profile of a child who comes from a home where loving and caring are not expressed, where discord is common, and where there is frequent physical abuse and drug abuse. This is the making of a child involved in the child porn industry.

❖ THE INTERNET AND CHILD PORNOGRAPHY

When the first edition of this book was published in 1991, the Internet was becoming a viable means of sharing all kinds of information. Certainly those interested in child sex were likewise interested in becoming experts in retrieving information about child pornography and other types of information about sex with children. The nonabuser population may not be aware of how the Internet serves the purposes of abusers in their search for victims (McCabe, 2000). Despite the numbers who agree that child pornography is a gross social problem, the traffic in child pornography has grown dramatically. Also, the revolution in child pornography enabled by digital cameras and published on the World Wide Web is presenting the criminal justice system with a monumental problem of enforcement (Williams, 1997).

What are the goals and objectives of child abusers who use the Internet? Durkin (1997) reports that child abusers use the Internet to

- Traffic in child porn with others
- Have sexual communication with children
- Locate children to abuse
- Communicate with others

The vast majority of information on the Internet is entertaining, informative, and educational. But the "Net" can have a dark side.

The growth of the Internet into a powerful, worldwide medium has increased the danger to youths throughout the world and complicated law enforcement capabilities. It has simplified the method of exchanging child pornography, allowing an individual to receive pornography instantly. In a matter of minutes a viewer can access images, pedophiles can use the Internet, with no precautions, to exchange names and addresses of other pedophiles and of potential child-victims.

SOURCE: Internet Related Child Exploitation, February 2001 www.missingkids.com/ncmec_default_ec_internet.html

John Karr

John Mark Karr was arrested in Thailand on 16 August 2006 in connection with the 1996 killing of JonBenet Ramsey. Ramsey was found strangled in her Boulder, Colorado, home on 26 December 1996; the killing was heavily covered in the media, bolstered by photos of the young victim's many appearances in junior beauty pageants. No one was charged in the case until Karr's arrest nearly a decade later. According to the Associated Press, Karr told reporters after his arrest that "I was with JonBenet when she died" and that the death "was an accident." Karr's connections to the victim and the Ramsey family were not clear, and almost immediately after his arrest questions arose as to the veracity of his confession. The *Bangkok Post* reported that Karr had been in Thailand for two months prior to his arrest and "appears to have lived a solitary, nomadic life roaming across the world surviving by teaching, without returning to the United States for several years." Karr had been arrested in California for possession of child pornography in 2001.

The Internet provides the child abuser and many others who have as a common interest their sexual attraction to children and who have collections of child pornography to share and trade. Such sharing has become very easy with the advent of digital photographic technology. In the same way that some adults are involved in triolism, those child abusers interested in trading pictures can attach a picture or a series of pictures and e-mail the attachment to another within a matter of seconds. Trading occurs over the Internet despite the best efforts of those opposed on various grounds (legal, moral, religious, etc.). Photographs taken by an individual, and pictures or slides scanned on a desktop or handheld scanner can all be used to send child pornography across the nation and across the world instantly. Those interested in child pornography can receive such images from those they know as well as complete strangers, some of whom are law enforcement personnel working child porn stings.

The Internet provides a source for adults to establish a link with children who are in chat channels. Frequently a pedophile or child molester will visit a chat channel where youth are "talking." Asking and answering questions, telling the child about himself or herself, courting and seducing with careful words, the abuser will often never make personal contact with the child. From the abuser's point of view, it may be sufficient to carry on a lengthy relationship over the Internet and use the connection as a means to become sexually aroused and culminate in masturbation. With others, there is an attempt to make a personal connection with the child. An effort is made to meet the child at an arcade, mall, or somewhere where children often gather. Sex is obviously the goal, but in some instances there are more serious intentions, such as homicide.

Some abusers use the Internet to inform themselves on locating children to abuse. They may enter chat rooms to see what children's latest activities are. They also may establish connections with other abusers who will share information about successful sexual abuse they have conducted. Names, addresses, pictures, and other information may be shared among the various abusers who have established connections over the Web.

Child abusers establish relationships with others of the same kind over the Internet. They may share not only the information they have learned from others, but arrange times and places to personally meet. In this way, information sharing becomes a part of the networking element of the Internet and the child abusers. Within a short time, the abuser, within the safety of a password and a nickname (which can be changed as often as desired, hourly, daily, weekly), can make statements, ask questions, make requests, seek information, and take other actions within relative safety and anonymity. The Internet becomes a vital tool in the abusers' repertoire for the eventual abuse of children.

Cyberspace is a reservoir for child-abuse activity. For example, on-line bulletin boards dedicated to special sexual predilections, including sex with children, are readily available to child abusers. These computer communications include not only an exchange of photos (usually containing scanned pictures, digital photos in JPEG format) but also shared messages of an erotic content, which may range from mild flirtations, exchanging information about sexual services available, and specific varieties of deviant behavior, including sex with children (Durkin & Bryant, 1995).

In the first edition of this book, we mentioned publications such as the *Broadstreet Journal*. These magazines and forms of child pornography have all but disappeared since the appearance of the World Wide Web. Enforcement against the material on the Web is more difficult than against print pornography if for no other reason than the character and anonymity of the material itself.

There is no reason to assume that the law enforcement community will be completely effective and eradicate child pornography on the Internet. One detective, Walt Parsons, of the Arvada, Colorado, Police Department, has utilized the Web to attract child abusers. One man from New Mexico answered his note on a chat channel about having a 12-year-old-daughter whom he would make available to the abuser for a price. The man drove to Colorado with money, a teddy bear, ropes, chains, dildos, and other sexual paraphernalia. Parsons videotaped the initial interview with the man and asked about the teddy bear. The man responded that this was a good way to win the child's attention before he would tie them up and insert objects into various orifices of the child's body. The man was arrested and sentenced to prison.

This is only one case. There are many others. But how many escape detection is unknown. The eradication of the Internet as a tool for abusers is the goal; how successful it will be, only time will tell. Law enforcement professionals must be careful in their zeal to apprehend child abusers. Agents of the U.S. government tried to entice Keith Jacobson, a 56-year-old Nebraska farmer, to buy child pornography through the mail. Government agents posed as representatives of groups advocating freedom of expression and opposing the moral majority and government censorship. Finally Jacobson bought a packet of child pornography. He was arrested and convicted in federal court. The U.S. Supreme Court ruled that the government's law-enforcement efforts had constituted entrapment. The court stated that there was no evidence that Jacobson was inclined to commit this violation before the government initiated its actions and made him a target in their investigations. The key issue here is what restrictions should be placed on the government in its investigations of this type of crime, which the court did not address (Piccarreta & Keenan, 1993).

❖ CONCLUSION

Child pornography is a social problem that affects a significant number of people, our children. It has been demonstrated that exposure to child porn does fuel the fantasy for many sex abusers, including incest offenders, pedophiles, and other types of child abusers. While it has been shown that incestuous perpetrators are not as likely to view child pornography, this is also not to say that child porn does not fuel the fantasy of those who view children in a sexual manner. The effects upon the child involved are also not well documented, but nothing positive could be the product of exposure to this form of abuse, something that the child may never recover. American society will also not tolerate child sexual abuse in any form, sexual abuse from a pedophile or child molester or child pornography

❖ DISCUSSION QUESTIONS

1. This chapter discussions two major forms of child pornography, commercial (those made by businesses and commercial outlets), and relational (those made by individuals, normally for their own use. Which of these two do you consider the most serious? Why?

2. What would you consider some of the problems in the enforcement of child pornography laws in this country?

3. How has the Internet contributed to the proliferation of child pornography? Should the federal government take a more active role in enforcement against this form of pornography on the Internet?

4. What would you consider to be some of the effects on children involved in the child pornography industry? How did you develop your conclusion?

5. There have been several cases in which parents or grandparents have taken pictures of their child or grandchild in the bathtub nude. The adults have been arrested and charged with the manufacturing and possession of child pornography. What is your position on this scenario?

❖ REFERENCES

Bahlmann, D., & Thomas, H. (1979). *Children and youth as victims of violence.* Paper presented at the Sixth National Conference on Juvenile Justice, Reno, NV.

Baker, C. (1978). Preying on playgrounds: The sexploitation of children in pornography and prostitution. *Pepperdine Law Review, 5,* 809–846.

Burdiit, T. (1978). *Social abuse of children and adolescents.* Houston: Texas House Select Committee on Child Pornography.

Densen-Gerber, J., & Hutchinson, S. (1978). *Medico-legal and societal problems involving children, child prostitution, child pornography, and drug-related abuse.* Baltimore: University Park Press.

Durkin, K. (1997). Misuse of the Internet by pedophiles: Implications for law enforcement and probation practice. *Federal Probation, 61*(3), 14–18.

Durkin, K., & Bryant, C. (1995). "Log on to sex": Some notes on the carnal computer and erotic cyberspace as an emerging research frontier. *Deviant Behavior, 16*(3), 179–200.

Holmes, R. (1983). *The sex offender and the criminal justice system.* Springfield, IL: Charles C Thomas.

Holmes, R. (1984). Children in pornography. *Police Chief,* 42–43.

Holmes, S., and R. Holmes. Sex Crimes. Patterns and Behavior. Thousand Oaks, CA: Sage Publications.

Holmes, R., & Holmes, S. (2001). *Murder in America* (2nd ed.). Thousand Oaks, CA: Sage.

Illinois Legislative Investigative Committee. (1980). *Sexual exploitation of children: Report to the Illinois General Assembly*. Chicago: Author.

McCabe, K. (2000). Child pornography and the Internet. *Social Science Computer Review, 18*(1), 73–76.

Mitchell, K., Finkelhor, D., & Wolak, J. (2005). Internet and family and acquaintance sexual abuse. *Child Maltreatment, 10*(1), 49–60.

Piccarreta, M., & Keenan, J. (1993). Entrapment targets and tactics: *Jacobson* v. *United States. Criminal Law Bulletin, 29*(3), 241–252.

Pope, R. (1978). Child pornography: A new role for the obscenity doctrine. *University of Illinois Law Forum, 47*, 711–757.

Quayle, E., & Taylor, M. (2001). Child seduction and self-representation on the internet. *CyberPsychology and Behavior, 4*(5), 597–608.

Quayle, E., & Taylor, M. (2002). Child pornography and the internet: Perpetuating a cycle of abuse. *Deviant Behavior, 23*(4), 331–362.

Schultz, L. (1980). *Sexual victimology of youth*. Springfield, IL: Charles C Thomas.

Strange, C., Doyle, K., & Miller, L. (2000). Traditional and new challenges in responding to difference and deviation. *Studies in Law, Politics, and Society, 20*, 159–238.

Taylor, S. Jr., & Clemetson, L. (2001). Is it sexual exploitation if victims are 'virtual'? *Newsweek, 137*(12), 51.

Walsh, W. A., & Wolak, J. (2005). Nonforcible Internet-related sex crimes with adolescent victims: Prosecution issues and outcomes. *Child Maltreatment, 10*(3), 260–271.

Wheeler, D. (1996). The relationship between pornography usage and child molesting. *Federal Probation, 15*(2), 34–48.

Wolak, J., Finkelhor, D., & Mitchell, K.J. (2005). Child Pornography Possessors Arrested in Internet-Related Crimes: Findings from the National Juvenile Online Victimization Study. National Center for Missing & Exploited Children, Alexandria: VA

Williams, P. (1997). Illegal immigration and commercial sex. New York: Frank Case Publishers.

8

Pornography

❖ ❖ ❖

There are few more difficult moral social issues confronting Americans than pornography and obscenity. There are many arguments over the effects, both positive and negative, of exposure to erotica. National organizations such as Citizens for Decency Through the Law (CDTL) have been established to lobby for legislation to combat the perceived dangers of pornography and obscenity.

What is lacking in this debate is any thorough empirical examination of pornography and obscenity and their effects. On the one hand, it is often suggested that exposure to pornography leads those exposed to serious sex crimes. Data presented in this chapter suggest that such exposure does not necessarily lead to the commission of sex crimes by someone who is otherwise a socialized human being. The content of the sexual messages, the amount and character of personal violence, the debasement of women, and so on may have more to do with the predilections of the viewer than with the pornography itself. Other studies will suggest a direct relationship between exposure and sex crimes. The reader must judge whether it is the exposure to pornography alone that accounts for the deviance or whether there are more concrete experiences that would account for serious and illegal sexual transgressions.

❖ PORNOGRAPHY AND OBSCENITY

In any examination of pornography there emerges immediately the issue of definitions. This should be the first thing addressed by any decisive examination. The word *pornography* literally means "the writings of harlots." In the early history of humankind, paintings that depicted men and women in sexual scenes were found on the walls of caves. In ancient Mesopotamia, for example, Baal and Ishtar, Marduk, humans, animals, and others were depicted in sexual scenes on dinner plates, wash basins, water holders, and other household goods. Today, a debate exists over whether this type of material can be classified as pornography. Were the plates kilned to arouse the citizens or were they depictions of religious rites, rituals, and ceremonies?

What is obscene and what is not? On the one hand, pornography is not difficult to define. Pornography is *not* a subjective evaluation from the point of view of the customer who buys *Playboy* magazine. Pornography is material produced for the manifest purpose of arousing erotic feelings. The primary motive for producing a painting, a book, a statue, a movie, or a music album may be to make money, but if a secondary reason is to arouse erotic feelings within the buyer or the viewer, it is pornography. Works of art that include nudity, such as Michelangelo's statue of David or the Venus de Milo, are never defined by serious critics as pornography. Medical textbooks that show sexual organs and parts of the body that normally are sexual in nature are seldom viewed as pornographic. But when one views the centerfold of a *Playboy* magazine, there is little doubt about the motivation of the model, the photographer, or the publisher. The depiction of the Playboy Bunny of the Month is intended for arousal of the viewer as well as to make money. The deliberate exposure of certain body parts is intended to arouse sexual feelings and also obviously to make money.

The definition of obscenity is more subjective. Obscenity can be defined as anything that is disgusting to the senses. This is a question that is very difficult to address and debate adequately (Abraham, Hill, Sass, & Sobel, 1980). There are issues and behaviors that are obscene but not pornographic—war, for example. For many, war is obscene under any circumstances. The conflict in Vietnam was judged to be obscene by untold thousands of people in the United States. Child sexual and physical abuse is obscene. Poverty, spouse abuse, and many other social problems that have nothing to do with sexual arousal are judged by many to be obscene.

Obscenity's subjective character causes a great deal of consternation among groups lobbying for action against pornography. A standard has been developed to measure what qualifies as pornography. But obscenity is an entirely different story.

❖ STANDARDS OF OBSCENITY

There have been numerous attempts to regulate obscenity throughout U.S. history. Some groups, such as Citizens for Decency Through the Law, are involved in pushing for legislation against pornography. CDTL was founded by Charles Keating, who is currently being sued by the state of California for alleged fraud in the sale of $250 million in now worthless junk bonds, particularly victimizing the elderly (*USA Today*, June 28, 1990, p. B1). Many would judge the bilking of the elderly, many on fixed incomes, as obscene. The beating of Rodney King, despite his criminal past, is judged to be obscene by many. The killings of Nicole Simpson and Ron Goldman are thought obscene. The list is really endless.

Obscenity is not protected by the First Amendment and may be forbidden and regulated by government (Gardner, 1989). The case of *Miller v. California* (413 U.S. 15, 93 S.Ct. 2607, 1973) was an attempt to settle once and for all the debate over what is obscene. There are three standards used to determine what is pornographic and obscene:

1. Whether "the average person applying contemporary community standards" would find that the work, taken as a whole, appeals to prurient interest (i.e., appeals to sexual interest, causing a person to become sexually aroused)

2. Whether the work or communication depicts or describes, in a patently offensive way, sexual conduct specifically defined by applicable state law

3. Whether the work of communication, taken as a whole, lacks serious literary, artistic, political, or scientific value

❖ CUSTOMERS FOR PORNOGRAPHY

It appears that most consumers of pornography are young married males. The majority are college-educated white-collar workers. Approximately 25% of all consumers of pornography have been exposed to some sadomasochistic material.

John B, an incarcerated pedophile who used to work as a counter salesperson at an adult porn bookstore, said in an interview that his store kept the child pornography under the counter and would sell the material only to customers who had become fairly well known. He stated that there were no distinguishing factors he could ascertain when selling the kiddie porn other than the customers were mostly white businessmen who came into the shore during their lunch hours.

Most consumers of adult pornography have sex partners and use pornography to enhance their own sex lives with those partners. Younger consumers and many others use pornography for masturbatory purposes (Nawy, 1973; Wilson & Abelson, 1973).

The viewing of pornography is not completely a male endeavor. Pearson and Pollock (1997) found that women also view pornography, although not to the same extent as men. Women who volunteer to view sexually explicit scenes appear to be more aroused by scenes that are produced from a female perspective than by those produced from a traditional male perspective. Their arousal also seems to be connected to the amount and extent of their previous experiences with pornography, their masturbation history, and the amount of guilt they feel about sex in general.

❖ PORNOGRAPHY, RESEARCH, AND THE SEX CRIMINAL

The central issue here is the relationship between sex crimes and exposure to erotica. Various studies have examined the relationship. In 1970, the President's Commission on Obscenity and Pornography failed to reach a firm conclusion on the relationship between exposure to pornography and sex offenses. Discounting the possible (some might say probable) relationship between child pornography and sex crimes against children, principally because of the lack of child pornography materials and observations that existed in U.S. society 20 years ago, the statements this commission made on pornography were directed toward adult pornography. The majority statement made by the commission members was that adult erotic materials should be available for all those persons over the age of 18 who want to look at said materials. Since there was no finding of a causal relationship between exposure to erotic materials and sex crimes, the commission believed that banning such materials would not serve a positive societal function.

Of course, not all members of the group believed this position. Charles Keating, then a congressman from Ohio, stated that pornography should be banned for all persons regardless of age. His classic statement, "Those who wallow in filth will get dirty," has been quoted and misquoted many times since he uttered it almost 40 years ago.

Kant and Goldstein (1973) studied three groups of men: "normals" (occasional viewers of pornographic material), "users" (regular purchasers and viewers of pornography), and "sex offenders" (incarcerated rapists, child molesters of young boys, and child molesters of young girls who had been free at least one year prior to the study). Two particularly important questions were asked of all the groups. One question was, "As an adolescent, how much pornography did you see?" Carefully measuring quantity, Kant and Goldstein found that sex offenders all reported less exposure to pornographic material than did the other two groups. A second question addressed the men's exposure to pornography "last year." The time frame was important because the sex offenders had all been free the previous year. Again, the sex offenders reported seeing less pornography than the other two groups. One finding of this study is that exposure to pornography may play a positive role in the maturational process of nonoffenders. The most important finding is that sex criminals, not only as adolescents but also as adults, see less pornography than do normals or users. Similar findings were reported by Khoury (1988) in her study of men who were abusive and men were not abusive in their relationships with the significant women in their lives. No difference was found.

The debate over the effects of pornography still rages. Jensen (1995) reports that there is a connection between pornography and the manner in which men view women. Jensen's study suggests that pornography can be a factor in shaping a male-dominant view of sexuality and in creating a difficulty in the separation between a sexual fantasy—mental imagery that is sexually arousing or erotic (Byrne & Osland, 2000)—and reality. Jensen further found that pornography can be used in a victim-selection process and create a learning manual for the viewer.

❖ PORNOGRAPHY AND VIOLENCE

McCarthy (1982) believes that the findings of the President's Commission noted above are no longer valid, since the character of pornography has changed a great deal since the early 1970s, with more violence, more attacks directed against women, and less consensual sexual acts shown. How pornography has changed certainly has some effects upon the persons who view it. But what is the effect? Is it always negative? Many believe that exposure to pornographic materials necessarily leads a person to commit sex crimes against women. Russell (1998) voiced a grave concern and concluded that there is a direct and causal relationship between pornography and sex crimes against women, a conclusion not shared by Cramer, McFarlane, Parker, Soeken, and Reel (1998). Harris and Staunton (2000) state that there does appear to be some relationship between exposure to pornography and violent crime but also suggest other antecedents: a poor family environment, a history of psychological disturbances, sexual abuse in the family, and substance abuse in the family. Levin and Fox (1999) report that serial killers are inspired by pornography.

Fishbach and Malamuth (1978) suggest a link between exposure to violent pornography and sex crimes against women. Their position has been validated by others (Goode, 1984, for example). In a study of 54 college-age males, Heilbrun and Seif (1988) found that men who viewed violent erotic pictures of women in physical distress in bondage found it to be more sexually stimulating than a female model displayed in a more positive setting. Linz (1989) found that long-term exposure to violent pornography (slasher films) resulted in consistently less sensitivity toward rape victims among a male sample. Cramer et al. (1998) surveyed 198 abused women and asked them if they had been asked or forced to look at, act out, or pose for pornographic scenes or pictures. Almost 60% of the white females had responded in the affirmative to this question, 27% of the blacks, and almost 40% of the Hispanics. The conclusion of the study was that there were a multitude of factors that accompany an abusive relationship, and pornography is just one of these elements. The report added that there was no relationship found between the severity of violence among the couples and the exposure to pornography. Norris, George, Davis, Martell, and Leonesio (1999) add alcohol abuse as a contributing element to the viewing of violent pornography resulting in the abuse of women, whether it is perpetrated within the family or on strangers. Caron and Carter (1997) also found that attitudes toward pornography were unrelated to attitudes (not necessarily actions) toward rape. There also appears to be no statistical relationship between the number of videos that are rented by a person and negative attitudes toward women that result in the sexual or physical abuse of women culminating in the violent crime of rape (Davies, 1997; Jansen, Linz, Mulac, & Imrich, 1997). This same finding was reported by Barak, Fisher, Belfrey, and Lashambe (1999) in their study of Internet pornography. They reported that they could not ascertain a statistical relationship between one's exposure to Internet pornography and negative attitudes toward women.

Padgett and Brislin-Slutz (1989) report that patrons of adult theaters who view more pornography than college students who were also studied, have more favorable attitudes toward women than the college students, and attitudes toward women are not influenced by type of exposure. In addition, pornography may become for some a source of sex education. This hypothesis is supported by research conducted by Tjaden (1988) and Gardos and Mosher (1999), who found significant differences between young men's and young women's uses of pornography as a sex education tool and gender differences in the arousal level from exposure to pornography. In perhaps a more controversial finding, Bogaert, Woodard, and Hafer (1999) reported that arousal might also be a factor of intelligence. They reported that the less intelligent viewer tended to be more sexually aroused by viewing pornography than the more intelligent in their sample.

Unfortunately for some women, their exposure to some pornography may present them with images of women that are exaggerated. This appears especially true among women who view pornography early in their lives (Keihani, 1999.). This false picture may leave them with a self-image that does not measure up to the physical displays of the actresses in the videos or in the movies. Siegel (1998) found that women who were interviewed after viewing pornography discussed their feelings about their own bodies in comparison to the women in the pornographic video or movie and how lacking the women viewed themselves in this physical regard. Walsh (1999) reports that women who view pornography are more likely to come from a family of divorce, more likely to have been divorced themselves, and had a poor personal relationship with their parents. These factors may also have had as much impact upon their poor self-image as the factors that Siegel (1998) found.

The central issue in the relationship between sex crimes and exposure to pornography is the long-term effect that this exposure may have on a person. Long-term effects have yet to be found in the research done by serious social and behavioral scientists. It may be that "exposure to violent pornography does not necessarily cause such callous attitudes, but may simply reinforce and strengthen attitudes that people already hold" (Conklin, 1989). Exposure to sexually explicit materials does not in itself foster negative attitudes or behavior in men's relationships with women. But there is some evidence that repeated exposure to pornography coupled with violence may decrease inhibitions for some and lead to some victimization (Donerstein, Linz, & Penrod, 1987).

❖ PORNOGRAPHY AND THE INTERNET

Perhaps the largest collection of pornography today resides within the Internet. The pornography there is varied in character and the content is immense. Sexual chat channels deal with a variety of topics. Pictures are available in a variety of formats depicting an equally wide variety of interests and practices.

Chat Channels

To have a conversation about sex within the comfort and safety of one's own home or office, the chat room is available. This is a software "location" where visitors meet to exchange messages (Mills, 1998). Meeting others to talk about sex is nothing new. Singles bars, phone sex, escort services, massage parlors, and houses of prostitution have historically been places where people to meet to talk or "chat" about sex. But what is different about Internet chat channels is that there is a geographical and personal distance among the persons who talk. There is a feeling of anonymity. It is "safe sex," with no fear of disease, little possibility of public exposure, and the ability to speak of whatever one wishes without the fear of reprisals. Each chat room has a title that alerts the visitor to the general topic to be discussed. Some have such names as "teenage chat room," "olders," and "S&M." These chat rooms cater to people with various sexual interests. The stories, notes, and so forth are exchanged for the express purpose of sexual titillation and arousal.

Photo Exchange

In many chat channels and other sources on the Internet, photographs are exchanged that depict models (often enough professional, but apparently most often amateurs) in a variety of scenarios. Holmes, Tewksbury, and Holmes (1998) examined the types of pictures exchanged and developed labels for the types.

Categories of JPEGs

Innocents

In this category, an "innocent" person is caught unaware that a picture is being taken when a part of the body of the victim is exposed. This may occur when a gust of wind blows up the skirt of a woman and exposes her panties, for example. There is no cooperation between the victim and the person taking the picture. Often the scene is outdoors, around a pool or the ocean, but sometimes it appears someone is taking a picture through an open window into the bedroom or bathroom of a victim. In this category, there is no overt sexual activity depicted.

Cartoons

Various cartoon characters, e.g., Snow White, Cinderella, or Mickey Mouse, are shown in sexually explicit scenes. Snow White, for example, may be depicted topless and engaged in an obscene verbal exchange with another cartoon character. Some scenes show a single character while other scenes will depict a group scene with various characters. There does not appear to be a preference. In one picture we viewed, Snow White was being molested by the Seven Dwarfs. Most often, the cartoon character is a female.

Oddities and Bizarre

This category will depict scenes of various sexual activities. Many will show some type of anal insertion with items as bowling balls, handguns, and other such objects. An examination of these pictures shows a pattern in which the inserter is a male and the insertee is a female.

Sexual Activities

This is one of the largest areas of contributions. The scope of sexual activities is wide. Some is will show acts of bestiality in which a female is usually the one having sex with an animal, often a dog. Others will depict animals having sex with each other. Yet others will show a male carrying an unconscious (or dead) female to a bed. How truthful these pictures are is unknown at this point. Other examples show regurgitation, urination, defecation, and self-fellation.

Bondage and Discipline

Within this category, women are often seen in various poses of submission. The women are often at the mercy of a male. Other times, the woman is seen alone. This is especially prevalent at a commercial address of www.smutworld.com. At times, women are shown in obviously posed scenes of lesbianism and sadism.

Cheerleaders

This collection contain images of young women, often adolescents, dressed in cheerleader uniforms. Usually the women are alone and involved in some form of masturbatory activity. The cheerleader uniform represents those worn by high school women, that is, with a school letter. Sometimes the women pose, but there is another side to this category. Sometimes parts of the body can be seen (sometimes clearly, sometimes not, as they raise their arms, kick, or jump.

Incest

Perhaps the most troubling of all the categories identified and downloaded are the images of adults with children. Many titles suggest a relationship between the adult and the child. Some titles suggest a father-daughter, mother-daughter, mother-son, or a brother-sister relationship. One title was "sis," and another was "my 9-year-old daughter." These findings are immediately reported to the police. (Holmes et al., 1998)

Holmes et al. (1998) offer the following findings: From a longitudinal perspective, Internet pornography has increased in

- Photographic professionalism
- The number of places to find it
- Specialization of the sites
- Extremism in the scenes depicted
- Amateur participation
- Blatancy in the chat rooms and photo exchanges

Simultaneously, the number of underage models seems to have decreased.

It appears that the Internet will continue to serve as a pool of pornography for those interested in this material. As more homes connect to the Internet, we are likely to see an increase in interest and the spread of digitalized voyeuristic materials. Those who are interested in pornography but have not sought it out to a great extent may find the Internet to be an avenue of opportunity. They may in fact become active in the securing and trading such pictures, stories, and so forth. For some, this may become a way of erotic arousal resulting in some crimes of sexual abuse. However,

> Contrarily to the assumption of some, who would believe that the voyeur will be driven to pursue more and more viewing opportunities, or might be "given ideas about these kinds of behaviors" by online exposure, there is essentially no data that supports such a contention. Voyeurs are interested primarily—if not exclusively—in viewing others, not in contacting them or interacting. Also, as is well known, many voyeurs also masturbate while viewing their targets. For them, computer images can be more attractive than live targets. The risks that the voyeur runs when viewing others (and masturbating) in public can be extreme; to view images on a computer screen while masturbating is clearly a safe (for all parties) activity.
>
> In the end, the vast world of on-line sexual images, especially in the form of hidden JPGs, provides a safe and rewarding sexual outlet to sexual voyeurs (Holmes, Tewksbury & Holmes, 1998).

Thus, the Internet provides to those who are interested in pornography an easy access to materials that are pornographic and, in some cases, obscene. The effects of what is on the Internet needs to be studied in great detail to ascertain any possible effects that exposure to erotica has on the human condition.

❖ CONCLUSION

The issue of pornography remains a serious one. Much energy is expended on developing social policies and programs to deal with the effects of pornographic material. Legislation should be enacted prohibiting the involvement of children in pornography. Since children are vulnerable and helpless, special attention needs to be paid to finding ways to protect them. Vigorous social action needs to he directed at those adults who victimize children and involve them in any form of child pornography.

In the case of adult pornography, a different approach may be warranted. Many Americans are not in favor of government censoring of reading and viewing materials for any reason. They feel they have the right to view and to read anything they desire and are vehemently opposed to any infringement on that right. In any case, it is clear that additional research needs to be done on the effects of adult pornography on sexual behavior.

❖ DISCUSSION QUESTIONS

1. What are the differences between pornography and obscenity?
2. Do you believe that the viewing of pornography contributes to the commission of sex crimes? Why or why not?
3. How has the character of pornography changed over the years?
4. Review some of the earlier writings on pornography, for example, Kinsey et al (1948), or Brownmiller. (1975). How accurate would their positions be today?
5. With chat channels, photo exchange channels, and other forms of pornography on the Internet today, how pervasive is pornography in today's world.

❖ REFERENCES

Abraham, S., Hill, R., Sass, S., & Sobel, L. (1980). *Pornography, obscenity, and the law.* New York: Facts on File.

Barak, A., Fisher, W., Belfrey, S., & Lashambe, D. (1999). Sex, guys, and cybersex: Effects of Internet pornography and individual differences on men's attitudes toward women. *Journal of Psychology and Human Sexuality, 11*(1), 63–91.

Brownmiller, S. (1975). Against our will: Men, women and rape. New York: Simon and Schuster.

Bogaert, A., Woodard, U., & Hafer, C. (1999). Intellectual ability and reactions to pornography. *Journal of Sex Research, 36*(3), 283–291.

Byrne, D., & Osland, J. (2000). *Sexual fantasy and erotica/pornography: Internal and external imagery.* New York: Wiley.

Caron, S., & Carter, D. (1997). The relationships among sex role orientation, egalitarianism, attitudes toward sexuality, and attitudes toward violence against women. *Journal of Social Psychology, 137*(5), 568–587.

Conklin, J. (1989). *Criminology* (3rd ed.). New York: Macmillan.

Cramer, E., McFarlane, J., Parker, B., Soeken, S., & Reel, S. (1998). Violent pornography and abuse of women: Theory to practice. *Violence and Victims, 13*(4), 319–332.

Davies, K. (1997). Voluntary exposure to pornography and men's attitudes toward feminism and rape. *Journal of Sex Research, 34*(2), 131–137.

Donerstein, E., Linz, D., & Penrod, S. (1987). *Question of pornography: Research findings and policy implications.* New York: Free Press.

Fishbach, S., & Malamuth, N. (1978). Sex and aggression: Proving the link. *Psychology Today, 12*, 111–122.

Gardner, T. (1989). *Criminal law: Principles and cases.* St. Paul, MN: West.

Gardos, P., & Mosher, D. (1999). Gender differences in reactions to viewing pornographic vignettes: Essential or interpretive? *Journal of Psychology and Human Sexuality, 11*(2), 65–83.

Goode, E. (1984). *Deviant behavior* (2nd ed.). Englewood Cliffs, NJ: Prentice-Hall.

Harris, V., & Staunton, C. (2000). *The antecedents of young male offenders.* London: Whurr.

Heilbrun, A., & Seif, D. (1988). Erotic value of female distress in sexually explicit photographs. *Journal of Sex Research, 24*, 47–57.

Holmes, R., Tewksbury, R., & Holmes, S. (1998). Hidden JPGs: A functional alternative to voyeurism. *Journal of Popular Culture, 32*(3), 17–29.

Jansen, L., Linz, D., Mulac, A., & Imrich, D. (1997). Men's interaction with women after viewing sexually explicit files: Does degradation make a difference? *Communication Monographs, 64*(1), 1–24.

Jensen, R. (1995). Pornographic lives. *Violence Against Women, 1*(1), 32–54.

Kant, H., & Goldstein, M. (1973). *Pornography and sexual deviance: A report of the legal and behavioral.* Berkeley: University of California Press.

Keihani, K. (1999). Pornography and female sexual socialization. Dissertation. Pacific University, Palo Alto, CA.

Kinsey, A., Pomeroy, W. and C. Martin. (1948) Sexual Behavior in the Human Male. Philadelphia: W.B. Saunders.

Khoury, B. (1988). Women survivors of childhood sexual abuse: Attitudes toward pornography and its effect on their committed relationships. *Dissertation Abstracts International, 58*(8-B), 4454.

Levin, J., & Fox, J. (1999). *Serial murder: Popular myths and empirical realities.* Thousand Oaks, CA: Sage.

Linz, D. (1989). Exposure to sexually explicit materials and attitudes toward rape: A comparison of study results. *Journal of Sex Research, 26*, 50–84.

Lynn, B. (1986). *Polluting the censorship debate: A summary and critique of the final report of the attorney general's commission on pornography.* Washington, D.C.: American Civil Liberties Union.

Marshall, L. (1988). The use of sexually explicit stimuli by rapists, child molesters, and non-offenders. *Journal of Sex Research, 25*, 267–288.

McCarthy, S. (1982). Pornography, rape, and the cult of macho. In J. Skolnick & E. Currie (Eds.), *Crisis in American institutions* (pp. 218–232). Boston: Little, Brown.

Mills, R. (1998). Cyber: Sexual chat on the Internet. *Journal of Pop Culture, 32*, 32–46.

Nawy, H. (1973). In pursuit of happiness: Consumers of erotica in San Francisco. *Journal of Social Issues, 29*, 147–161.

Nobile, P., & Nadler, E. (1986). *United States of America vs. sex: How the Meese Commission lied about pornography.* New York: Minotaur.

Norris, J., George, W., Davis, K., Martell, J., & Leonesio, R. (1999). Alcohol and hypermasculinity as determinants of men's empathic responses to violent pornography. *Journal of Interpersonal Violence, 14*(7), 683–700.

Padgett, V., & Brislin-Slutz, J. (1989). Pornography, erotica, and attitudes toward women: The effects of repeated exposure. *Journal of Sex Research, 26,* 479–491.

Pearson, S., & Pollack, R. (1997). Female response to sexually explicit films. *Journal of Psychology and Human Sexuality, 9*(2), 73–88.

Russell, D. (1998). *Dangerous relationships: Pornography, misogyny, and rape.* Thousand Oaks, CA: Sage.

Scott, J. (1988). Book reviews of attorney general's commission on pornography and related works. *Journal of Criminal Law and Criminology, 78,* 1145–1165.

Siegel, S. (1998). *Applying social comparison theory to women's body image and self-esteem: The effects of pornography.* Dissertation. Pacific University, Palo Alto, CA.

Tjaden, P. (1988). Pornography and sex education. *Journal of Sex Research, 24,* 208–212.

Walsh, A. (1999). Life history theory and female readers of pornography. *Personality and Individual Differences, 27*(4), 779–787.

Wilson, W., & Abelson, H. (1973). Experience with and attitudes toward explicit sexual materials. *Journal of Social Issues, 29,* 19–39.

9

Sex and the Internet

❖   ❖   ❖

Perhaps no one thing has opened the door for sexual information, misinformation, fantasy enhancement, sexual sharing, predation, and even murder than the Internet and cyberspace. DiMarco (2003) reported in her study that the Internet and cyberspace have liberated Internet users in providing an anonymous arena where the users can express their sexual desires and interests. This seems to be especially true for women. Chat rooms, for example, provide a relatively safe place for women to discuss their sexual fantasies without fear of reprisals or predations. The personal secrecy of the Internet also provides a space where the woman can explore fantasies of same-sex practices, a practice space for sexual dialogues that they may use later in life in real-life interactions, and other sexual matters they may not be comfortable addressing in interpersonal communications.

As a counterpoint, Hughes (2003) reports that the Internet and cyberspace offers males a worldwide medium for the sexual exploitation of women and children. She stated that the medium offers privacy for the men as well as an anonymous place for ready communication. There is little doubt that the Internet offers a unique opportunity for predation by sexual offenders. It has made volume large number of men, women, and children available to sexual predators. Sometimes, though infrequently, victims contribute to their own victimization. (This is not meant to excuse the predator for the victimization.) There is one case, for example, of a woman who corresponded with a man on the Internet. She wanted someone to murder her. They met; he complied.

The military originally started Internet as a plan to share information among a community of computers. In June 1969, the Advanced Research Projects Agency (ARPA), in conjunction with the Stanford Research Institute (SRI), started developing a computer system to accomplish the mission. Within months, they established communication between the University of California at Los Angeles and SRI: the letter *I* and the word *Owens* were transmitted. Not yet called the Internet, ARPSNET was born, and now more than 3 million Internet hosts serve 900 million users communicating with each other across the world today.

❖ THE INTERNET

From the beginning of the Internet in 1969, the Internet has grown immensely. It gives us almost instant information on an immense variety of subjects. Search engines such as Google, Ask.com, Yahoo, Dogpile, and many others respond to our queries in fractions of a second.

What is a chat room?

Chat rooms are places on the Internet where people with similar interests can

- Send electronic messages to one another
- Converse by typing messages in real time
- Exchange ideas, messages, and other information
- Preserve anonymity with "screen names"
- Arrange to meet in personal at another time

(Jaffe & Sharma, 2001)

There is a sinister side of the Internet. This darker side deals with subjects judged by many to be replete with aberrant sexual behaviors, violent sexual predation, and a reservoir of potential victims for violent sexual predators.

How many victims fall prey to sexual predators on the Internet? This is not an easy question to answer. One source, the Texas Office of the Attorney General (2001), suggests that 1 young person in 5 has been sexually solicited over the Internet and 1 in 17 has experienced threats or harassment. How accurate these numbers are is unknown; but we believe that sex on the Internet and cyberspace is a real problem.

In this chapter we will discuss the role of the Internet and cyberspace in sexual predations and predators. We will examine the Internet as a world that sexual predators use to identify potential victims and meet each other to share exploits and information. We will also discuss spaces on the World Wide Web that cater to those with interests that are normal and those that are perverse.

❖ HISTORY OF THE INTERNET AND SEX

There is little doubt that sex became a part of Internet content very early in its existence. In 1971, the world's first e-mail system was created. In 1989, the World Wide Web was created. In 1992, the first audio and video were broadcast over the Internet; in 1994, the first commercially available web browser was created. When the first pornography site was made available is unknown. It is safe to assume that the last several years have seen a dramatic rise in the number of Internet sexual venues. While there is no manner in which to accurately determine the exact number of websites that predators may visit to locate potential victims, they will number in excess of a million. Fantino (2003) estimates that there are more than 100,000 websites that contain strictly child pornography. These sites cater to those with an interest in children from the very young to teenagers, perhaps the most vulnerable populations on the Internet (Magid, 2006), and young people between the ages of 12 and 24 compose the largest population for using the Internet for communication purposes (Boles, Knudson, & Young, 2004). Certainly there are many more sites that feature adult pornography.

Over the years innumerable sites have emerged that utilize the Internet for sexual purposes. These sites cater to various sexual preferences and paraphilias. For example, two sites cater to older men who are homosexual or bisexual, silverdaddies.com and maturemen.com. Another website is voyuerweb.com, which contain sections within itself that deal with exhibitionism, voyeurism, triolism, and other paraphilias. Some sites on the web have been published for several years. For example, the North American Man/Boy Love Association (NAMBLA) has its own website and address.

❖ USERS OF THE INTERNET AND CYBERSPACE

Who are the ones who use the Internet and cyberspace for sexual purposes? Obviously, the motivations and anticipated gains vary from one person to the next. The persons may include

1. People with normal sexual interests who use the Internet and cyberspace for educational and personal reasons to gather information on society's proscribed behavior

2. Couples who use the Internet and cyberspace to enhance their own sexual lifestyles and physical and sexual behaviors and techniques for mutually satisfying behavior

3. People who post and exchange erotic photographs for sexual purposes

4. Members of child molester and pedophile groups

5. Adults seeking partners for sexual exchanges

6. Sexual predators, including rapists and lust killers

The predatory users of the Internet and cyberspace are many and varied. The motivations and anticipated gains of each will differ, but a psychological profile of such a user does emerge. Deirmenjian (1999) offers such a profile. The person involved in looking for victims on the Internet has the following traits and characteristics:

1. Emotionally disturbed

2. Often conceals gender and identity

3. Is computer-sophisticated

4. Is financially able to subscribe to various online services

Quayle, Vaughn, and Taylor (2006) report that Internet users often have psychological problems and use the Internet to avoid negative emotions (boredom, anxiety, and depression). The Internet and cyberspace offer a means to avoid personal confrontations and unpleasant emotional states. This trait will have obvious implications for treatment, which we will discuss later in this book.

Lanning (1998) stated that the pedophile, for example, has historically visited places where children gather. What better place would there be than the Internet for today's sexual predator? They can communicate their own sexual interests and validate their interests. After all, it may seem to the predator that many others are writing the same things and verbalizing the same thoughts, and this in some fashion validates the predator.

With the various kinds and groups on the Internet looking for adults and children to victimize, we believe it is important to come to some kind of understanding about the personality of those who stalk victims. Perhaps the anonymity of the Internet provides an ideal place for the user to act out and perform thoughts, actions, words, forms of coercion, and so on.

As difficult as it may be to understand, it is not only strangers that use the Internet to solicit strangers for victimization. Mitchell, Finkelhor, and Wolak (2005) report that family members are just as apt to use the Internet to victimize family members. They may use the Internet to seduce the selected family member to post intimate pictures of the victim, to arrange meetings with the victim while the latter thinking he or she is meeting someone else, or to sell or exploit the victim for financial or psychological gain.

Of course, there has to be a system for the user to utilize. Cyberspace and cybertechnology offer an accessible reservoir of information on sexual behavior, paraphilias, and other information limited only by what the industry itself can imagine (Chatterjee, 2001).

❖ A MODEL OF INTERNET AND CYBERSPACE PREDATION

It is obvious when one is dealing with Internet and cyberspace sexual predators that not all predators are alike. The way they make contact, the manner in which they will court their victims, and so on, will differ from one to the other. But there are some similarities among the various types of predators and the manner in which they proceed toward the acts of victimization. For example, let us consider the following stages in the solicitation of children over the Internet for sexual purposes.

Initially, the predator will make some type of contact with the victim. This contact can be made through a chat room, a website devoted to conversations on a topic of interest, or some other form of content.

In this stage, the predator can fabricate personal information. For example, he can misstate his age, use a false name or lie about his race or gender, or any other information the predator believes will enhance his chances of moving to the next stage of contact.

The predator may send photos that are not of the predator, but of someone else. The victim is encouraged to send photographs of herself or himself. One killer we interviewed encouraged young girls to send him nude pictures of themselves, and many actually did. This was after he had sent them picture of himself wearing only jogging shorts (author's files). The exchange of photos over the Internet through cyberspace becomes an integral part of the seduction process. But as Grienti (1997) pointed out, pedophiles or other types of sexual predators, for example, may misrepresent their ages, genders, appearance, and special interests in order to attract their potential victims.

After the initial contact, the predator moves on to a more intimate and personal contact. The predator will make efforts to determine the specific likes and dislikes of the victim. If a child, the predator may find out the victim likes a particular musical group. If that group comes to town, the predator makes every effort to secure tickets to that concert and give them to the victim as a special favor. The predator may purchase gifts for the victim, such as athletic shoes or athletic event tickets. All this is meant to ingratiate the predator with the victim.

Personal phone calls may take place at this stage. The predator may call the victim on the telephone or send instant e-mail messages to the victim's cell phone, along with a picture of himself or herself. This method of personal contact can be done in some private form with no one, including the victim's parents, knowing of the transmissions.

After the personal contact is made, the direct contact is the next stage. In this stage, the predator and the victim meet in person. At this time, the predator makes some action toward a sexual assault and predation. The molestation of a child then begins.

Protect the Kids website reports that

- More than $34 billion is generated annually from child pornography.
- 40% of child predators had some form of child pornography in their possession at the time of their arrests.
- The number of child pornography images has increased 1500% in the last twenty years.
- Almost 20% of all cases of pornography on the Internet involves child pornography.
- More than 20,000 images of child pornography are posted in the Internet weekly.
- There is an increasing demand for child pornography that depict babies and toddlers on the Internet.
- Rape and sexual assaults against adult victims and murders of victims all follow a similar pattern of victim predation.

SOURCE: www.protect the kids.com/dangers/stats.htm 5–16–06.

The Internet pornography industry generates victims for the fixated offender. The seduction process has a manifest goal of making a direct contact with the victim, whether child or adult. The ultimate goal is sexual predation, and the Internet and cyberspace are tools to make contact and accomplish the predation.

❖   ADULTS, SEX, AND THE INTERNET

There is no doubt that the Internet and cyberspace have replaced more traditional methods and modes of meeting people. Bars and social occasions are still popular places to meet someone for a personal relationship or just casual sex. But the Internet offers an avenue to meet people economically and from a safe position. Where else can someone from the safety of their own home contact thousands of people with a touch of a key? Where else can someone talk to others from a safe position? Where else can someone meet others without the trying experience of bar hopping?

Discussion Groups

There are thousands of places where one can go on the Internet to meet people or to simply discuss various topics. If one is interested in history, there are hundreds of discussion groups one can join all day, every day. If one is interested in football, weaving, travel, politics, and other innumerable topics, there are others who are within reach of you.

The discussion groups that center on the topic of sex are the most popular. There are discussion groups entitled "sex and you," "meat me," and other such graphic titles. The titles are deliberately named to draw attention to the persons interested in discussing sex with others. By entering the web address, you are almost immediately into the action of the discussion site.

There are obvious drawbacks to discussion groups. For example, there is the issue of honesty. Are you really talking with a person with the social traits and interests as advertised by the other person? Is a certain amount of exaggeration tolerated as normal on the discussion scene? Is the person really the stated age, with the true physical attributes, education, or profession claimed? Some type of dishonesty is to be expected. After all, as the person entering the discussion group, how honest are you?

Introduction Agencies

Some have greatly profited by designing introduction agencies for a fee. If we look at some of these for-profit introduction agencies there is a common theme.

First, all the introduction agencies usually feature young people. The advertisements appearing on the Internet show attractive men and women usually in their 20s and, at the oldest, early 30s. They appear to be professional people, with great looks and perfect teeth. There are also testimonials to attest to the way that this particular agency has found them their perfect mates, including the reasons why others should use this agency rather than others on the Internet.

Who would use such a service? From their advertisements, it appears that they cater to persons who are educated, above average in income, and with well paying jobs. Their financial standing appears above average. One wonders, if this were all true, why would they need to use an introductory group.

❖ GAYS AND THE INTERNET

Just as the Internet provides a service for the straight population, gays and lesbians are equally served. There are sites for young gays, older gays, and senior gays. For example, one site, silverdaddies.com, is a site that caters to seniors. It contains a gallery of photos of men in various stages of dress, many nude, some by themselves, and others with a partner, often engaged in oral or anal sex. There is another gallery of young men who have an interest in older men.

On MySpace, with its 33 categories and 24,782,000 automobile, hobby, music, food, and other groups within the categories, there are 4,182 gay, lesbian, and bisexual groups. One group is called GirlsKissGirls, started in 2005, at present with more than 29,000 members. Another site, BoysMakeOut, started in 2004, has approximately 15,000 members. How many are active members is unknown; it may be that there are many who just visit the site never to return again.

❖ CHILDREN, SEX, AND THE INTERNET

The Internet sites that cater to children have received a great deal of attention not only from law enforcement but from concerned parents, school administrators, and mental health professionals.

Myspace.com has come under specific scrutiny. Often explicit adds and provocative photos are displayed, despite the declaration by MySpace that explicitly sexual photos and sexually provocative words will not be published. There is some evidence that some child predators use the Internet and MySpace and other Internet sites to communicate, stalk, and seduce children for sexual purposes.

There are other sites that depict children in pornographic postures, but most websites on pedophilia deal with the problems of pedophilia. They discuss, among other things, the etiology of the pedophile, the definitions of pedophilia, the clergy and the pedophile problem, and other such concerns. In Chapter 6 we discussed pedophile organizations such as the North American Man/Boy Love Association (NAMBLA). There are many hyperlinks to NAMBLA, but most cannot be opened. Those that open are sites that are critical of the pedophile organization. The Rene Guyon Society used to have a website homepage, but when one attempts to locate Rene Guyon Society or NAMBLA, the hyperlink will not connect, and instead a message will appear and state that the file is not found. This same is true of the Howard Nichols Society, the Childhood Sensuality Circle, and the Pedophile Information Exchange.

Personal Ads

Children often place ads on blogs, discussion channels, and chat channels with personal information about hobbies and likes and dislikes. Too often, the young person will respond to messages from others who are posing as children or young people to strike up a conversation. The poser has the final goal of a personal meeting and a sexual encounter. This is no better illustrated than in the television series *Dateline: To Catch a Predator*. In this series, an adult, posing as a child of 13 or 14, will correspond with someone who is interested in having sex with a girl or boy of those ages. The conversations may extend over several occasions until finally the predator will come to the child's "home." Once inside the home, a reporter will emerge from another room accompanied by a camera crew. The reporter will talk with the predator asking personal questions accompanied by copies of the predator's conversation with the child actor. Upon leaving the home, the predator is immediately arrested by the local police.

The *Dateline* series illustrates perfectly how personal ads work. The predators have places where they can easily locate victims in a touch of a computer key stroke.

The Effects of the Internet and Cyberspace on Sexual Predation

A crucial concern to all would be the possible and direct effects of the Internet and cyberspace on the victimization rates of both adults and children. How would one obtain the data for victimization? What would constitute victimization? How would it be measured? These and other questions would have to be addressed.

It may be that the use of the Internet and cyberspace is too new to know the effects it has on the predation of our citizens (Kopelev, 1999). Those within the criminal justice system must be proactive in investigating the Internet and cyberspace and its possible effects. Undercover operations would be one important proactive step in police investigation of child predation. For example, if MySpace becomes an important source of sexual predation of children and young adults, investigators must learn to present appropriate victim credentials in sting operations (Kopelev, 1999).

The National Center for Missing and Exploited Children recommends that children be informed of the dangers of the Internet and chat rooms. See the box for some of the center's recommendations.

Chatrooms let you have a conversation with people around the block or around the world. It's like being on a party line, only you type instead of talk. Everyone in the chatroom can see everything you type.

Types of chatrooms tend to be different. Some chatrooms are just open conversations where everyone has an equal role. Some rooms are moderated where a "speaker" leads the chat and tries to keep everything in order. Some rooms have chaperones or monitors who try to make sure things don't get out of hand and can kick people out of the room if they don't behave. Even so, in some of these rooms what you type is seen right away by everyone. And the monitor can't prevent you from going off to a private chat area with a person who may want to hurt you or type information that may put you in danger (Interview with Julliard Chatterman, June 21, 2006).

You may want to get together with someone you meet in a chatroom, but remember—people are not always who they seem to be.

Never give out personal information and never arrange a face-to-face meeting with someone you first "meet" in a chatroom unless your parents or guardians have said it's OK. Even then you need to follow the precautions in "Do Not Meet in Person."

Stay away from chatrooms that get into subjects associated with sex or cults or groups that do potentially dangerous things. It may seem interesting or fun, but some people may take you seriously or try to convince you to do something you don't want to do. Be particularly suspicious of anyone who tries to turn you against your parents, guardians, teachers, or friends.

On some services and websites you can enter into a private chat area. Once there you can arrange to meet people. In some cases those rooms are truly private, but in other cases they may be listed in a directory of rooms. If so, there is nothing to stop others from entering those rooms. So be extra careful in these rooms, or avoid them altogether.

A smart way to avoid harassment in a chatroom is to choose a name that doesn't let people know if you're a girl or guy. Just make sure the name doesn't let anyone know anything about you or mean something that may encourage others to bother you.

Some websites ask for information about you. The site may ask for your name, your mailing address, your e-mail address, and other information before letting you in. It may ask you to provide information in exchange for sending you a gift or entering your name in a contest. Never enter any information about yourself without first checking with your parents or guardians.

Obviously, some of the same advice is equally appropriate for adults who use the Internet. And when one considers that the Internet is primarily used by juveniles and young adults for communication, such advice is important and meaningful. Technologies will increase over the next several years, and Internet sites will proliferate at an increasing rate (Bowker & Gray, 2004).

The use of the Internet for sexual predation has important implications for those involved both in and outside the criminal justice system. For example, police and parole and probation officers should acquire a special expertise in dealing with online sexual predators. They should learn everything available about the traits and etiology of the predator from the case files of all agencies that have had some contact with the predator. They can include police files, social service files, medical reports, and correctional reports. Examining the predator's computer system can not only inform the investigators and others of how deeply the offender was involved—with potential evidence and identification of the persons contacted—but also the computer sophistication of the offender.

The information on the computer can alert the investigators and others to the history of the offender's activities. A history of the real-life activities of the predator and possible identifying information of meeting sites, related websites, and other information (Bowker & Gray, 2004).

In the family setting, parents and caregivers should provide safeguards for children and other juveniles in their access and use of the computer in accessing websites that contain objectionable material. This should be the first line of defense and a role that should be assumed by adults who have any suspicion of the misuse of the Internet by others.

❖ CONCLUSION

Victimization by adult predators is real and significant. The Texas Office of the Attorney General (2001) reports that 1 young person in 5 has been solicited sexually over the Internet, and 1 in 17 has experienced threats or harassment, including unwanted e-mails that are abusive, threatening, or obscene, junk e-mail messages, and the infection of another's computer with a virus (Ellison, 2001; Williams, 2001). More efforts need to be directed toward the treatment of online predators. It is our opinion, verified by research (see Buttell & Carney, 2001), that those within the criminal justice system are lacking not only in resources to fight victimization but also to monitor the predators or to offer pertinent and helpful counseling.

Efforts must be taken. Victimization, whether of a child or an adult, must not be tolerated. The technology of the Internet provides opportunities for victimization as well as for the legitimate gathering of needed knowledge. Free speech must be protected, but we must have ways of knowing when victimization is occurring and clarify what the responsibility of our community is. This is really the least we can do.

❖ DISCUSSION QUESTIONS

1. What is your personal belief about the specific role of the Internet and sexual abuse of the youth and adults in this country?

2. Much has been said about My.Space.Com as an aid in identifying potential victims for sexual predators. What is your opinion?

3. Should the venue of the Internet be a forum for *complete* free speech?

4. If a predator has been identified and found guilty of sexual child abuse and used the Internet as a tool for predation, should

he/she be forced to abandon the use of the Internet in the future for all forms of use?

5. Chat rooms and blogs are becoming more and more popular. Can they be used as tools for predation?

❖ REFERENCES

Boles, S., Knudson, G., & Young, J. (2004). Internet, sex, and youths: Implications for sexual development. *Sexual Addiction and Compulsivity, 11*(4), 343–363.

Bowker, A., & Gray, M. (2004). Introduction to the supervision of the cybersex offender. *Federal Probation, 68*(3), 3–8.

Buttell, F., & Carney, M. (2001). Treatment provider awareness of the possible impact of the Internet on the treatment of sex offenders. *Journal of Child Sexual Abuse, 10*(3), 117–125.

Chatterjee, B. (2001). Last of the rainmacs: Thinking about pornography in cyberspace. *Crime and the Internet*, 74–99.

Deirmenjian, J. (1999). Stalking in cyberspace. *Journal of the American Academy of Psychiatry and the Law, 27*(3), 407–413.

DiMarco, H. (2003). Electronic cloak: Secret sexual deviance in cyberspace. In Y. Jewkes (Ed.), *Dot.coms: Crime, deviance, and identity on the Internet* (pp. 53–67). Englewood Cliffs, NJ: Prentice hall.

Ellison, L. (2001). Cyberstalking: Tackling harassment on the Internet. In D. Wall (Ed.), *Crime and the Internet* (pp. 141–151). London: Routledge.

Fantino, J. (2003). *Child pornography on the Internet: New challenges require new ideas, 70*(12), 28–30.

Grienti, V. (1997). Pedophiles on the Internet. *Gazette, 59*(10), 14–15.

Hughes, D. (2003). Prostitution online. *Journal of Trauma Practice, 3*(3–4), 115–131.

Jaffee, M., & Sharma, K. (2001). Cybersex with minors: Forensic implications. *Journal of Forensic Sciences, 46*(6), 1397–1402.

Kopelev, S. (1999). Cyber sex offenders. *Law Enforcement Technology, 26*(11), 46–48.

Lanning, K. (1998). Cyber pedophiles: A behavioral perspective. *APSAC Advisor, 11*(4), 12–18.

Magid, L. (2006). *Teen safety on the information highway.* Washington, DC: National Center for Missing and Exploited Children.

Mitchell, K., Finkelhor, D., & Wolak, J. (2005). Internet and family and acquaintance sexual abuser. *Child Maltreatment, 10*(1), 49–60.

Quayle, E., Vaughn, M., & Taylor, M. (2006). Sex offenders: Internet child abuse images and emotional avoidance: The importance of values. *Aggression and Violent Behavior, 11*(1), 1–11.

Texas Office of the Attorney General. (2001). Cybercrimes. *Criminal Law Update., 8*(3), 4–11.

Williams, M. (2001) Language of cybercrime and the Internet. In D. Wall (Ed.), *Crime and the Internet* (pp. 152–166). London: Routledge.

❖ INTERNET REFERENCES

Anti-Pedophilia Webring, http://j/webring.com/hub?ring=stoppedos
CBCNEWS—Indepth, http://cbc.ca/news/background/internet/
Pedowatch. Com, http://pedowatch.com/
ProtectKids.com, http://www.protectkids.com

10

Dangerous Sex Crimes

❖ ❖ ❖

M any sex crimes that are dangerous to societal members as well as to the individual practitioners themselves. Necrophilia, lust murder, anthropophagy, autoeroticism, pyromania, and sexually motivated serial murder are such crimes. These crimes are responsible for the victimization and death of an untold number of people year in and year out (Barlow, Barlow, & Stojkovic, 1995; S. Holmes, Hickey, & Holmes, 1998; Meloy, 2000; Terry, 2003).

The tales of Edmund Kemper, who decapitated his victims, Ed Gein, a grave robber and necrophile, Jeffrey Dahmer, serial killer and cannibal, Ottis Toole and Henry Lucas, lust killers both, and other sex offenders fill the media with their stories. It is these types of crimes that we will cover in this chapter. These are dangerous crimes, dangerous to unsuspecting victims, and sometimes dangerous to the practitioner.

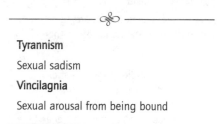

Tyrannism

Sexual sadism

Vincilagnia

Sexual arousal from being bound

❖ NECROPHILIA

Once thought to be especially rare and a male perversion only (A. Ellis, 1986), necrophilia is now being seen more and more often.

——————— ✥ ———————

Necrochlesis

Sex with a female corpse

Necrocoitus

Sexual penetration of a corpse

Necrophagia

The cannibalism of a corpse

——————— ✥ ———————

Brachioproticism

Insertion of the arm into the rectum of another person for sexual pleasure (also known as brachioprotic eroticism)

Buggery

Anal sodomy

——————— ✥ ———————

Autassassinphilia

Sexual gratification from arranging one's own death at the hands of another

Case

A woman was killed by a man after corresponding with him for a short time on the Internet. They exchanged correspondence on a chat channel and she informed him that she had a fantasy of being murdered by a stranger. They decided to meet close to his home in a far distant state. After exchanging pleasantries, she repeated her desires and he accommodated her wish.

It is also viewed as one of the most serious of sex crimes, often more serious than rape and child molestation (Wasby, 1980). The use of dead bodies as vaults of sexual desire has been well documented for some time (Brill, 1941). Burg (1983) disagrees with the assumption that necrophilia is rare, arguing that many cases are simply not discovered or reported. We have found a number of serial killers whose dangerous crimes are motivated by bizarre sexual fantasies. Bartholomew, Milte, and Galbally (1978) report two cases of necrophilia. One case was that of a 22-year-old male who had homosexual tendencies that varied in intensity over the years. He carried out his fantasy of taking a male friend into the mountains, shooting him in the head, and then sexually molesting the corpse. The other case concerned a 47-year-old single male who sodomized a 9-year-old boy and then killed him with a blow to the head. He then returned to the body after several hours and sodomized the boy again. Freire (1981) presents a case of a 28-year-old female who had sexual relations with a corpse, and Foerster, Foerster, and Roth (1981) relate a similar story of a 17-year-old girl. Schlesinger and Revitch (1997) relate the case of a 16-year-old male who committed a sexual matricide after years of mother-son incest. After murdering the mother by strangulation, which the youth admitted was sexually arousing, the youth engaged in both vaginal and anal sex. When I interviewed a serial murderer on San Quentin's death row, he admitted to me that he had cut the heads off several prostitutes and that he and his accomplice, a female, performed sexual acts with these heads.

As with any sex crime, fantasy plays an important role in the necrophiliac's actions (Baker, 1983). For this reason, Goldenson (1970) reports that funerals, cemeteries, morgues, and autopsies hold great interest for necrophiliacs. DSM-III-R describes necrophilia as an atypical paraphilia and defines it as having sexual intercourse with a corpse (American Psychiatric Association, 1987). This definition is too limited. As this chapter will make clear, there is more to necrophilia than having intercourse with a dead body. We have talked with incarcerated serial killers who sexually assaulted their victims after death. Ed Gein robbed graves to have sex with corpses (Gollman, 1981). A syndicated columnist often repeats a letter that she received from a woman whose husband demanded that she take a cold shower, douse herself with powder, and lie completely still in bed while he had intercourse with her. If she moved in response to his advances, he lost his ability to perform sexually. Certainly this man has a fantasy that centers on sex with a dead person, a form of necrophilia.

Bug Chasing—A Dangerous Sex Practice

In a study that examined the practice of "bareback sex"—unprotected sex—the researchers discovered a bizarre and very dangerous, even fatal, form of sexual practice. Bareback sex is practiced by both heterosexuals and homosexuals, the practice of having sex with another and not using any protection against sexually transmitted diseases.

Accompanying the use of barebacking, a new form and sociologically unknown form of sexual deviance has been discovered. This is known as "bug chasing."

Bug chasing is the sexual practice in which HIV-negative gay men seek to become infected with the deadly disease. The immediate question comes to mind why someone would deliberately choose to have sex with another person who is known to be diseased and such a copulation could result in one's own death. In our own research with serial killers, we have found several say "the greater the risk, the greater the thrill." Could this same feeling be present with men who seek out infected men to run the risk of being themselves infected with the AIDS virus? One man stated, "I now view AIDS as both a gift and a blessing. . . . You go through this amazing kind of transformation. You look at things for the first time, in a powerful new way that you've never looked at them before in your whole life."

So, the infection with AIDS may be for some infected gay men a status-granting position.

How prevalent is this form of dangerous sex? Unknown, is the only answer. There are certainly those who will continue to seek out sexual partners to contract the AIDS virus. We hope this number will be small. (Gauthier and Forsyth, 1999)

Levels of Necrophilia

The practice of necrophilia should be envisioned as a culmination of a pattern of multiple and increasing practices. It is not simply one act and then no other actions of this type will be practiced again. Other types of problems exist with the necrophile: alcoholism, impotency, hypersexuality, and severe mental problems, as well as hallucinations, interest in black magic, and paranoid grandiosity (Janik & Chromy, 1979; Riveria, 1995).

There are at least three types of necrophiles. The first type is similar to the husband described above. This person "only" fantasizes about having sex with a corpse. His partner is alive but, in a cooperative sex relationship, pretends to be dead. One prostitute stated that she had two clients with this type of "trip." Both men were professional types, one a lawyer and the other a dean of a local university, who were frequent customers; the attorney only wanted to look at her while she lay on the bed, while the latter customer would have intercourse with her (authors' files).

The second type of necrophiliac is a person who has sex with a person who is already dead. This person will sometimes place him- or herself in an occupational role where he or she has access to dead bodies: morgue attendant, funeral home personnel, or coroner. Often a disorganized offender (Ressler, 1986), this paraphiliac gains easy access to corpses, so the fantasy that demands sexual activity with a corpse can be easily realized.

———————— ✤ ————————

Necrosadism

Sadism or mutilation of corpses. Necrosadistic killers murder to have sex with the dead.

The third type of necrophile is the necrosadistic offender. This person murders to have sex with a dead body. There are many examples of this type, including Ted Bundy (see chapter 1), Albert Fish, and Ed Gein. In this form, as well as the second type, necrophilia must be viewed as the ultimate and most extreme form of erotic eligibility distancing—that is, the partner must be dead (Money, 1984).

A similar typology has been developed by Rosman and Resnick (1989) (see Table 10.1). The pseudonecrophiliac has a transient attraction to corpses and, although the fantasy includes having sex with a person just killed, corpses are not the object of the sexual fantasy—living partners are preferred. The second type is the genuine necrophiliac, and this is divided into three subtypes: the homicidal necrophiliac, who murders to have sex with a dead body; the regular necrophiliac, who uses already-dead bodies for sexual pleasure; and the necrophiliac fantasy offender, who merely fantasizes about having sex with the dead. Rosman and Resnick studied 122 necrophiles and found that the sex of the corpse desired mirrored the sexual orientation of the necrophile. Some 79% were heterosexual, 64% had histories of prior sadistic sexual acts, 86% had non-necrophilic intercourse, more than half were diagnosed with personality disorders, 17% were psychotic, and most were of above-average intelligence. The subjects in this research gathered their bodies through their work: hospital orderly, cemetery employee, morgue attendant, funeral parlor assistant, soldier, cleric, pathologist, anatomy student, and ambulance driver. Only a few committed homicide; the majority simply took advantage of chance opportunities.

Etiology of Necrophilia

No one knows the precise etiology of necrophilia. Since there are widespread differences among types of necrophiliacs, from those who merely fantasize to those who kill, explanations will certainly vary. Calef and Weinshel (1972) and Faguet (1980) state that the fantasies that accompany the necrophile act express a desire to reenter and explore the maternal body. Further elaborating, according to this view, the necrophiliac desires also to replace a rival fetus and to replace the paternal phallus. Other psychodynamic considerations may lie in the areas of a neurotic mother fixation, preoccupation with the mother's death, alcohol abuse, and social personality deprivation (Janik & Chromy, 1979). Of course, it would be most difficult to validate this theory.

H. Ellis (1946) has reported that necrophiliacs are often feebleminded or possess a high degree of psychopathology. (See also Katchadourian & Lunde, 1975.) Of course, this is not always true, and later studies show this may be indeed in error. Lancaster (1978) reports the case of a male with an IQ of 153 and with no signs of psychopathology reported prior to the incident. This necrophiliac broke into a mortuary on two separate occasions to have sexual intercourse with a corpse but was unsuccessful each time. Deciding to obtain a corpse by his own hand, this sex offender then broke into a home, where he stabbed a woman to death and had sexual intercourse with her.

Table 10.1   Typology of Necrophiles

Category	Characteristics
Pseudo-necrophile	Transient attraction to a corpse, but living partners are the preferred choice.
Homicidal Necrophile	Murders to have sex with the dead (the necrosadistic offender).
Regular Necrophile	Uses already dead bodies for sex. This person may work in a place where the offender will have access to dead bodies, e.g., such as a morgue, cemetaery, or funeral home.

SOURCE: Adapted from Rosman and Resnick (1989)

Selected Cases of Necrophiles

Edmond Kemper

In the 1970s in California, Kemper killed as many as 6 college coeds in addition to his mother. After murdering the young women, he would masturbate in their faces, cut off their heads, sometimes took their bodies home with him, and "planted" their heads in his mother's garden with their faces facing her window. Kemper is in prison in California.

Ed Gein

A grave robber as well as a killer, Gein kept skulls on his bedpost, made skin into lampshades, and admitted to having sex with corpses. These acts took place in the 1950s in Wisconsin. Gein died of natural causes in a mental hospital in Wisconsin.

Ted Bundy

Bundy admitted to keeping one young woman in his apartment for 4 days and another for 9 days while he dressed, undressed, and had sex with them. These murders occurred in the 1970s. Bundy was executed in Florida in 1989.

Jeffrey Dahmer

In Milwaukee, this homosexual killer desired to change his victims into zombies for his sexual cravings. He also practiced cannibalism as well as necrophilia. His victims were all males. Dahmer died in prison of a physical assault.

John Wayne Gacy

This killer in Chicago had more than a score of young men buried in the crawl space under his home. Often in advanced stages of their decay he would retrieve the skeletons and have sex with their remains. He was executed in prison.

Jerry Brudos

This killer from Oregon admitted to having sex with 2 of his 4 victims after they were dead. He also mutilated the bodies, cutting off one woman's foot and another's breasts, and from a third he cut off both breasts. Brudos died in prison of natural causes

Douglas Clark

The Hollywood Strip Killer, Clark is thought to be responsible for killing a as many as 60 victims some with a female accomplice, Carol Bundy. Clark said in an interview that he would masturbate into the face of a decapitated female victim and at least on one occasion was receiving oral sex from a victim as the victim was shot in the head. Clark is on death row in California.

John Christie

Christie killed at least 8 victims. The victims were found in his house and yard. All the victims were sexually abused after death. The medical examiner stated that some of the victims were dressed in diapers covering their genitals, some had their faces covered with a pillow case, and others had their stockings still on.

Many necrophiliacs are insensitive to others and have a great hatred for women. The mutilation that occurs to the (dead body of the female reduces the worth of the corpse and increases the emotional excitement of the act itself. Because the victim is dead—in the case of the necrosadistic offender and the one who has sex with corpses—the sex criminal does not risk rejection; the helplessness of the corpse could certainly enter into the decision to assault the body sexually (R. Holmes, 1983; Weeks, 1986).

Some necrophiles mention their attraction to vampirism. The mention of vampires arouses popular attention in print or in the film media. The bestselling Anne Rice novels are examples. Horror movies often depict a crazed killer and vampire. The "true" vampire involves necrophilia (unless that person is an "autovampire," one who only fanaticizes about having a dead body (Bourguignon, 1997; Schlesinger & Revitch, 1997). Sadism, cannibalism, and a fascination with blood all combine in the integral elements of a vampire (Jaffe & Dicataldo, 1994). One practitioner mentioned that vampirism is an experience that suggests draining the energy life force from the victim (Wilson, 2000). In therapy, the compulsion in this dangerous practice must not be overlooked. The therapist must consider the propensity for the vampire activity to continue (Kelly, Abood, & Stanley, 1999). What one must realize is that the vampire has blended a pathological fantasy that is composed of blood, sexuality, and death. The "active" vampire would be considered the necrosadistic offender. Bundy said in our interview that sometimes he felt like a vampire; he was more likely a cannibal. For example, he bit off and ingested the nipple of one victim, and bit several others.

The vampire is a dangerous person if left unnoticed. His mental pathology is of a disturbed person, often schizophrenic, sometimes delusional, and often under the compulsion of a blood lust. To obtain that blood, the person may kill, as in the case of Richard Carpenter (Dr. Joseph Davis, personal communication, September 2000).

❖ SADISM

Sadism is a paraphilia in which the will to exercise power over someone is sexually accentuated. This behavior is sexually enhanced and in some fashion, the sadist has learned that the inflicting of the pain (or even the anticipation of the infliction) is erotic. Power appears to be a integral element with the sadist (Holt, Meloy & Strack, 1999).

———— ❧ ————

Flagellationism

An intense desire to beat, whip, or club someone

From this activity, sexual gratification is achieved.

What are some of the characteristics of the sadist? Allnutt, Bradford, and Greenberg (2006) report that more than half their subjects who were sadists were also alcoholics. Geberth and Turco (1997) related that in their study of 68 serial killers who were sadists, their traits included

1. Domination over their victims

2. Total control over their victims

3. Humiliation of their victims

4. Sadistic sexual violence committed against their victims

5. Lack of guilt or shame during their acts

6. Lack of remorse over what they had done

Firestone, Bradford, and Greenberg (1998) found in their study of homicidal sex offenders who were previously diagnosed as sexual sadists that many suffered from psychosis, antisocial personality disorder, and several paraphilias, with more than 3 of 4 in their sample having three of the elements mentioned above. Meloy (2000) adds that sexual sadists are emotionally detached from others, psychopathic, and surprisingly suffered no early trauma.

———— ❧ ————

Algolagnia

Sexual satisfaction derived from the anticipation of inflicting or suffering pain; a manifestation of sadomasochism

———— ❧ ————

In Atlanta, police arrested a 19-year-old male who had been posing as a music producer to gain the confidence of young women. Then he would force the women to bite his navel. He threatened to kill them if they refused to service him.

SOURCE: APBnews.com 12–8–2000

While we will cover the lust and serial killers later in this chapter, we have found with several of the types of serial murderers (lust, thrill, and power/control types) that sexual sadism plays a vital part. Brudos, Bianchi, Bundy, Yates, and others needed the sadistic element in their crimes to reach some part of their sexual satisfaction. Did they behave like this as children? None of the above serialists did, but there may be warning signs manifest in juveniles who are potential sexual sadists that those in the helping professions may spot.

Hunter, Hazelwood, and Schlesinger (2000) report that juveniles who are sadists often offend against females, often offend against strangers, offend with a group of their peers, and commit their sexual crimes while committing other crimes, and the injuries they commit against others are usually quite severe. In rare cases, the injuries may even lead to death (Silberstein, 1998).

❖ INFIBULATION

Infibulation, an inward-directed dangerous sex crime, is torture of one's own body for sexual pleasure. This sex act is masochistic; often it involves piercing the flesh of one's own genitals. Albert Fish, a serial killer and mysoped in New York in the early 20th century, was an infibulator. After he was electrocuted in New York's electric chair, the autopsy showed that he had twenty-nine sewing needles inserted into his scrotum and penis.

Mazoperosis:

Sexual gratification received from the mutilation of female breasts

Erotic tattooing is viewed by some as one form of infibulation. Tattooing is an art form of body adornment developed in Japan and Polynesia. Among some men in the United States, tattoos serve as symbols of masculinity and toughness. In some other cultures, scarification is held to be an absolutely necessary for manhood (A. Ellis & Abarbanel, 1967).

Other forms of infibulation include the insertion of rings into the nipples, labia, clitoris, or penis. In one case, a 28-year-old female admitted repeatedly to a psychiatric hospital for acute depression was evaluated because of her insertion into her urethra of an ejectable razor blade that then lodged in her bladder. The patient had done this on numerous occasions when she felt lonely and "needed to feel alive." In another case, a 47-year-old man admitted to masturbating intraurethrally with a thin wooden stick. While masturbating, he fantasized about being a woman having sexual intercourse with a man (Wise, 1982). In another case, a man died on the operating table while the physicians attempted to remove a jar of pickles from his rectum (author's files).

Traumaphilia

Sexual arousal from wounds or injurious trauma

Etiology of the Infibulator

This form of sexual abuse has not received the serious research study that many other forms of behavior have. One study, however, lists six etiological factors in the background of the infibulator: abuse by relatives as a child, long and intense sexual confusion, masochistic relations with and submission to women, strong female identification, penis repudiation, and depression that is relieved by mutilation (Bourgeois, 1983). Conacher and Westwood (1987) believe that infibulators are often not paranoid schizophrenics—a position not accepted by Hall, Lawson, and Wilson (1981) or Silva, Leong, and Weinstock (1989)—but that they have a deeply hidden doubt about their sexual identity and a previous history of self-abuse. Another motivation may be an urge to rid oneself of unacceptable sexual urges that are viewed as dirty and evil (Fisch, 1987; Greenberg, Bruess, Mullen, & Sands, 1989). It may be that a combination of biological, psychological, and social factors, as well as the culture in which the person is reared, account for a propensity to infibulation (Favazza, 1989).

❖ AUTOEROTICISM

The term *autoeroticism* means involvement in a sexual behavior without a partner. There are several types of autoeroticism, including masturbation, erotic asphyxiation, chemical eroticism, and aquaeroticism. The study of masturbation has largely been ignored (Groenendijk, 1997). Simple masturbation poses no danger to the person who practices it. Despite the claims made years ago regarding "self-abuse," there is no evidence of any relationship between masturbation and physical injury. Davidson (1984) discovered some differences among the subjects in his study. Those who had masturbated were more likely to enjoy the experience and have more sexual partners than those who did not, but they did not find any statistical difference in sexual adjustment between those who did and those who did not masturbate.

Erotic hanging, chemical eroticism, and aquaeroticism are quite a different story. These solitary sex acts are practiced predominantly by males and are quite dangerous (Innes, 1997). As many as 1,000 accidental deaths a year may he attributed to erotic asphyxiation (Burgess & Hazelwood, 1983; Mimer & Dwyer, 1997). The person who practices this form of sex typically uses some type of mechanism to impede the flow of oxygen to the brain in order to heighten sexual pleasure. This oxygen deficiency somehow enhances feelings of sexual excitement (although there is no clear understanding of how this works). The enhancement mechanism can be a rope, a plastic bag, or an inhalant such as gas or a chemical aerosol (Lowery & Wetli, 1982; Polson & Gee, 1973). A rope is the most common method used to induce asphyxia. Luke (1967) reports that many men and women use some type of padding (towels, scarves, sweaters) under the ligature to prevent abrasions on the neck when a rope is used. This sex act has been practiced for centuries, unfortunately frequently resulting in the deaths of its practitioners.

Often, deaths resulting from erotic asphyxia are misclassified. For example, a young person is found hanged from a tree in a public park, nude, with clothing neatly folded near the tree. It may well be that the young person committed suicide, but it is also possible the person was involved in erotic hanging and the release mechanism malfunctioned. In one recent reported case, a gentleman was found hanging from a rafter in his office at a construction site. He was nude except for a semen guard (common among practitioners of erotic asphyxia), and his hands and feet were tied. In front of him was a collection of pornography that aided in his fantasy. In examining his personal effects, his mother found magazines and letters that he had written to members of the Eulenspiegel Society, a national organization for erotic asphyxiates. This was a classic case, and of course there was no misclassification. (For a list of typical elements found in erotic hanging, see Table 10.3.) In another case, a young man was found by his mother in the parent's attic. He had a garbage bag over the top half of his body, covering his face. Duct tape was placed around both thighs and he had wrapped his midsection with the coiled tube from the family's vacuum machine. He had tied a rope around his ankles and wrists after he placed the rope over a rafter in the ceiling. Perhaps placing the plastic bag over his face for the first time, he accidentally suffocated. The thought in these cases is that the person accidentally died. Our personal opinion is that this is the case in an overwhelming number of instances. But in some small percentage, it may not be (Johnston & Huws, 1997). Some cases may be suicides, and this is why the alert investigator must know what to look for in scenes like these.

Sheehan and Garfinkel (1988) studied nine young male paraphiliacs who had died as a result of erotic hanging. These researchers identified some common features of erotic asphyxiation, including the presence of partial or total undress, cross-dressing, the presence of pornographic material, evidence of penile enlargement, and some form of bondage.

Further examples illustrate these common elements. In one case, on arriving at work one morning, the owner of a gay bar found the bar

Table 10.2   Typical Profile of Erotic Asphyxia

- Young, white male; usually under 30
- Overachiever in school, work
- Shy with the opposite sex
- Neat and clean in appearance
- Typically in good physical condition
- May have some suicidal tendencies
- Often a churchgoer
- Upwardly mobile socially and occupationally
- Introvert and introspective
- A social loner
- Feels shame about his/her behavior
- May be viewed as intelligent and an intellectual

Table 10.3   Crime Scene Elements

In a case of erotic asphyxiation, the following may be present:

- Mirrors viewing back to the corpse
- Pornography at the scene in view of the practitioner
- Evidence of symmetrical bonding
- Collateral evidence of diaries, videos, and writings
- Rope burn evidence on door frames, knobs, etc., from past episodes
- In the case of males, cross dressing is often present
- Position of the knot in the middle of the back of the neck
- Object insertion in the anal opening
- Videos of self-practice

manager (a male) dead in the women's restroom. The manager was lying on the floor, dressed in a woman's slip. There was an opened newspaper on the floor in front of him and an amount of semen on the floor. The rope around his neck had not slipped as designed and he had died of asphyxia. Cesnik and Coleman (1989) report the case of a 24-year-old male who sought treatment for depression; his ritualized and compulsive autoerotic behavior included putting plastic bags over his head, binding his head with duct tape, tying himself up, and wearing a diving suit.

In another example, an optician was found in his home by a neighbor who had not seen him in a few days. His newspapers and mail had not been picked up in three days. The neighbor looked through the kitchen window and saw the man dead in his kitchen. He was dead, panty hose wrapped around his neck and fastened to a shop vacuum, which was in the "on" mode. There was a tube with one end attached to the shop vacuum and the other to his penis. There was also child pornography on his computer monitor and trash in the home. There was a collection of child pornography and videos of the decedent practicing his autoerotic activities.

❖ CHARACTERISTICS OF EROTIC ASPHYXIATES

Lowery and Wetli (1982) report that the overwhelming majority of those involved in erotic asphyxia are young, white, middle-class, unmarried males. Saunders (1989) found that of 43 persons who had died by autoerotic asphyxia, 35 were men under the age of 30 (the age range was 14–75), two-thirds were single, and most were white. One in three practiced transvestitism at the time of their death.

Because few persons will openly admit to the practice of erotic asphyxiation, the characteristics of those who indulge in these acts are gleaned from those who have failed in their practice—that is, from those who have died. The characteristics that Haydn-Smith, Marks, and Repper (1989) report from their study were youth, transvestitism, and masturbation; most practitioners are male, and only a few seek help. Burgess and Hazelwood (1983), in a study of 132 cases of erotic asphyxiates, found that 96% were males, 65% were less than 30 years of age, 94% were white, and almost 60% were single.

Schlesinger and Revitch (1997) report that there is a strong connection between these paraphiles and an attraction to masochism. In Schlesinger and Revitch's study, for example, many had made a connection between sexual gratification and humiliation.

Whatever may be the primary etiology of those who participate in this form of autoeroticism, we do not have a firm understanding of the basic reason for involvement in this most dangerous form of sex practice. It may have something to do with the risks involved in placing oneself at the door of death to have some form of sexual gratification.

❖ AQUAEROTIC ASPHYXIATION

In a case reported in a southern state, a man came home from work in the afternoon to find his 21-year-old wife dead. She was dressed in a jogging suit, with a heavy knit tie around her neck, and her hands were bound in front of her. Her face was in three inches of water; she had drowned. Upon interrogation, the husband admitted that his wife had been involved in erotic hanging. She had usually practiced this form of solitary sex in the bathroom, a fact that was verified by various rope burns on the top of the bathroom door. Apparently, she had tried to induce partial drowning to enhance sexual excitement. The results were fatal.

Sivaloganathan (1984) describes aquaeroticum (autoerotic drowning) in the case of a 36-year-old male, who was found at the bottom of a river encased in a bag. His wrists and ankles were tied loosely together, and his right forefinger was passed through the small loop of a pair of scissors. Upon investigation, it was determined that the man was practicing aquaeroticism and apparently had accidentally drowned before he could cut himself free.

In a midwestern town, a man's body was found inside a sleeping bag. The bag was attached to a rope which was tied to the neck of the man inside the bag with the other end having been severed by a blade from a speed boat.

Upon the investigation of the body and the scene by the police and the coroner's office, it was ascertained that the man was practicing aquaeroticism. The investigation showed that the man had climbed into the sleeping bag nude, bound his feet with plastic ties, handcuffed his wrists and placed one end of the rope around his neck and the other around a branch on the river's edge. Inside the bag itself, he had placed scissors close by his hands, zipped up the bag from the inside up to his chin, and then jumped into the river. Unfortunately the rope snapped and he floated onto the river. On this busy Sunday, there were many boats riding on the river. One speed boat sped over him, slashing his bag and portions of the body itself. His body suffered multiple injuries and he was killed. Eventually the body bag rested on the shore of the river and his body was discovered. His death was ruled an accident by the coroner's office. Jefferson County (KY) Coroner's Office, Louisville, KY., 2007

This form of autoeroticism appears to be very rare, but the elements in the practice are not too different from those found in erotic asphyxiation: a complicated use of ligatures involving the genitals and neck, pornography, and so on.

Forms of autoerotic behavior other than those discussed above have been recorded as well. Sivaloganathan (1984) reported cases of devotees to the practice of inserting objects—lamps, electrical cords—into their bodily orifices, which resulted in fatal electrocutions. Although some forms of autoerotic behavior are potentially lethal, little is known about the characteristics of persons who become involved in this form of sexual activity. Additional research needs to be done in this area.

Because there is such a dearth of information, there is a great need for social action programs designed to inform the public as well as practitioners of these potentially dangerous sexual acts. There must be an added effort to inform mental health professionals of the growing numbers of persons who practice aquaerotic asphyxiation and of methods developed to enable them to deal with this form of sexual activity.

❖ PYROMANIA

There are approximately 20,000 incidents of arson per year in the United States. There are many types of arson (see Table 10.4). Fire setting for revenge or for commercial purposes are two forms of arson. Pyromania is yet another. Pyromania is an eroticized form of arson. It is a pathological condition characterized by a compulsion that becomes very strong, until there is an inability to refrain from it. As Grant, Levine, Kim, and Potenza (2005) report in their study of psychiatric inpatients using the Minnesota Impulsive Disorders Interview instrument, it may be that pyromaniacs suffer from a compulsive impulsive control disorder. Where that particular disorder arises is unknown.

Unfortunately, pyromania is not a well-understood form of arson. Pyromania is misunderstood not only among the mental health professionals but also among police and fire protection experts (Geller, McDermeit, & Brown, 1997). It must also be acknowledged that there is no one clear motive for firesetting; the motivations and anticipated gains are many and varied. But as Doley (2003) stated, there must be a clear pattern of impulsive firesetting behavior that is preceded by a feeling of tension and followed by a sense of psychological release once the act has been committed. Couple this with a sexual motivation and a sexual release, and then the true picture of the pyromaniac will arise.

Masters and Robertson (1990) estimate that about 40% of firesetters are pyromaniacs, although that statistical figure the authors feel is too high. Revenge is a much more common motive, not to mention that some fires are started by the homeless in an attempt to keep warm.

Pyromaniacs commit arson, but their motivation is different from that of other types of firesetters; theirs is an erotic motive. In some instances, the pyromaniac ignites a fetish (e.g., shoes, panties), and, although the fire is initially specific in character, it may spread to an entire building (Haas & Haas, 1990), sometimes resulting in the deaths of innocent people.

As with many sex offenders, there appears to be a situational impulse that sets the pyromaniac into action. Bourget and Bradford

(1987) relate the case of one young adult as follows: As a child he was fascinated with fire, but his first experience of arson occurred when he was a young adult. He went into a bar, felt rejected and angry when he was not able to meet anyone, and left the bar to set a fire. This became a pattern of firesetting behavior in his residential neighborhood. His firesetting involved both an erotic component and one of revenge. When he was unsuccessful with females, he abused alcohol, only to become more angry and resentful. In this state of mind he would set a fire. He would see images of women in the fire and become sexually aroused. He would then masturbate, watching the fire. Then he would go home and masturbate again while reading pornography. As the behavior continued, it led to erotic feelings of power and sexual arousal.

The pyromaniac experiences sexual excitement at the sight of a fire or smoke, and this leads to urination, erection, masturbation, and sometimes spontaneous orgasm. This sex offender often sets a fire and then stands apart and watches not only the fire but the calamity the fire has produced (Money, 1985). When we talked with Ottis Toole, a serial killer who was also a pyromaniac, his eyes glistened with excitement as he talked about his firesetting escapades. He said that there was a sense of power and excitement in setting a fire and watching people as they responded to the fire. The citizens in the neighborhood who came to the fire, the professional firefighters who fought the fire, and the police at the site of the fire. They are all there because of what he had done. Of course, there was a sexual component to the fire, and he masturbated in response to the fire, the smoke, and the excitement (authors' files).

Characteristics of the Pyromaniac

Dooley (2003) reports that there is a great deal of misunderstanding about firesetting, arson, and pyromania. She stated in her article "Pyromania: Fact or Fiction," for pyromania to be considered pyromania, there must be a clear pattern of impulsive firesetting behavior that

Table 10.4   Types of Arson

Type	Characteristics
Organized	crime loan sharking. extortion, strippers, and other crime concealments
Insurance	overinsurance, blockbusting, parcel clearance, housing fraud
Commercial	inventory depletion, stop-loss, and modernization
Residential	public housing, relocation, automobile, and redecorating

SOURCE: Macy (1979)

is preceded by a feeling of tension and followed by a sense of relief or pleasure once the act has been completed. We would add that the pleasure, to be considered the work of a pyromaniac, must involve a sense of sexual release.

Almost 30 years ago, McCary (1978) stated that pyromania affects only males. This same assertion was made in the older studies of kleptomania. There have been several newer studies that refute this conclusion. For example, this point is contested slightly by the research of Crossley and Guzman (1985), who state that the pyromaniac is "primarily a male." Even older studies refute the position, For example, Karpman (1957) states that sometimes the pyromaniac is a female, and she will set fires "either prior to or during menstruation or during pregnancy" (p. 140).

The pyromaniac is typically young and experiences sexual frustration and tension that leads to a compulsion to start a fire.

Characteristics of Pyromaniacs

Age: The heaviest concentration is between ages of 16 and 28; highest frequency at age 17.

Sex: Most are male.

Race: Most are white.

Intelligence ranges from mentally defective to genius. (Approximately 22% of those with no explanation for their firesetting are low-grade defectives.)

Physical Defects are frequently found to be present.

Enuresis is present in some.

Mental Disorders: Psychopathy, as well as psychotic disorders, have been identified within this category; the compulsive urge also appears to reflect a neurotic obsessive-compulsive pattern of behavior.

Academic Adjustment: Poor educational adjustment, although some pyromaniacs are intellectually bright. Their academic performance is marginal or scholastically retarded—underachievers.

Rearing Environment: Pathological, broken, and harsh rearing environment with inconsistent discipline and parental neglect. Pyromaniacs note unhappy home life.

Social Class Structure: Pyromaniacs come from all social classes

Marital Adjustments: Although some pyromaniacs are married, their marital adjustments are poor.

Sexual Adjustments: Sexually maladjusted and inadequate; limited contact with women.

(Continued)

(Continued)

Occupational/Employment History: Most frequently unskilled laborers, if employed. They accept subservient positions and become resentful when they realize their work is degrading.

Personality: May be described as misfits and feeble persons, physical cowards with feelings of inadequacy, inferiority, insufficiency, and self-consciousness; introverted, reclusive, aloof, frustrated, and lonely. Often pyromaniacs have unconscious fears of being unwanted and unloved and suffer from wounded self-esteem and lack of pride and prestige. They often project an image of calm and indifference (anxiety and tension are present nonetheless). They have vague feelings, however, that their defenses will fail them and that these repressed impulses will emerge. They tend to be defensive and obstinate in attitude and ambivalent toward authority, they also have contempt for authority. Although they have an inner dependency on authority, they also have contempt for it. In fact, they have repressed their rage toward society and authority figures. They lack ambition and aggressiveness. Some state that they had no desire to hurt anyone. They may be apologetic but are ashamed of being apologetic. They seek expression through excitement. Some pyromaniacs have been found to be quite intelligent, neat, and methodical in their behavior. They have a need to be recognized and have a sense of worth. They have a craving for power and prestige. They fail to express remorse or to accept responsibility for their firesetting.

Criminal History: Many have histories of delinquency and criminal behavior, including running away from home, burglary, theft, and various property offenses.

Use of Alcohol: Pyromaniacs frequently use alcohol as a method of escape and to remove social inhibitions, but they do not set fires because they drink.

Suicide: Some attempt suicide after arrest and incarceration.

Motives: Exact motivation in each case is unknown, but the following motives have been identified: (1) desire to be a hero and the center of attention (craving for excitement and prestige)—playing detective at the fire, rendering first aid, helping to rescue victims, assisting firefighters; (2) desire to show themselves sufficiently clever to cause the "experts" (firefighters and detectives) problems and render them helpless—grandiose ambitions to be the executive who directs the firefighting activity and puts the firefighters into action; (3) enjoyment of the destruction of property (vagrants exhibiting pyromania receive sadistic pleasure in watching the destruction of buildings); (4) irresistible impulse (unable to offer any other explanation); (5) revenge, although not consciously present, is a possible factor; (6) sexual satisfaction (noted in a relatively small percentage of cases).

Irresistible Impulse: No single precipitating factor produces this impulse. It is believed to be the result of sexual desires, loss of employment, refusal of employment, death of parent or loved one, threats to personal security and masculinity, explosive protest over imagined immorality or promiscuity of mother or spouse, and fear of impotence.

Types of Fires: Generally made in haste and in a disorganized fashion; often set in rubbish, basements, and in and around inhabited dwellings, office buildings, schools, hotels, and other structures in thickly populated sections of cities. Fires frequently set in rapid succession. Matches, newspapers, and other available materials are used in starting the fires.

Number of Fires: May start numerous fires, sometimes hundreds, until caught.

False Alarms: Some pyromaniacs also set off false alarms.

Time of Day: Firesetting is often nocturnal.

Regard for Life: No regard for life exhibited; fires are frequently set in and around occupied buildings.

Emotional State and Behavior During Firesettting: Many feel the act of firesetting is outside themselves; some describe the emergence of a sort of dissociative state (a transient sensation of being controlled by an internal force—a feeling of being automated). They recognize the firesetting is senseless but do not have the control to prevent it. To a casual observer, the pyromaniacs appear normal.

Emotional State and Behavior After Fire Setting: Relief and even exaltation; tensions released. Few express sexual satisfaction in setting fires. Many stay at or near the fire as a spectator or to assist responding firefighters by rendering first aid or rescuing victims. Some enjoy playing detective at the fire scene. Some, after setting a fire and ensuring firefighters' response, go home to a restful sleep.

Arrest: Some pyromaniacs ensure that they will be identified and arrested; some even turn themselves in to the police. Many continue to set fires until apprehended. For some, arrest seems to release them fro their irresistible impulses to set fires. It is a relief for them to be stopped.

Confession: Many readily confess or admit guilt, though they express no remorse or regret for their behavior; neither do they generally accept responsibility for their firesetting. They are most often quiet and cooperative under arrest.

Selection of Target: Firesetting targets are often randomly selected, no apparent reason.

Ritualism: Like many sex offenders, pyromaniacs are ritualistic. They are often the first to arrive at the scene of the fire they have set. They often act as "traffic guards" helping the police with the inevitable traffic snarls that develop around the fires. Also, they will often be in the crowd observing the fire, the reactions of the onlookers, and the work of the fire personnel and the police. (Lewis & Yarnell, 1951, cited by Rider, 1980; and authors' personal files)

There appear to be some common characteristics that the majority of known pyromaniacs possess. For example, many suffered physical abuse as children, poor parental relationships, and severe conduct disorders (Lowenstein, 1989). Oliver (1974) believes that many pyromaniacs are mentally retarded, severely paranoid, schizophrenic, alcoholic, or sexually sadistic.

Pyromania, while sexually motivated, is a very dangerous sexual practice because of the real peril it presents to unaware citizens. Treatment programs directed toward this type of arsonist must be expanded if the statistics that have been reported are at least remotely accurate.

❖ CONCLUSION

This chapter has focused upon very dangerous sex offenders. The reader will notice that, while sadism and masochism have not been explored directly as distinct topics, sex behaviors that inflict pain and suffering upon hapless and helpless victims are an integral part of dangerous sex crimes. Every year, thousands of victims are targets of offenders who commit the crimes discussed in this chapter. New names are continually coming to our attention—Gary Heidnik, Gerald Gallego, John Story, Cameron Hooker, Randy Craft—graphically illustrating that victimization is not declining. It may be a more serious problem than we have originally envisioned.

❖ DISCUSSION QUESTIONS

1. What do you believe is the role of our society and its culture in the formation of a dangerous sex offender? Does society share some culpability?

2. Recognizing that not all serial killers kill for sex, how much of a potential danger to society is the sexually motivated male or female serial killer?

3. Among all the dangerous sex offenders discussed in this chapter, which one do you believe to be the most dangerous?

4. Discuss the major differences between the organized and disorganized offender. Recognizing that the FBI has never made their methodology public, how much credence should we pay to the results they report?

5. Select a major character from a work of fiction, such as Sherlock Holmes, Dr. Kay Scarpetti, or Clarice Starling. Now select an infamous killer, either real or fictional. Using the typology of organized and disorganized, how would your first character investigate the crimes of the killer?

❖ REFERENCES

Allnutt, S., Bradford, J., & Greenberg, D. (2006). Co-morbidity of alcoholism and the paraphilias. *Journal of Forensic Sciences, 41*(2), 234–239.

American Psychiatric Association. (1987). *Desk reference to the criteria from DSM-III-R.* Washington, DC: Author.

Baker, N. (1983). Some considerations arising from the treatment of a patient with necrophilic fantasies in late adolescence and young adulthood. *Revista de Psicoanálisis, 40*(1), 157–173.

Barlow, M., Barlow, D., & Stojkovic, S. (1995). The media, the police, and the multicultural community: Observations on a city in crisis. *Journal of Crime and Justice, 17*(2), 133–165.

Bartholomew, A., Milte, K., & Galbally, F. (1978). Homosexual necrophilia. *Medicine, Science, and the Law, 18*(1), 29–35.

Bourgeois, M. (1983). Genital self-mutilation in humans. *Annales Medico-Psychologiques, 141*, 522–532.

Bourget, D., & Bradford, J. (1987). Fire fetishism, diagnostic and clinical implications: A review of two cases. *Canadian Journal of Psychiatry, 32*(6), 459–462.

Bourguignon, A. (1997). Vampirism and autovampirism. In L. Schlesinger & E. Revitch (Eds.), *Sexual dynamics of anti-social behavior* (Vol. 2, pp. 271–293). Springfield, IL: Charles C Thomas.

Brill, A. (1941). Necrophilia. *Journal of Criminal Psychopathology, 2*, 51–73, 433–443.

Burg, B. (1983). *Sodomy and the perception of evil.* New York: New York University Press.

Burgess, A., & Hazelwood, R. (1983). Autoerotic asphyxial deaths and social network response. *Journal of the American Orthopsychiatric Association, 53*(1), 166–170.

Calef, V., & Weinshel, E. (1972). On certain equivalents of necrophilia. *International Journal of Psychoanalysis, 53*(1), 67–75.

Cesnik, J., & Coleman, E. (1989). Use of lithium carbonate in the treatment of autoasphyxia. *American Journal of Psychotherapy, 43*, 277–286.

Conacher, G., & Westwood, G. (1987). Infibulation. *British Journal of Psychiatry, 150*, 565–566.

Crossley, T., & Guzman, R. (1985). The relationship between arson and pyromania. *American Journal of Forensic Psychology, 3*(1), 39–44.

Davidson, H. (1984). Protecting children. *ABA Journal, 70*(5), 160–182.

Doley, R. (2003). Pyromania: Fact or fiction. *British Journal of Criminology, 43*(4), 797–807.

Ellis, A. (1986). *Time encyclopedia of sexual behavior.* New York: Hawthorne.

Ellis, A., & Abarbanel, A. (1967). *Sex behavior.* New York: Hawthorne.

Ellis, H. (1946). *Psychology of sex: A manual for students.* New York: Emerson.

Faguet, R. (1980). Munchausen syndrome and necrophilia. *Suicide and Life-Threatening Behavior, 10*(4), 214–218.

Favazza, A. (1989). Infibulation. *Community Psychiatry, 40*(2), 137–145.

Firestone, P., Bradford, J., & Greenberg, D. (1998). Homicidal and nonhomicidal child molesters: Psychological, phallometric, and criminal features. *Sexual Abuse, 10*, 305–323.

Fisch, R. (1987). Genital self-mutilation in males: Psychodynamic anatomy of a psychosis. *American Journal of Psychotherapy, 31*, 453–458.

Foerster, K., Foerster, G., & Roth, E. (1981). Necrophilia in a 17 year old girl. *Schweizer Archiv für Neurologie und Psychiatrie, 199*(1), 97–107.

Freier, A. (1981). The necrophiliac character according to Erich Fromm: The case of Amanda. Psiquis: Revista de Psicologia yes Psicosomatica, 2(1), 23–32.

Gauthier, D. K., & Forsyth, C. J. (1999). Bareback sex, bug chasers, and the gift of death. *Deviant Behavior, 20*(1), 85–114.

Geberth, V., & Turco, R. (1997). Antisocial personality disorder, sexual sadism, malignant narcissism, and serial murder. *Journal of Forensic Science, 42*(1), 49–60.

Geller, J., McDermeit, M., & Brown, J. (1997). Pyromania? What does it mean? *Journal of Forensic Science, 42*(6), 121–135.

Goldenson, R. (1970). *Encyclopedia of human behavior: Psychology, psychiatry, and mental health.* Garden City, NJ: Doubleday.

Gollman, R. H. (1981). *Edward Gein: America's most bizarre murderer.* C. Hallberg: Minneapolis, MN

Grant, J., Levine, L., Kim, D., & Potenza, M. (2005). Impulse control disorders in adult psychiatric inpatients. *American Journal of Psychiatry,* 2184–2188.

Greenberg, R., Bruess, C., Mullen, K., & Sands, D. (1989). *Sexuality.* Dubuque, IA: William C. Brown.

Groenendijk, L. (1997). Masturbation and neurasthenia: Freud and Stekel in debate on the harmful effects of autoeroticism. *Journal of Psychology and Human Sexuality, 9*(1), 71–94.

Haas, L., & Haas, J. (1990). *Understanding sexuality.* Boston: Mosby.

Hall, D., Lawson, B., & Wilson, L. (1981). Command hallucinations and self-amputation of the penis and hand during a first psychotic break. *Journal of Clinical Psychiatry, 42,* 322–324.

Haydn-Smith, P., Marks, H., & Repper, D. (1989). Behavioral treatment of life-threatening masochistic asphyxiation: A case study. *British Journal of Psychiatry, 150,* 518–519.

Hazelwood, R., Dietz, P., & Burgess, A. (1983). *Autoerotic fatalities.* Lexington, MA: D.C. Heath.

Holmes, R. (1983). *The sex offender and the criminal justice system.* Springfield, IL: Charles C Thomas.

Holmes, S., Hickey, E., & Holmes, R. (1998). Female serial murderesses: The unnoticed terror. In R. Holmes & S. Holmes (Eds.), *Contemporary perspectives on serial murder* (pp. 59–73). Thousand Oaks, CA: Sage.

Holt, S., Meloy, Strack, S. (1999). Sadism and psychotherapy in violent offenders. Journal of American Academy of Psychiatry and the Law. 27(1), 23–32.

Horley, J. (1995). Cognitive-behavioral therapy with an incarcerated exhibitionist. Iinternational Journal of Offender Therapy and Comparative Criminology. 29, 335–339.

Hunter, J., Hazelwood, R., & D. Schlesinger,. (2000). Juvenile perpetrated sex crimes: Patterns of offending and predicting violence. *Journal of Family Violence, 15*(1), 81–93.

Innes, R. (1997). Autoerotic asphyxia and art psychotherapy. In E. Welldon & C. Van Velsen (Eds.), *A practical guide to forensic psychotherapy* (pp. 172–181). London: Jessica Kingsley.

Jaffe, P., & Dicataldo, F. (1994). Clinical vampirism: Blending myth and reality. *Bulletin of the American Academy of Psychiatry and Law, 22*(4), 533–544.

Janik, A., & Chromy, K. (1979). A case of necrophilia. *Československe Psychiatrie, 75,* 305–306.

Johnston, J., & Huws, R. (1997). Autoerotic asphyxiation: A case report. *Journal of Sex and Marital Therapy, 23*(4), 326–332.

Karpman, B. (1957). *The sexual offender and his offenses.* New York: Julian.

Katchadourian, H., & Lunde, D. (1975). *Fundamentals of human sexuality.* New York: Holt, Rinehart, and Winston.

Kelly, B., Abood, Z., & Stanley, D. (1999). Vampirism and schizophrenia. *16*(3), 114–115.

Lancaster, N. (1978). Necrophilia, murder, and high intelligence: A case report. *British Journal of Psychiatry, 132,* 605–608.

Lowenstein, L. (1989). The etiology, diagnosis, and treatment of the fire-setting behavior of children. *Child Psychiatry and Human Development, 19*(3), 186–194.

Lowery, S., & Wetli, C. (1982). Sexual asphyxia: A neglected area of study. *Deviant Behavior, 4,* 19–39.

Luke, J. (1967). Asphyxial deaths by hanging in New York City. *Journal of Forensic Sciences, 12,* 359–369.

Macy, J. (1979). *To the reader. In arson: The federal role in arson prevention and control (report to congress).* Washington, D.C.: Office of Planning and Evaluation.

Masters, R., & Robertson, C. (1990). *Inside criminology.* Englewood Cliffs, NJ: Prentice-Hall.

McCary, J. (1978). *McCary's human sexuality.* New York: D. Van Nostrand.

Meloy, J. (2000). The nature and dynamics of sexual homicide: An integrative review. *Aggression and Violent Behavior, 5*(1), 1–22.

Mimer, N., & Dwyer, S. (1997). The psychosocial development of sex offenders: Differences between exhibitionists, child molesters, and incest offenders. *International Journal of Offender Therapy and Comparative Criminology, 41,* 63–44.

Money, J. (1984). Paraphilias: Phenomenology and classification. *American Journal of Orthopsychiatry, 38,* 164–179.

Money, J. (1985). *The destroying angel.* Buffalo, NY: Prometheus.

Oliver, J. (1974). *Clinical sexuality.* Philadelphia: J.B. Lippincott.

Polson, C., & Gee, D. (1973). *The essentials of forensic medicine* (3rd ed.). Oxford, UK: Pergamon.

Ressler, R. (1986). Murderers who rape and mutilate. *Journal of Interpersonal Violence, 1,* 273–287.

Rider, A. (1980). The firesetter: A psychological profile. *FBI Law Enforcement Bulletin, 49,* 14–15.

Riveria, D. (1995). Necrophilia. *Journal of Criminal Justice. 32*(11), 11–21.

Rosman, J., & Resnick, P. (1989). Sexual attraction to corpses: A psychiatric review of necrophilia. *Bulletin of the American Academy of Psychiatry and the Law, 17*(2), 153–163.

Saunders, E. (1989). Life-threatening autoerotic behavior: A challenge for sex educators and therapists. *Journal of Sex Education and Therapy, 15,* 82–91.

Schlesinger, L., & Revitch, E. (1997). *Sexual dynamics of anti-social behavior.* Springfield, IL: Charles C Thomas.

Sheehan, W., & Garfinkel, B. (1988). Adolescent autoerotic deaths. *Journal of the American Academy of Child and Adolescent Psychiatry, 27,* 367–370.

Silberstein, J. (1998). A paradigmatic case in family violence. *International Journal of Offender Therapy and Comparative Criminology, 42*(3), 210–223.

Silva, J., Leong, G., & Weinstock, R. (1989). Infibulation. *Psychosomatic, 30*(20), 228–230.

Sivaloganathan, S. (1984). Aqua-eroticum: A case of autoerotic drowning. *Medical Science Law, 24,* 300–302.

Terry, K. (2003). *Sexual offenses and offenders: Theory, practice, and policy.* New York: Wadsworth.

Wasby, S. L. (1980). The impotency of sex policy: It's not all in the family (or: A non-voyeuristic look at a coupling of sex and policy). *Policy Studies Journal, 9*(1), 117–120.

Weeks, J. (1986). *Sexuality.* New York: Harwood.

Wilson, N. (2000). A psychoanalytic contribution to psychic vampirism: A case vignette. *American Journal of Psychoanalysis, 60*(2), 177–186.

Wise, R. (1982). Urethral manipulation: An unusual paraphilia. *Journal of Sex and Marital Therapy, 8,* 222–227.

11

Sexually Motivated Homicides

❖ ❖ ❖

O n June 27, 2006, Angel Resendiz was executed in Texas. The Mexican drifter known as the Railroad Killer was executed for the slaying of physician Claudia Benton almost eight years earlier. She was killed during a deadly spree in 1998 and 1999 that earned Resendiz a spot on the FBI's Most Wanted list as authorities searched for a murderer who slipped across the U.S. border and roamed the country by freight train. Ottis Toole, 1947–1997, was another serial killer motivated by lust. At one time he confessed that he and his partner, Henry Lucas, killed more than 600 people. He later retracted that number and confessed to 6 murders. He died in prison in Florida.

There are other serial killers who killed for sexual purposes. Douglas David Clark, presently on death row in California, is the infamous Hollywood Strip Killer. On death row for the murder of 6 young women, and a suspect in more than a score of other murders, Clark allegedly decapitated several of his victims and sexually assaulted them after death. Jerry Brudos, another lust killer, killed 4 women, mutilated them after they were dead, committed acts of necrophilia on them, and cut off their breasts (mazoperosis) and an ankle and foot. He died in prison in Oregon while serving multiple life sentences. John Wayne Gacy, a serialist from the Chicago area, killed 33 young men, buried some under his home and under his driveway, and dumped others in the local river. There are many other examples of lust-motivated killers. Some murder their victims and commit gross acts of necrophilia; other can torture and mutilate and commit other sexual assaults, but once the victim is deceased, the activity ends. The acts of the latter example is more typical of the thrill-type sexually motivated killer.

What is it about this type of killer who fatally dispatches sometimes a sequentially large number of people for sexual gain? What is the mentality of those of kill for sexual gratification?

❖ LUST MURDER

Holmes and DeBurger (1988; see also Holmes & Holmes, 1998b) have developed a typology of serial murderers that differentiates visionary, mission, hedonistic, and power/control types. The visionary and mission types kill typically not for sexual purposes. In contrast, the hedonistic types (of which there are two subtypes, *lust* and *thrill)* and power/control killers certainly are impelled by sex to kill, and in some cases for power and control as well. John Gacy, Ted Bundy, Douglas Clark, Ottis Toole, Gerald Stano, Carol Bundy, Kenneth Bianchi, and Angelo Buono are all examples of hedonistic killers, an extremely dangerous offender. Lust killers often kill with weapons that demand skin-to-skin contact, such as knives, fists, or hands. Kirby (1999), however, suggested that the choice of weapon for the sexual attack may be due more to the occupation and gender of the killer. Women use more covert weapons such as poisons, suffocation, and lethal injections. And occupation may affect weapon choice by providing ready access to suitable weapons. In our experiences, though, occupation would probably be more important in weapon choice for the female killer, lust or not.

The sexually motivated serial killer is one who has made a vital connection between sexual gratification and fatal violence. This type of serial killer is motivated by the hunger for sexual gratification. Unfortunately, many such killers are sadistic to the extent that their sexual pleasure depends on the amount of torture and mutilation they can administer, and ultimately on the killing of their victims. These killers are typically in touch with reality and can establish

—— ✄ ——

"I'm the coldest mother fucker you ever put your eyes on. I didn't give a shit about those people." (author's interview with Bundy, 1986)

relationships with other persons, but their sexual gratification comes from the use and the abuse of people they view as sexual objects. Elaborate stalking, carefully planned activities surrounding the extermination of the victim, and sexual experimentation after death (necrophilia) are often elements in lust killings; mutilation of the victim is often perpetrated as well.

Lust killers often select women and children as victims for many different reasons, often to fulfill their sexual and fatal fantasies. They seek an ideal victim type, often seek victims with certain physical characteristics such as body style or hair style. Often diagnosed as an antisocial personality, this

Agonophilia

Sexual excitation from a pretension that one's partner is involved in a struggle to be free

killer represents a very real danger to society. Consider the following from an interview conducted with a serialist who is currently in prison for the murder of several young women

> Almost 15 years have passed since the little blond named Becky died alone in the darkness of my bedroom closet. And perhaps more appalling than the raw brutality surrounding her demise is that she was not my only victim that fateful day. Less than two hours after Becky's life had ended, there was yet another, slightly older girl lying naked and bound inside my bedroom. This second girl's name is long forgotten now, but it was she who was forced to endure all the sadistic cruelties that I'd failed to carry out on her dead predecessor. While she lay tied down to my bed, I terrorized and battered and tortured this girl for more than an hour, covering up the sound of her gag-muffled screams with music from a loudly blaring radio. Next, after becoming intensely aroused by the sight and sound of her agony, I lowered myself onto the bed and started raping her, continuing with this assault until I wanted her no more. Finally, then, having no further need of this second victim, I wrapped an extension cord around her neck and pulled hard on the ends, strangling her until I was certain that she, like the blond-headed Becky before her, was dead.

> So began my career as a killer. I had only recently celebrated by 20th birthday when these, my first two murders, were carried out inside my home. Several years would pass and I'd be just under

24 before capture and imprisonment finally put an end to my habit of killing. Throughout the years in between, however, I would succeed at luring a multitude of unsuspecting young women into the front seat of my car and on into the house where I lived. Most of these young females were hitchhikers, some were stranded motorists whose cars had broken down along uncrowded highways, and others were lone pedestrians who were just naive or incautious enough to follow me to the moon on the promise of a free high. And, in almost every instance, I ended up torturing and raping and murdering these young women, filling their last hours with pain and agony. (authors' files)

The lust killer often combines aberrant sexual practices, including picquerism, flagellation, anthropophagy, and necrosadism. Picquerism is the intense desired to stab, wound, or cut the flesh of another person. One inmate in Utah State Prison admitted liking to see people suffer. He liked to cut people, and he related that "knifing someone is like cutting through foam rubber" (authors' files). Often these stab wounds are inflicted near the genitals or breasts in a lust killing (De River, 1958). Henry Lucas was another lust killer who apparently had a deep need to confess. Whatever the reason for his confession, be it a poor self-image, eagerness to please, or a need for notoriety (Gudjonsson & Sigurdsson, 2000), Lucas's confessions enabled many police departments to close their cold cases.

Flagellationism is an intense desire to beat, whip, or club someone. This form of sadism often leads to severe beating and sexual abuse of victims.

Vampirism is rare, but it does occur. We recently completed a profile for a police department in a southern state in which 8 young women were found, all nude, with no blood left in their bodies. There were puncture wounds in the left arm of each victim. Immediately, the police suspected some type of occult group operating in the area. There were no other forms of abuse, victims had not been sexually abused, and there were no signs of satanic involvement (bum marks, tattoos, or the like). The evidence indicated a sex criminal with a propensity for vampirism. The police finally arrested an engineer who had abducted 9 women, tying each to his kitchen table and draining her blood. He kept the blood in mason jars in his refrigerator to drink when he wanted it. The 9th victim managed to loosen her bonds after he went to work; she escaped and went to the police.

John Haigh killed 9 women in 1949. After killing one victim, Haigh remarked

I shot her in the back of the head. Then I went out to the car and fetched a drinking glass and made an incision, I think with a penknife, in the side of the throat and collected a glass of blood, which I then drank. (Blundell, 1983, p. 74)

Ted Bundy admitted to having feelings of vampirism. He also, on at least one occasion, bit off the nipple of one victim and ingested it.

Female Cannibalism

The *Rocky Mountain News* reported that Carolyn Blanton, 41, was charged in the shooting death of Peter Green, 51. The police reported that some bodily remains were found in cooking pans in Blanton's apartment. Evidence was presented in court that included bite-size chunks of human flesh.

The police also reported that Green's torso was found in the closet at his home, and his legs were found in a nearby trash container. They also stated that the flesh was removed from his legs from the ankle up.

Cannibalism, a form of anthropophagy, appears to be more common than vampirism. Jack the Ripper, for example, was said to have sent a kidney of one of his victims to Scotland Yard, with a note saying that he had eaten the other (Chesser, 1971; Shuster, 1975). Fritz Haarman kidnapped, murdered, butchered, and stored the remains of young boys. Only recently, Gary Heidnik was arrested in Philadelphia with the body parts of one victim cooking on his kitchen range. Ed Gein, Albert Fish, and other lust killers are also examples of cannibals.

Sometimes anthropophagy is inner-directed. Stoller (1985) reports one patient who, after failing in relationships with women, would eat parts of his own flesh. Each time he ate his own skin, he discovered that he received pleasurable orgasms.

❖ CHARACTERISTICS OF THE LUST KILLER

Ressler, Burgess, and Douglas (1988) report that fantasy plays an important role in the murderous acts of the lust killer. Many of these killers come from homes where there was abuse—physical, sexual, verbal, emotional—and had sociopathic behavioral traits displayed as a child. Holmes and Holmes (1998) noted that serial killers are usually white males between the ages of 20 and 40 whose early crimes sometimes involved cruelty to animals. Hensley and Wright (2003) found in their research that many serial and lust killers, for example, Jeffrey Dahmer, Edmund Kemper, Henry Lucas, and Arthur Shawcross, suffered episodes of great personal humiliation both as children and as adults, and in a psychological state of powerlessness and low self-esteem coupled with rage, the offender formed a pattern of killing animals and later adults to resolve these intolerable feelings. Lust killers also tend to be introverted and friendless because they are strange, weird, or bizarre (the Henry Lucas type) or because no one is good enough for their friendship (the Ted Bundy type).

Lust killers often live in a world where fantasy plays a major role. In the beginning of their killing careers, many lust killers have fantasies about what they are going to do. After they kill, the fantasies revolve around what they have done. They relive their acts of predation and the sexual thrill of their actions and the termination of human lives.

The lust killer will often take souvenirs or trophies with him as he leaves a crime scene. These will play into his fantasies of what he has done and what he has "won." But in addition to what he has taken, these trophies and souvenirs to symbolically commit the sexual acts again. But as with many fantasies, the compulsion or sexual urge becomes strong and with it the need to try it again, this new time with more rage and a fantasy of a better sexually arousal and sexual thrill, a fantasy doomed to fail to achieve reality.

One lust killer we talked with in the death row visiting room at San Quentin Prison in California told us of his fantasy to have a sex with a decapitated head. He carried out his fantasy with several victims; he was successful in realizing his fantasy but unsuccessful in evading apprehension by the police. He is under a death sentence.

Myers (2002) reported that in a 10-year study of 16 males who either completed or attempted sexual homicides, most were average in intelligence—IQ mean of 102—and came from dysfunctional families in which physical abuse was common, moves by the family were frequent, at least one parent abused drugs, family members were incarcerated, and domestic violence occurred. The psychological reports indicated a great inability to experience guilt feelings, serious school

———————— ✣ ————————

"I blindfolded my victims ... because, you know, eyes scream at you."

(authors' files)

Table 11.1   Traits of the Organized and Disorganized Lust Killer

Organized Lust Killer	Disorganized Lust Killer	
High Intelligence	Below Average Intelligence	May Turn to Religion
Socially Adequate	Socially Inadequate	Father's Work Unstable
Charming, Charismatic	Anxious Mood During the Crime	May Keep Diary
Situational to the Crime	Lives Alone	May Change Jobs
Controlled Mood During the Crime	Lives/Works Near the Crime	Minimal Use of Alcohol
Masculine Image	Usually Does Not Date	May Have Personality Change
Geographically Mobile	Returns to the Crime Scene	Minimal Interest in the Media
Occupationally Mobile	Secret Hiding Places	Significant Behavioral Change
High Birth Order Status	Low Birth Order Status	Nocturnal
Harshly Disciplined as a Child	May Attend Funeral/Burial	High School Drop-Out
Sexually Competent	Unskilled Work	
Lives With a Partner	May Place Memorial in Media	

SOURCE: Crime Scene and Profile Characteristics of Organized and Disorganized Murderers. (1985). *FBI Law Enforcement Bulletin, 54*(8), 18–25.

NOTE: Interview techniques useful with this kind of offender include using empathizing and introducing evidence indirectly. Nighttime interviews may be most productive.

problems, sadistic fantasies, and psychopathic personality traits. Such a background seems to be a perfect breeding ground for a violent personal offender. Pakhomou (2004) nevertheless found a great deal of diversity among the backgrounds of lust killers. Some were from loving backgrounds, others had been abused greatly by caretakers. The psychological mechanisms for how one moves from a similar juvenile background to an adulthood of fatally violating others sexually is a fruitful avenue for serious professional research. The end result is that most serial killers have no gross history of mental illness and truly understand the consequences of their actions but for one reason or another are not able or at least not willing to control their compulsion to sexually assault and murder. Their repetitive acts of aggressive and sadistic behaviors have been framed by their fantasies and the symbols within their fantasies give a face and character to the sources of their frustration and anger as well as sexual antagonisms (Singer & Hensley, 2004).

It has been hypothesized that lust killers who have organized personalities are generally of above-average intelligence, are socially competent, plan their killings, and move the bodies of their victims so that the crime scene is usually not where the body was found. If the lust killer's personality is disorganized, the opposite appears to be true (Crime Scene and Profile Characteristics of Organized and Disorganized Murderers, 1985, see Tables 11.4 & 11.5). Revitch and Schlesinger (1989) add another item to the traits of the lust killer from a psychodynamic perspective: displaced anger toward females, originally directed toward the killer's mother.

It is important to avoid confusing causes of lust killing with the characteristics of some lust killers. One expert (Norris, 1988) in the area of serial murder has developed a list of traits of serial killers: white, male, intelligent, travels continually in his search for victims, and so on. These are not causes, but they are indeed traits of some serial lust killers. At the same time, there are so many exceptions that such a list becomes almost meaningless. Lust killers are real and present dangers, and there is no real advance protection against them.

❖ THE NUMBER OF LUST AND SERIAL KILLERS

How many serial and lust killers are there? This is an impossible question to answer. The FBI at one time estimated there were 35 lust/serial killers operating at one time. This number may be low. We believe the correct number is much higher. Robert L. Yates Jr. was arrested and suspected of at least a score of killings. He has admitted to 13 murders, that of two young people, Patrick Oliver and Susan Savage, among them. He was arrested in 1998, and he finally entered a plea bargain agreement that resulted in a sentence of 447 years in prison.

There is no one explanation for the making of a serial and lust offender. Gerberth and Turco (1997) cite early childhood experiences of extreme aggressiveness and antisocial activities as

—— ✃ ——

Types of Male Serial Killers

Visionary

Mission

Hedonistic
  Lust
  Thrill
  Comfort

SOURCE: (Holmes & Holmes, 1998)

behaviors that might indicate an emerging serial murder personality. Delia (1999) reports that serial killers suffer from an Achilles complex, a defect that renders the serial killer into a sadistic personality without the inner personality traits to counteract the violent behaviors. This hypothesis is based on a small sample, 6, with 2 of the 6 apparently not completing the profile or the actions of the serial murderer personality. Obviously, this hypothesis needs further study. Claus and Lidberg (1999) report that serial killers possess personality traits of omnipotence, sadistic fantasies, ritualized performance, and dehumanization of the victims. They do not fully address the issue of etiology. Other hypotheses and questions deserve some serious study by those interested in the subject of serial murder (Holmes & Holmes, 2001). Myers, Husted, Safarik, & O'Toole (2006) report that the main reason to kill, the anticipated gain, is in excitement and pleasure, not anger, as others may expect. It may be that to the serial killer the exercise of control over the victim and the victim's pain to the extreme extent of taking a life are what are of utmost importance in the killing process. Without the complete domination of a hapless victim, there is no sexual thrill or sexual pleasure. With the mass killer, anger and rage is more prevalent and is integral in the decision to take the lives of many. Sex is not a part of the mass killer's mentality and reason for action (Holmes and Holmes, 1998b).

❖ THE FEMALE SERIAL KILLER

Little has been written about the female serial killer. Kelleher and Kelleher (1998) reported that the female serial killer is more deadly, rarer, and far more determined that her male counterpart, as well as more complexly motivated. The authors further stated that these women's crimes makes personality profiling by homicide detectives a difficult, if not impossible, task, a position with which the present authors do not agree. But knowledge is the first step toward the understanding and the possible apprehension of the female predator. (R. Holmes & S. Holmes, 1998) offer a typology of female serialist.

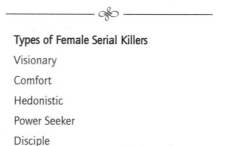

Types of Female Serial Killers

Visionary

Comfort

Hedonistic

Power Seeker

Disciple

Usually, women do not kill serially for sexual purposes. Hickey (2002) reports that most kill for creature comfort reasons: money is the main reason; Holmes and Holmes (1998b) state that the main motivation is money, business holdings, or other financial reasons. Sex plays a minor role in most killing for women, less than 10%. There are obvious exceptions to this general rule. For example, Carol Bundy killed with Douglas Clark for sexual reasons and also as a means to get even with a former lover. Ms. Bundy only recently died (authors' files).

Aileen Wuornos killed 7 men in Florida in the early 1990s. Each of the killings started out as a sexual episode with Wuornos, a prostitute. She would have sex with the men and then rob and kill them. She hid their bodies along the I-95 Interstate. She was executed in Florida for her crimes.

How do female sexual predators kill? Our few examples of female serial killers most often kill by poison, then by shooting, bludgeoning, suffocation, stabbing, and drowning (Holmes & Holmes, 1998b).

There needs to be additional research on the female serialist, especially the female lust killer. The research is so sparse that most sources will list only two lust female killers, Aileen Wuornos and Carol Bundy. With the female gender becoming more like the male in many areas, it may be that females are becoming more like men even in this area.

❖ CONCLUSION

Sexual homicide is always a topic that is popular and most interesting to the general public. The popularity of certain television programs illustrates that interest. The *CSI* programs, *Cold Case,* and other weekly program feature case after case of sex crimes. Even more "serious" programs such as *20/20, Dateline,* and *48 Hours* feature cases of sex crimes often unsolved. A Showtime program, *Dexter,* features a blood-spatter expert associated with a police department in Miami who not only investigates crimes but also murders the guilty who killed the innocent.

There is no doubt about the interest and the prevalence of serial and lust killers. What can be said with some reliability is that both men and women kill sometimes for sex, although women rarely do. Women's motivating factors more often are money, revenge, and cult involvement (e.g., the "girls" in the Charlie Manson "family").

It may be that some of the powerful causative factors are childhood abuse, cruelty to animals, arson, and truancy, and the pathology only usually comes to the attention of society when their crimes are later detected. Bundy killed for 17 years before he was apprehended by the police. Henry Lucas told the police he had killed for more than 20 years before he was discovered.

❖ DISCUSSION QUESTIONS

1. List and desribe the four different types of serialist. Which type do you think is the most dangerous and why.

2. Why do you believe that many experts deny the existence of female serial killers?

3. It is estimated that at any given time there are 35 serial killers operating in the United States. Do you believe this estimate to be to low or too high?

4. Do you agree with Kirby (1999) that the weapon often used by serialist often times depends on their occupation. Why or why not.

❖ REFERENCES

Blundell, B. (1983). *The world's most infamous murders.* New York: Berkeley.

Chesser, E. (1971). Strange loves: The human aspects of sexual deviation. New York: William Morrow.

Claus, C., & Lidberg, L. (1999). Serial murder as a "Schahriar syndrome." *Journal of Forensic Psychiatry, 12*(2), 427–435.

Crime Scene and Profile Characteristics of Organized and Disorganized Murderers. (1985). *FBI Law Enforcement Bulletin, 54*(8), 18–25.

Delia, D. (1999). The Achilles complex: A paradigm for understanding impulses and their manifestation (serial murder). *Dissertation Abstracts International, 59*(10-A), 3968A.

De River, P. (1958). *Crime and the sexual psychopath.* Springfield, IL: Charles C Thomas.

Gerberth, V., & Turco, R. (1997). Antisocial personality disorder, sexual sadism, malignant narcissism, and serial murder. *Journal of Forensic Science, 42*(1), 49–60.

Gudjonsson, G., & Sigurdsson, J. (2000). Difference and similarities between violent offenders and sex offenders. *Child Abuse and Neglect, 24*(3), 363–372.

Hensley, C., Wright, J., Tewksbury, R., & Castle, T. (2003). The evolving nature of prison argot and sexual hierarchies. *Prison Journal, 83*(3), 289–300.

Hickey, E. W. (2002). Serial murderers and their victims. Belmont, CA: Wadsworth.

Holmes, R., & DeBurger, J. (1988). *Serial murder.* Newbury Park, CA: Sage. No space

Holmes, R., & Holmes, S. (1998b). *Serial murder* (2nd ed.). Thousand Oaks, CA: Sage.

Holmes, R., & Holmes, S. (2001). *Mass murder.* Englewood Cliffs, NJ: Prentice-Hall.

Kelleher, M., & Kelleher, C. (1998). *Murder most rare: The female serial killer.* Westport, CT.: Greenwood.

Kirby, P. (1999). The feminization of serial killing: A gender study of male and female serialists using covert methods or murder. *Dissertation Abstracts International, 59*(7-A), 2727A.

Myers, W. (2002). *Juvenile sexual homicide.* San Diego, CA: Academic Press.

Myers, W. C., Husted, D. S., Safarik, M. E., & O'Toole, M. E. (2006). The motivation behind serial sexual homicide: Is it sex, power, and control, or anger? *Journal of Forensic Sciences, 51*(4), 900–921.

Norris, J. (1988) *Serial Killers.* New York: Bantam Doubleday.

Pakhomou, S.-M. (2004). Serial killers: Offender's relationship to the victim and selected demographics. *International Journal of Police Science and Management, 6*(4), 219–233.

Ressler, R., Burgess, A., & Douglas, J. (1988). *Sexual homicide: Patterns and motives*. Lexington, MA: Lexington Books.

Revitch, E., & Schlesinger, L. (1989). Sex murder and sex aggression: Phenomenology, psychopathology, psychodynamics, and prognosis. Springfield, IL: Charles C Thomas.

Shuster, S. (1975). Jack the Ripper and the doctor identification. *International Journal of Psychiatry, 6*, 385–402.

Singer, S. D., & Hensley, C. (2004). Applying social learning theory to childhood and adolescent firesetting: Can it lead to serial murder? *International Journal of Offender Therapy and Comparative Criminology, 48*(4), 461–477.

Stoller, R. (1985). *Observing the erotic imagination*. New Haven, CT: Yale University Press.

12

Rape

❖ ❖ ❖

I t is commonly agreed that rape is a crime of violence, and sex is the weapon used. It directly and indirectly affects more than a million people a year. Both women and men are victims. Some victims feel they were to blame for their attack, that they were in the wrong place at the wrong time, they should not have dressed in such a provocative fashion, that because they were intoxicated they could not ward off their attackers, and many other such reasons. But it is our position that despite the words, actions, dress, or location, there is no excuse for the rape. "No" means "no" in a shout or a whisper.

❖ STATISTICS OF RAPE

Because there are no reliable statistics on the incidences of rape because of reporting failures and other data collection problems, the exact extent of rape is unknown. There are many circumstances of rape—such as date rape, stranger-to-stranger rape, jail and prison rapes—and we will never know the complete statistical and human suffering of this horrific crime (Gaes & Goldberg, 2006). But what is known is that rape is a human problem that is devastating to the victim as well as their significant others.

Masters and Robertson (1990) stated that more than a million women are raped each year. Spitzberg (1999) estimates that about

Rape

Nonconsensual sex involving coercion, empowerment, and anger

13% of women and 3% of men have been raped sometime during their lifetimes. Johnson and Sigler (2000) report that 19% of their female subjects admitted that they were forced to have sex with someone during their lifetimes. Saunders, Kilpatrick-Dean, & Hanson-Rochelle (1999) stated that 8.5% of females and males have been victims of a completed rape sometime before age 18. They estimated that this would amount to about 8.33 million women who have such a history.

The U.S. Department of Justice (2006) reports a general decrease in the rape rates in the last several years. For example, in 1991 the rape rate was 2.2 persons per 100,000 population. This has progressively dropped to .09 persons in 1999 and continues the decline to this date.

Newer statistics suggest even a further drop. The Bureau of Justice Statistics (2005) reported 247,990 rape/sexual assaults in 2001–2002. That number decreased to 204,370 in 2003–2004, a rate of 1.1 per 100,000 dropping to 0.9 per 100,000. This becomes even more significant when one compares the victimization rate from 1993, 2.5 per 100,000. Lisak (2006) reports only on percentages: 14.8% of women were victims of rape sometime during their lifetimes; 2.8% of women were victims of attempted rape at some point during their lifetimes; 0.3% of women had been victims of rape during the previous 12 months.

The data gathered on rape is for reported rapes. Many rapes are not reported. While we discuss some of the reasons later in this chapter, let us say here that the reasons are varied: does not want the family to know, does not want other people to know, embarrassment,

---

Sexual Harassment in the Military

A colonel in the U.S. Air Force was sentenced to 4 months in prison and fined $50,000 for sexually abusing a lieutenant under his command. The colonel, Alvin L. Hicks, was arrested after he had kissed the officer on her neck and mouth, groped her genitals, and partially unbuttoned her blouse.

Hicks was found guilty of this crime after an 8-day trial. He was allowed to retire, collecting his military retirement of nearly $4,000 a month. He is to serve his sentence in Fort Leavenworth.

This is not the first time Hicks was in trouble for sexual misconduct. In 1997, he was accused to mistreating a civil service worker on an Air Force base in Mississippi.

SOURCE: Associated Press, April 5, 2001.

not understanding the legal definition of rape, not reporting someone they know as being a rapist, lack of proof that a rape did occur, fear of being victimized by the police or the court system a second time, and other reasons.

Warshaw (1988) stated that 1 in 4 women is a victim of completed or attempted rape; women knew their assailant 84% of the time; only 5% reported the crime to the police; and 1 man in 12 reported that he had committed such an act! To further muddy the waters on the statistics of rape, a study by Tjaden and Thoennes (2006) reported that 1 in 6 women (compared to 1 in 4 by other researchers) has been raped at some time, more than 300,000 women and 93,000 men are raped in a single year, and women who reported being raped as a juvenile are more likely to be raped as an adult. And last, they found that 1 in 5 adult women who was raped report the rape to the police.

Table 12.1   Selected Types of Victimizations

Types of Victimization	Definition
Completed rape	Unwanted completed penetration by force or the threat of force. Penetration includes penile-vaginal, mouth on your genitals, mouth on someone else's genitals, penile-anal, digital-vaginal, digital-anal, object-vaginal, and object-anal.
Attempted rape	Unwanted attempted penetration by force or the threat of force. Penetration includes penile-vaginal, mouth on your genitals, mouth on someone else's genitals, penile-anal, digital-vaginal, digital-anal, object-vaginal, and object-anal.
Completed sexual coercion	Unwanted completed penetration with the threat of nonphysical punishment, promise of reward or pestering/verbal pressure. Penetration includes penile-vaginal, mouth on your genitals, mouth on someone else's genitals, penile-anal, digital-vaginal, digital-anal, object-vaginal, and object-anal.
Attempted sexual coercion	Unwanted attempted penetration with the threat of nonphysical punishment, promise of reward, or pestering/verbal pressure. Penetration includes penile-vaginal, mouth on your genitals, mouth on someone else's genitals, penile-anal, digital-vaginal, digital-anal, object-vaginal, and object-anal.

(Continued)

Table 12.1 (Continued)

Types of Victimization	Definition
Completed sexual contact with force or threat of force	Unwanted completed sexual contact (not penetration) with force of the threat of force. Sexual contact includes touching (grabbing or fondling the breasts, buttocks, or genitals, either under or over your clothes); kissing (licking or sucking); or some other form of unwanted sexual contact.
Completed sexual contact with force or threat of force	Any type of unwanted completed sexual contact (not penetration) with the threat of nonphysical punishment, promise of reward, or pestering/verbal pressure. Sexual contact includes touching (grabbing or fondling the breasts, buttocks, or genitals, either under or over your clothes); kissing (licking or sucking); or some other form of unwanted sexual contact.
Attempted sexual contact with force or threat of force	Unwanted attempted sexual contact (not penetration) with the threat of nonphysical punishment, promise of reward, or pestering/verbal pressure. Sexual contact includes touching (grabbing or fondling the breasts, buttocks, or genitals, either under or over your clothes); kissing (licking or sucking); or some other form of unwanted sexual contact.

SOURCE: Fisher, B., Cullen, F., & Turner. (2000). *The sexual victimization of college women.* Washington, DC: Bureau of Justice Statistics.

It is not certain how accurate any of these numbers are. Koss, Gidycz, and Wisniewski (1987) considers self-reported figures more accurate than statistics reported by police departments because of the various reasons for not reporting the rape to the legal authorities.

The mass media constantly represent males in superior social and physical positions and women as helpless and vulnerable. In films, for example, women are often depicted only as vulnerable victims, but as victims who, once raped, degraded, and dehumanized, come to accept their treatment and to "grow to love" their attackers (Wilson, 1988). *Tie Me Up, Tie Me Down, Boxing Helena, 9 ½ Weeks, Red Dragon, The Silence of the Lambs,* and *Hannibal* are examples of films that show men who dehumanize women and the women later show affection for their abusers.

Table 12.2   Rape Statistics

Rapists usually have raped approximately 14 times for each time they are caught.

Rapists are on an ascending scale of violence with each assault.

More than 50% of all rapes occur in the home of the victim.

1 in 4 rapes take place in a public area or a parking garage.

More than 93% of the time, the assailant and the victim are of the same race.

Somewhere in the United States, a woman is raped every 2 minutes.

Almost half of rapists were under the influence of alcohol or drugs.

In almost 1 in 3 rapes, a weapon of some type was used.

In almost half of all rapes, the victim sustained injuries other than rape injuries.

SOURCE: Rape Relief Center, Louisville, KY, and RAINN (Rape, Abuse, & Incest National Network, 2006).

Legal Degrees of Rape and Sodomy

Rape in the first degree
510.040
A person is guilty of rape in the first degree when
He engages in sexual intercourse with another person by forcible compulsion; or
He engages in sexual intercourse with another person who is incapable of consent because he:
    Is physically helpless; or
    Is less than twelve (12) years old.
Rape in the first degree is a Class B felony unless the victim is under twelve (12) years old or receives a serious physical injury, in which case it is a Class A felony.

Rape in the second degree
510.050
A person is guilty of rape in the second degree when, being eighteen (18) years old or more, he engages in sexual intercourse with another person less than fourteen (14) years old.
Rape in the second degree is a Class C felony.

Rape in the third degree
510.060
A person is guilty of rape in the third degree when

(Continued)

(Continued)

He engages in sexual intercourse with another person who is incapable of consent because he is mentally retarded or mentally incapacitated; or
Being twenty-one (21) years or more, he engages in sexual intercourse with another person less than sixteen (16) years old.
Rape in the third degree is a Class D felony.

Sodomy in the first degree
510.070
A person is guilty of sodomy in the first degree when
He engages in deviate sexual intercourse with another person by forcible compulsion; or
He engages in deviate sexual intercourse with another person who is incapable of consent because he:
Is physically helpless; or
Is less than twelve (12) years old.
Sodomy in the first degree is a Class B felony unless the victim is under twelve (12) years old or receives a serious physical injury, in which case it is a Class A felony.

SOURCE: Kentucky Revised Statutes, 2007.

❖ MYTHS ABOUT RAPE

Many myths have a manifest purpose of legitimating aberrant behavior. This is especially true when rape is concerned. There are many such myths that center on the commission of rape, be it date rape, marital rape, or stranger rape. Mayerson and Taylor (1987) stated that women a well as men believe in many rape myths and are aroused by rape depictions. Men, for example, may believe that a women will respond positively to sexual force if she initially refuses sexual advances: "she says no, but really means yes."

One Definition of Rape

Forced sexual intercourse

May or may not include penetration by the offender(s) and includes attempted rapes, male as well as female victims, and both heterosexual and homosexual rape.

Attempted rape includes verbal threats of rape.

SOURCE: The U.S. Department of Justice 2006*

Such myths may play a role that in determinations of guilt or innocence of a defendant. For example, Gray (2006) found that jurors who received statements in a court hearing that profiled rape myths were significantly more likely to find the defendant innocent of the charges. The court officers should be most careful in any statements voicing these myths in a trial, since profiling rape myths were more consistent with finding a person innocent and, alternatively, those biased anti-rape statements were more consistent with the jurors finding the defendant guilty.

Rape Is a Crime Controlled by an Uncontrollable Sex Drive

Some men incarcerated for serial rape and serial murder with rape an integral part of the murder often claimed they felt such a compulsion to rape, or rape and then murder, that they could not control themselves. There is no verifiable evidence that men as a gender are under such a psychological sexual compulsion that they cannot control themselves. Moreover, many perpetrators either are married or have available sexual partners when they commit their crimes. This is one such example of a rape myth. The following section details many of the myths about the crime of rape and explains how dangerous the perpetuation of these myths can be to victims and the prosecution of offenders of this heinous crime.

A Woman Can Resist Rape If She Truly Wishes

This myth suggests that any woman can successfully ward off a rape if she wants to. Sometimes the argument is stated in a different way, however crudely, "You can't thread a moving needle." This is obviously untrue. First, men have been raised differently. Men have been trained to be more physical than women, and generally men are stronger than women. Historically women have been trained to be more passive (though that appears to be changing, for the better we believe). Such socialization no doubt enhances the possibility of a "successful" rape. In addition, it is the rapist who chooses the place and the time for the rape to occur—the victim has little to do with the situation other than being in the wrong place at the wrong time.

Strangers Commit Rapes

We will later address this myth when we examine the prevalence of date rape and intimate rapes. By suffice it to say at this point that rapes are often committed by persons who know the victims (Fisher, Cullen, & Turner, 2000). The Bureau of Justice Statistics (2005) found that a stranger raped or sexually assaulted a victim only 31% of the time. In 47% of the cases, it was a friend, 17% an intimate partner, and 3% another relative. It may well be that the family is the cradle of violence, and the adult members are often the victims of violence that is obviously not limited to rape.

"Why did I rape and murder? Because I wanted to. Women are there for me. It is what I am entitled to. I look at a woman like a meal. Just as I might have one type of meal one evening and another the next, I might select a blond one night, a redhead the next. It just came down to I wanted to."

(authors' files)

The Rape Abuse and Incest National Network (RAINN, 2006) found in their research that fewer than 1 in 3 rapists was a stranger to the victim. Bergen (1998) reports in a study of battered primarily African American women, almost half had been raped by their partners. Others have found that in most cases there was a relationship between the rapist and the victim (Foley, Evancie, & Karni-Karnik, 1995; Johnson & Sigler, 2000; Turner, 1988; Vicary, Klingaman, & Harkness, 1995; Walker, 1988).

Many Women Falsely Cry Rape

There is no doubt that some women report rape when it has not occurred (for revenge or some other reason), but it would be a gross mistake to assume that the majority of rape cases reported to the police are false. Historically, it has been more likely for women not to report rape that has occurred. Crooks and Bauer (1983) point out that, in the past, women who failed to report rape may have had good reasons. They often faced severe questioning from a defense attorney when the case went to trial. And the police often are less than sensitive when the investigation of the case commences. Bachman (1998) found in a study of adult females raped by males that the likelihood for reporting increased when two factors were present: first, if the victim sustained a serious physical injury; and second, if the offender used a weapon. It appears that the victim is more likely to sustain a physical injury when a rapist brings a weapon. If some women had not had the courage to face the queries of those inside and outside the criminal justice system, fewer rape cases today would be prosecuted successfully.

All Women Want to Be Raped

This myth has been romanticized in the media. The paperback romance story often starts with the female resisting the advances and even the sexual attack of the rapist, only to melt in passionate acceptance (Crooks & Bauer, 1983). It may true that some women do have a rape fantasy, but these fantasies typically do not center on the use of pain or force but on a feeling of being "swept off one's feet" by a tall, dark, and handsome stranger into a sexual liaison that one would not ordinarily entertain in real life.

It Can't Happen to Me

This is a delusional belief that many women hold. Accepting the myth that rape victims are always young and attractive, many believe that they are unlikely victims because they are too old, too thin, too heavy, or otherwise unattractive. But rape is a crime of violence and not of sex. Sexual attractiveness is not a selective trait used by most rapists when they are stalking their victims.

Kentucky State Police Sex/Criminal Offender Registry Website

THE KENTUCKY STATE POLICE DOES NOT GUARANTEE THE ACCURACY OF THE INFORMATION PROVIDED
   "UNDER KRS 525.070 & 525.080, USE OF INFORMATION FROM THIS WEBSITE TO HARASS A SEX OFFENDER IS A CRIMINAL OFFENSE PUNISHABLE BY UP TO 90 DAYS IN THE COUNTY JAIL. MORE SEVERE CRIMINAL PENALTIES APPLY FOR MORE SEVERE CRIMES COMMITTED AGAINST A SEX OFFENDER."

NAME:	EDGAR B. LUCAS	
ALIASES:	DANNY LEE LUCAS	Photo Unavailable
ADDRESS:	10510 LAGRANGE ROAD	
CITY/STATE:	LOUISVILLE/KY	
ZIPCODE:	40223	
COUNTY:	JEFFERSON	
SEX:	MALE	
RACE:	CAUCASIAN	
DOB:	08/10/1944	
HEIGHT:	5'10"	
WEIGHT:	170	
HAIR:	BROWN	
EYES:	BLUE	

DATE OF REGISTRATION: 03/28/1999
LENGTH OF REGISTRATION: LIFETIME

OFFENSE REQUIRING REGISTRATION:

510.060—RAPE 3RD DEGREE
510.040—RAPE 1ST DEGREE

❖ REASONS FOR NOT REPORTING RAPE

Myths abound about rape for other reasons, one of which is the lack of knowledge about such behavior. Rape is one of the most underreported crimes committed. The crime is one of degradation as well as violence, and fear of reprisal and embarrassment contributed to the victim's hesitation to report it. The investigation of the rape may prompt the offender to victimize the victim further.

Some estimate that only about 10% of all rapes are reported (Nelton, 1987). Thus little is known of the other 90%. Hagan (1990) reports that women are reluctant to report rape for the following reasons:

1. The stigma attached to being a rape victim

2. The sexist treatment given to women, who are in effect mentally raped a second time by the criminal justice system

3. Legal procedures that, in the past, have permitted courtroom prosecutors to probe the victim's sexual past, which can be both humiliating and embarrassing

4. The fact that the burden of proof is on the victim, who must prove that the attack was forced and against her will and that she resisted the attack

Another reason women do not report rapes is that they feel the incidents are too personal or that police will be insensitive (RAINN, 2006). The very interesting study by Monnier, Resnick, Kilpatrick, and Seals (2002) reported that there are differences among those who do report their victimizations. For example, they found that 75% reported stranger rape, 6% reported a rape by an ex-husband or ex-boyfriend, and 19% reported a rape by a friend or other nonrelative. Those who reported the rape were more likely to have experienced a history of physical and sexual attacks and were in a dangerous situation to experience further attacks.

Men too are raped, although male rape is less common in this society. Homosexual rape in prisons and jails is a means to establish power and control, and one warden remarked that this act was one of his most serious concerns as an administrator of a maximum-security institution (Parke, personal interview, June 21, 2006). But according to RAINN (2006), men are the least likely group to report rape, although they may constitute 10% of all cases.

The underreporting of rape leads to assumptions about rape that contradict current knowledge. It may also be true that since only a small percentage of all rapes are reported, and the knowledge that we have on rape, rapists, and rape victims is gleaned from crisis centers and the police, sampling bias may be present.

If we are to draw a "typical profile" of a rape victim, developed from reported rapes obviously, the following would be evident:

"He didn't kill me, but he killed the person I was."

SOURCE: —rape victim (authors' files)

- From a poverty household, less than $7,500 per household
- Divorced or separated
- A weapon, most often a knife, present at the time of the rape
- From the southeast region of the United States
- Lives in an urban area (Bureau of Justice Statistics, 2005)

❖ RAPE AND THE LAW

In ancient times, the rape victim was viewed as a fallen woman—one who invited, contributed to, and thus deserved the sexual assault upon her. She also deserved the punishment that followed the rape, in some cases stoning to death, in other cases, exile.

Rape prosecution in the United States is very difficult, to say the least. Often the woman herself is once again assaulted, emotionally, by the police (although we believe this is not the problem it once was), and the court system. Despite the rape shield law, which prevents the defense from bringing up the victim's sexual history in court, the judge and the jury often hear intimate personal details of her past sex life. This experience can have an unfortunate devastating effect on her self-esteem, her reputation, the successful prosecution of the case, and her successful reentry to physical and mental health.

The court has to deal with the legal issues of corroboration and consent in rape prosecution. The prosecution must prove that a rape did indeed occur, that there was sexual penetration, some type of force was used, and consent was absent. Some states still require the testimony of an eyewitness other than the victim, for a conviction. The jury must be convinced that sexual penetration took place, which demands some type of medical testimony. Detailed medical information is shared with the court on the physical condition of the victim when examined his/her clothing and other personal effects, the presence of semen or blood, and other items that must be preserved in some type of "chain of evidence."

As times have changed, so have laws on rape. Some states have moved away from the traditional point of view that sexual penetration is necessary for rape to occur. Oral sex is included in this new definition, as is object penetration; anal sex is also now included. Further, resistance in some jurisdictions does not have to be proven.

Newer laws use gender neutral terms for both offenders and victims. Even the definition of force has changed. For instance in Kentucky, the law reads:

physical force or threat of physical force, expressed or implied, which places a person in fear of immediate death, physical injury to self or another person, fear of the immediate kidnap of self or another person. . . . Physical resistance on the part of the victim shall not be necessary to meet this definition. (Kentucky Revised Statutes, 510.010 (2)

Thus, it appears that the essential elements of the crime of forcible rape include

1. Proof that a sex act has occurred (as defined by the statute)
2. Proof that force (actual or threatened) was used to perform the sex act
3. Proof that the sex act occurred "without the consent" and "against the will" of the victim (these terms being synonymous in the law of rape)

SOURCE: (Gardner, 1989)

Of course, there are good reasons for care to be taken in the prosecution of accused rapists. Only recently, one man was released from prison when DNA analysis demonstrated that he was not the rapist. He had been in prison for 7 years.

❖ CHARACTERISTICS OF RAPISTS

As in most cases of human behavior, different behavioral patterns and personalities are evident. This is also the case for rape. Rapists are typically young. Four of five rapists are under the age of 30, and 75% are under the age of 25 (Queen's Bench Foundation, 1976). They are most often of the lower socioeconomic class, are often minority group members, and typically choose victims of their own race. Koch (1995), for example, reports that blacks choose black victims, white perpetrators choose white victims.

Most rapists are unarmed at the time of their rape. When the rapist is armed, the weapon of choice is a knife (Holmes, 2001; Bureau of Justice Statistics, 2006). It appears that most rapists plan their attacks (Haas & Haas, 1990), a little fewer than half decided to rape on the spur of the moment. The study by Warren, Reboussin-Roland, and Hazelwood (1998) reports interesting findings on those rapes that are more likely to be planned. In their sample of 108 serial rapists,

1. Serial rapists traveled on average 3.14 miles to rape.

2. Half the offenders raped at least once within 0.5 miles of their homes.

3. Those rapists who used a scripted, ritualized type of act, those who used force, those who burglarized the victim during the rape, and those with extensive criminal records tended to travel farther to find the victim.

Violence during a rape may not be as prevalent as once thought. For example, Stevens (1997) reports that career rapists used violence very selectively and sparingly. But the use of violence by the rapist may be connected to the completion of the rape itself. For example, when rape was coupled with the use of alcohol, the likelihood decreased that the rape would be completed, but in those that were completed, injury to the victim was more likely (Martin & Bachman, 1998). Hazelwood and Warren (1989) interviewed 41 rapists in prison and found that the serial rapist more often than not comes from an advantaged home and as an adult is a well-groomed, intelligent, employed individual who is living with others in a family context. The greatest pathology is reflected in the rapists' developmental histories. Few of the men described close relationships with either of their parents, and 76% reported either observing sexual acts or being sexually abused as children or adolescents. As children, 15% of the rapists reported residing in orphanages, 41% in detention homes, 8% in foster homes, 26% in mental health facilities, and 4% in boarding homes or military schools. The majority of the rapist's victims were strangers who, in almost half the cases, were assaulted in their homes. As far as victim selection was concerned, "availability" was an important factor.

Vinogradov, Dishotsky, Dotyand Tinklenberg (1988) studied adolescent rapists and found that the typical adolescent rape takes place on a weekend night around the end of the summer vacation. This rape usually occurs in the victim's home or in an automobile. During the adolescent rape, it is common to have multiple rapists (gang rape). This rapist is typically a young male who is from the lower social class and who has a history of prior arrests. This rapist may also carry some type of weapon. The victim is usually a female who is a stranger to the rapists, and the rapist has no sexual interest in the victim. Many rapists, both adolescents and others, are under the influence of alcohol or drugs when they rape (Martin & Bachman, 1998; Rodenas, Osuna, & Luna, 1989). Moreover, the majority of adolescent rapists become involved in other crimes, though most did not continue to rape (M. Hagan & Gust-Brey, 1999).

——————— ✀ ———————

Date Rape

When a man enters into legitimate dating behavior that evolves into a situation where force is used to gain sex from an unwilling woman.

(Johnson and Sigler, 2000)

Date rape appears to be a growing concern. How prevalent is date rape? Johnson and Sigler (1996) found that about 1 in 5 of their female subjects reported that they were victims of forced sex with men with whom they were socially close.

Who are the women who fall victim to date rape? Vicary, Klingaman, and Harkness (1995) reported that slight more than 1 woman in 5 had been forced into unwanted touching, intercourse, oral sex, and other unwanted behaviors by their dates by the time they had reached their fourth year in college. Fifteen percent stated that they had been raped. Family background has no effect upon the predictors of unwanted sex. But the researchers found that early menarche, early sexual activity, sexually active friends, low self-esteem and poor peer relationships are associated with the likelihood of being a victim of date rape. Date rape victims were also more likely to have been sexually abused as children. The victim's use of alcohol often makes her vulnerable. Women victims who were drinking were less likely to classify their rape as a rape (Sanders & Moore, 1999; Schwartz & Leggett, 1999). Men, on the other hand, assign more responsibility to the female and less responsibility to the male in a rape date scenario. One of the considerations in the assignment of responsibility was the dress of the victim, that is, sexually provocative clothing. In other words, was the woman "asking for it" by the manner in which she dressed (Workman & Freeburg, 1999)? When the victim has used alcohol extensively, male peer support for the victimization of the woman rises (Schwartz & Nogrady, 1996).

Characteristics of Someone Who Commits Acquaintance or Date Rape

1. Is socially less mature that peers or others in his age group.

2. Has a quick and violent temper in his interaction with others

3. Speaks of his history of violent behavior

4. Has sociopathic or psychopathic behavior, wants his needs satisfied immediately without regard for the feelings of others

5. Wants to date without other couples; in other words, does not like to double-date

6. Is possessive of the relationship; is extremely jealous of other friends and friendships

7. Touches physically to an extreme, especially in public, placing his hands on intimate parts of the partner's body

8. Tries to make the other person feel guilty about inappropriate sexual behavior

9. Is physically and verbally abusive with the partners as well as in front of others

10. Is a male chauvinist in all manners of his behavior

SOURCE: Adapted from danet.wicip.org and author's files

❖ MARITAL RAPE

Marital rape is another form of rape that deserves review. Some believe that resources are bare for women who are raped by their husbands and partners. Moriarty and Earle (2000) suggest that relatively few cases of marital rape, even serial rape, are reported to law enforcement agencies throughout the United States. What kind of home environment exists where marital rape occurs? Two conditions seem to stand out: a high level of anxieties on both parties' part and a sense of distrust between the two (Mahoney & Williams, 1998). There are problems in the reporting of marital rape cases, starting with the spouse's refusal to report the crime. Sometimes the rapes are not reported because of fear of more violent reprisals in the future. Other times, the spouse is fearful that the husband-rapist will take the wife's children away.

Marital Rape

34% of married women reported they have been coerced to have sex with their husbands sometime during their married lives.

In talking with some marital rape victims, we were surprised that one additional reason, and a popular one, was that the spouse still loved the partner-rapist! Fortunately, many women raped by their husbands and partners cooperate with the criminal justice system and testify against the rapist by attending the trials and speaking at the sentencing hearings (Konradi & Burger, 2000).

Women's Reasons for Having Unwanted Sex With Their Husbands

She believed it was her duty, 43%
For romance, 29%
Husband begged, 26%
For money, 24%
The husband bullied her into having sex, 9%

(Basile, 2002)

Bergen (2006) offers the following traits of women who are highly at risk:

- Women married to domineering men who view them as "property"
- Women who are in physically violent relationships
- Women who are pregnant
- Women who are ill or recovering from surgery
- Women who are separated or divorced

Rape is considered a crime in all 50 states. The effects of such a violent crime among married and women living in committed relationships are multiple and severe:

- **Physical effects** include injuries to the vaginal and anal areas, soreness, bruising, torn muscles, broken bones, black eyes, bloody noses, and wounds from weapons, fatigue, and vomiting.
- **Gynecological effects** are vaginal stretching, inflammation of the pelvis, unwanted pregnancies, miscarriages, still births, and sexually transmitted diseases such as HIV and AIDS, among others.
- **Psychological effects** are posttraumatic stress disorder, shock, fear, short-term and long-term depression, sleeping problems, eating problems, intimacy issues, sexual dysfunctions, and suicide ideation (adapted from Bergen, 2006).

The Prevalence of Marital Rape

The research on marital rape is rather sparse in the last 20 years (Bennice, 2005). One problem with examining the statistics of marital rape is that very few officially reported the rape incidents (Moriarty and Earle, 2000). With that said, the Bureau of Justice Statistics (2005) reported that in 2004 there were 203,680 female victims of rape and sexual assault in the United States. Of this total, 35,340, or 17%, were committed by intimate partners. Of these intimate partners, how many were actually legally married is unknown. It is unlikely that most of these women were raped only once. One counselor at the rape crisis center in Louisville, Kentucky, says that their data suggest that many women are raped more than 20 times during their extant relationships (anonymous personal communication, June 21, 2006)! This presents a very different picture of marital rape, a picture of horror and anomie for many women living with an abusive and sexually violent partner.

Age also plays a significant role in the incidence of marital rape and sexual violence. For example, the Action Alliance (2006) reports that women of age 16 to 24 experience the highest per capita rate of intimate violence.

❖ CAMPUS RAPE

In a college dorm room at Boston University, a male raped a coed with a vibrator. On the campus of the University of Colorado, a young woman was knocked off her bicycle and sodomized and raped. At Yale University, a woman was knocked to the ground and physically assaulted, and the assailant attempted to rape her. In a startling report in the *Dartmouth*, the Dartmouth College newspaper, the coordinator of the Sexual Abuse Awareness Program estimated there were 109 completed rapes per year on campus (S. Cohen, 2006).

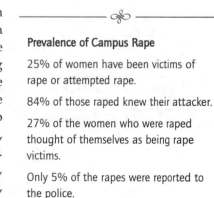

Prevalence of Campus Rape

25% of women have been victims of rape or attempted rape.

84% of those raped knew their attacker.

27% of the women who were raped thought of themselves as being rape victims.

Only 5% of the rapes were reported to the police.

SOURCE: (Action Alliance, 2006)

Estrich (1987) informs us that on a college campus, 1 in 5 women are forced to have sexual intercourse. Fisher, Cullen, and Turner (2000) report that "college administrators might be disturbed to learn that for every 1,000 women attending their institutions, there may well be 35 incidents of rape in a given academic year (based on a victimization rate of 35.3 per 1,000 college women). For a campus with 10,000 women, this would mean the number of rapes could exceed 350" (p. 11). This number could be much higher, because many coeds do not report their rapes or even characterize their assaults as rapes.

Often there is a relationship between the rapist and the coed victim. For example, when a coed is raped, 35.5% of the time the rape is committed by a classmate, 34.2% of the time committed by a friend, 23.7% of the time by a boyfriend or ex-boyfriend, 2.6% by an acquaintance, and 4% by "other." In 66% of the rapes, the rape was committed off campus (Fisher et al., 2000).

Recent Federal Laws on Campus Crime

In 1990, Congress acted to ensure that institutions of higher education have strategies to prevent and respond to sexual assault on campus and to provide students and their parents accurate information about their campus crime. The major federal laws pertaining to this study are

Student right-to know and campus security act of 1990 (the Clery Act) (20 U.S.C.1092). This law, Title II of Public Law 101–542, requires that schools annually disclose information about crime, including specific sexual crime categories, in and around campus.

Campus Sexual Assault Victims' Bill of Rights of 1992. This amendment to the 1990 act requires that schools develop prevention policies and provide certain assurances to victims. The law was amended again in 1998 to expand requirements, including the crime categories that must be reported.

(National Institute of Justice, 2005–2006).

❖ ETIOLOGY OF A RAPIST

There is no simple explanation for the etiology of a rapist. Moreover, not all rapists are alike. Motives, expectations, gains, and anticipations all vary from one rapist to another. But there are some studies that shed some light on the personality of the rapist. The relationship between the mother and the rapist has been a major focus of research. The father, on the other hand, appears to be less significant.

The mother is typically described as being rejecting of the rapist as a child, domineering, punitive, overprotective, and seductive. The father is described as uninvolved, aloof, distant, absent, or passive, but occasionally punitive and cruel. Paternal cruelty, inconsistency of discipline, envy, and sexual frustration also play a role in the development of a rapist (Holmes, 1983; Rada, 1978).

Many rapists also have histories of severe physical punishment by their dominating, sadistic, and castrating mothers. The father, because of his personality, may not lend support to the child when it is really needed. If the mother is cruel, dominating, and so on, the rapist's future hostility may be directed toward women in general because of the pain he has suffered from a woman Holmes & Holmes, 1996).

The research on rape shows generally that the rapist is not brain-damaged or possessed of a marked mental pathology (F. Hagan, 1990). Other research suggests a small percentage of the rapists are psychotic at the time of the rape (Groth, 1979).

Rapists Are Often

- Very attractive men
- In their late teens through mid-30s
- Married or with a sexual partner
- Fathers of small children still at home
- Of average or above-average intelligence
- In jobs that require travel
- Respected in their neighborhoods
- Insecure, with their childhood often marked by cruelty

SOURCE: Rape Relief Center, 2006

Types of Rapists

Many social scientists develop some typology to use as a framework for intellectual examination (Knight, Warren & Reboussin, 1998). Holmes and Holmes (1998) developed a typology with four major types of serial killers: visionary, mission, hedonistic, and power control. Several other studies have developed typologies in the academic research on rape (Amir, 1971; Becker & Abel, 1978; M. Cohen, Garofalo, Boucher, & Seghorn, 1971; Douglas, Burgess, Burgess, & Ressler, 1992; Knight & Prentky, 1987).

As we used loci of motivation and anticipated gain as integral elements in the typing of serial murderers, Knight and Prentky (1987), base their typology, on the elements of anger and power. We are mentioning several types of rapists in this section using the research done by others, to whom we are in debt for their efforts and scholarship.

The Power Reassurance Rapist

Power reassurance rapists, also termed compensatory rapists, are the least violent and aggressive of rapists. They are also the least socially competent, suffering from extremely low self-esteem and feelings of inadequacy.

As Knight and Prentky report, the overwhelming majority (almost 9 in 10) are from homes where either the mother or father was absent. Many had minor problems in school, and their average education is to the 10th grade. The compensatory rapist is most often single and lives with one or both of his parents. He is unathletic, quiet, and passive; he has few friends and no sex partner. Often he lives in a home where an aggressive and possibly seductive mother dominates him. He may spend some time frequenting adult bookstores in his own neighborhood. Because he has little education, he is often employed in some menial occupation and is viewed as a steady and reliable worker.

The power reassurance rapist may have a variety of sexual aberrations. He may be involved in transvestitism, for example, or in promiscuous sexual behavior, such as exhibitionism, voyeurism, fetishism, or excessive masturbation (Shook, 1990). The possible voyeurism in such rapists is an important element because often this rapist will victimize those within his own neighborhood (Kenney & More, 1994). Table 12.3 lists the social core variables of the power reassurance rapist. Of course, the variables in this table and the others in this chapter are meant as general guidelines; they will not fit perfectly every rapist who may be thought to be a certain type.

The main purpose of rape for the power reassurance rapist is to elevate his own status. The primary aim is sexual, in contrast to the general case, in which rape is not primarily a sexual behavior but a means of assault in which sex is secondary. For this rapist, the sex act validates his importance. He perceives himself as a loser, and by controlling another person, he hopes to make himself believe that he is important, if only temporarily. For this reason, he uses only enough force to control his victim.

Table 12.3   Social Characteristics of the Power Reassurance Rapist

Single	Menial occupation
Lives with parents	Frequents adult bookstores
No sex partner	Voyeur
Nonathletic	Exhibitionist
Quiet, passive	Transvestite
Social loner	Fetishist

Table 12.4   Elements in the Power Reassurance Rape

Neighborhood attack	Travels on foot
Believes victims enjoys the rape	Rapist may be impotent
Little use of profanity	Uses weapon of opportunity
Wants victim to "talk dirty"	Increasing violence as rapes progress in number
Victim asked to remove clothing	Possible later contact with victims
Only body parts essential for the rape are exposed	Possible covering of the victim's face
Victim of same age cohort of the rapist	Rapes continue until he is apprehended
Victim same race as rapist	Possible collection of souvenirs
Rape committed every 7–15 days	Possible keeping of a written diary by rapist

This kind of rapist's behavior during the commission of his crime is an expression of his sexual fantasies. For this reason, he is concerned with the physical welfare of his victim and will not usually harm her intentionally. He operates under the delusion that his victim actually enjoys the rape. He may request that his victim "talk dirty" to him, but he will use little

———————— ❧ ————————

Axillistic rape

Rape of the armpit

profanity himself in the verbal exchanges with his victims. He may politely ask his victim to remove her clothing and will often expose only the body parts necessary for the rape to occur.

The power reassurance rapist tends to choose victims from his own age cohort and within his own race (Koch, 1995). Also, he usually rapes within his own neighborhood or close to his place of menial employment. The rapes are usually committed at night, from midnight to 5:00 A.M. The time between the rapes tends to be between 7 and 15 days. Although his rapes generally begin with little violence, the violence may increase as the attacks continue. He will choose a weapon, if he needs one, from the home of the victim. He may also collect souvenirs from the victim's home.

A unique characteristic of the power reassurance rapist is that he may later contact his victim to inquire about her health or about whether she had any ill effects from the attack. This rapist may also be so convinced that his victims enjoyed the attack that he may promise to return. In one case that we know, the rapist promised to return the next day after the rape. The rapist and the victim sat on the edge of the bed, cried together, and both prayed. He asked her if she enjoyed the rape, and she said she did. He asked her if he was better sexually than her husband. She said yes. He asked her if he could come back tomorrow, and she said yes. The next day he climbed through her bedroom window, the same one he had entered the day before. He was crushed and devastated when the local police were waiting for him and arrested him on the spot.

Anger Retaliation Rapist

Unlike the power reassurance rapist, the anger retaliation rapist has as his general overarching purpose to hurt his victims. He wants to rape to get even with all women for the injustices, real or imagined, he has suffered at the hands of the females in his life. As the list in Table 12.5 makes clear, this violent personal offender is usually socially competent. Typically, the family situation from which he comes has been anything but pleasant or normal. More than half the men in this category were physically abused during childhood by one or both parents. Approximately 80% come from families where the parents are divorced; further, some 20% of the men in this group of rapists were adopted children, and 53% have spent some time in a foster home. Eighty percent were reared by a single female parent or other single female caregiver. Because of this rapist's experiences with his female significant other (mother, adopted mother, foster mother, or whatever), he has adopted a position of negative and hostile feelings toward women in general.

The self-perception of this offender is very important. He sees himself as athletic and masculine, and for this reason he often seeks recreation that centers on contact sports and may also be involved in an action-oriented occupation, such as police officer or racecar driver. He is likely to be married and, like many rapists, is not assaultive to his mate. Supporting his macho image, he may also be involved in a variety of extramarital affairs.

Table 12.5   Social Characteristics of the Anger Retaliation Rapist

Parents are divorced	20% are adopted
Ninth-grade education	Does not assault wife
Married	Athletic
Majority are physically abusive	Frequents bars
Socially competent	Likes contact sports
Hates women	Action-oriented occupations

Table 12.6   Elements in the Anger Retaliation Rape

Neighborhood attack	Rapes committed every 6 months to a year
Blitz attack	Possible ejaculation into face of the victim
Little planning	Anal and oral sex
Intent to harm the victim	Victim of same age or older than the rapist
Use of weapons of opportunity	Possible retarded ejaculation
Ripping off of victim's clothing	Increasing aggression
Use of excessive profanity	Situation-precipitated attack

Friends of this kind of rapist will often report that he has a quick, violent temper. He seems to have an uncontrollable impulse to rape, and his rapes tend to follow precipitating events with his wife, mother, or some other significant woman in his life. This event can send him into a rage, and rape is the action that follows.

Table 12.6 shows that the anger retaliation rapist tends to rape close to his home. His attacks are sudden, blitz attacks, which shows that there is little planning in his rapes. For this rapist, the rape is not a sexual act; it is primarily an expression of anger. The aggression in the rape is intended to harm the victim.

The aggression manifested in the rape ranges from verbal assault to physical assault to possible murder. The rapist usually uses a great deal of profanity toward his victims, and he will often rip off her clothing and assault her with weapons of opportunity, including his fists and feet.

The anger retaliation rapist has made a vital connection between sexual gratification and his expression of anger and rage. Once he secures his victim within his "comfort zone," he uses profanity got a dual purpose: to heighten his own sexual excitement and to instill fear and terror into the victim. He feels the need to express his anger and rage in many forms. For example, this rapist may rape his victim anally and then force her to perform oral sex upon him immediately afterward. Following oral sex, he may ejaculate in her face in a further attempt to degrade her.

This type of rapist tends to seek women of his own race and in his own age group or slightly older. He stalks his victims close to his home, and he tends to travel by car. Unlike the power reassurance rapist, after this attack he will make no further effort to contact the victim.

Power Assertive Rapist

For the power assertive, or exploitive rapist, rape is an attempt to express virility and personal dominance. This kind of rapist has a sense of superiority simply because he is a man, and he rapes because he believes he is entitled to—this is what men do to women.

For this offender, rape is not only a sex act; it is an impulsive act of predation. The aggression exhibited in the rape is intended to secure the compliance of the victim. The rapist is indifferent to the comfort or welfare of his victim; she is at his mercy, and she must do what he demands.

Table 12.7   Social Characteristics of the Power Assertive Rapist

Raised in single-parent family (69%)	Frequents singles bars
Lived in foster homes (31%)	Macho occupation
Physically abused in childhood (74%)	Domestic problems
High school dropout	Property crime record
Serial marriages	Athletic
Image conscious	Dishonorable discharge from the military

Some of the social core variables of the power assertive rapist are shown in Table 12.7. Approximately 70% of these rapists have been reared in single-parents families, and a third of them have spent time in foster homes. Approximately 75% were victims of physical abuse during childhood (Knight & Prentky, 1987). This type of rapist generally has many domestic problems and has often been involved in a series of unhappy marriages. He is very image-conscious and tends to be a flashy dresser. He is often a regular at singles bars, and probably most of the other regulars know him as one who is always trying to pick up women, is loud and boisterous, and is continually trying to validate his image as a macho individual.

Table 12.8   Elements of the Power Assertive Rape

Rapist cruises singles bars	Retarded ejaculation
Attacks occur from 7:00 P.M. to 1:00 A.M.	Rapist has no further contact with the victim
Victim's clothing likely to be torn	The victim conned or overpowered
There are usually 20–25 days between the rapes	There is no attempt by the rapist to hide identity
Multiple assaults	Very brutal attack
Anal, then oral assault	Victim of rapist's age group
Rapist is selfish in his behavior	Victim is of rapist's race

This type of rapist may be involved in some type of traditionally masculine occupation, such as construction worker or police work. A uniform of some kind may be part of his masculine image. He often drives a flashy car, perhaps a sports car or a particular model that is a favorite among his social crowd.

As Table 12.8 shows, the power assertive rapist often finds his prey in singles bars, where there are always an ample number of females from which to select.

The attack consists of a mixture of verbal and physical violence. If resisted, he will physically overpower his victim to get what he wants. This rapist will often rip or tear the clothing off his victim—after all, he believes, she will not need them and she is only there for him. So why take care in removing them?

This type of rapist may commit multiple assaults on a particular victim, and his victims are usually of the rapist's age group. Not only will this rapist assault his victim vaginally, he will also often commit anal assaults and then demand that she perform fellatio immediately after he withdraws. He may suffer premature ejaculation, so he may force the victim to perform oral sex upon him so that he can become aroused again so that penetration may occur. For this rapist, sex is expressed as an impulsive act of predation.

The power assertive rapist tends to commit rape in a 20–25 day cycle, a time span strangely similar to the length of a menstrual cycle. This contrasts with the tendency of the power reassurance rapist to assault within a 7- to 15-day cycle and that of the anger retaliation rapists to commit new offenses approximately every 6 months to a year.

The power assertive rapist does not rape for sex, but as an act of predation. He usually has a sex partner, a wife or a lover. This rapist feels the need to rape, and his aggression is intended to force the victim's compliance with his demands. The aggressions of such rapists tend to escalate as they continue to rape. He may often bring his own weapon to the rape, a behavior that shows forethought and planning.

The power assertive rapist does not hide his identity from his victims; masks, darkness, or blindfolds are not necessary. He has no intention of ever contacting his victims again. He will not apologize after the rape, nor will he usually collect trophies or souvenirs or keep a diary. He also usually rapes within his own race.

Sadistic Rapist

Of all rapists discussed thus far, the sadistic rapists are the most dangerous. The aim of this offender in raping is

Anthropophagolagnia
Rape with cannibalism

primarily the expression of his sexual-aggressive fantasies. His purpose is to inflict physical and psychological pain on his victims. Many of the rapists who fall into this category have antisocial personalities and are aggressive in their everyday lives, especially when criticized or thwarted in their quests for personal satisfaction. This rapist has made a vital connection between his aggressive behavior and his sexual gratification—in other words, he has eroticized aggression and violence.

Table 12.9   Social Characteristics of the Sadistic Rapist

Raised in single-parent home (60%)	Some college education
Parents were divorced	Married
Lived in a foster home (13%)	No arrest record
Physically abused in childhood (63%)	Age range 30–39
Raised in sexually deviant home	Compulsive personality
Middle-class family man	White-collar occupation

Table 12.9 displays the social characteristics associated with the sadistic rapist. As the table shows, some 60% have been reared in single-parent homes. The majority suffered childhood physical abuse, and many come from homes where there was evidence of sexual deviance (e.g., where the fathers were rapists themselves). Many sadistic rapists have histories of such juvenile pathologies as voyeurism, promiscuous sex, and excessive masturbation.

In his adult life, the typical sadistic rapist is married and is considered to be a good "family man." He often lives in a middle-class, residential neighborhood where crime rates are low, is viewed as an asset to his community, has a better than average education, and is in a white-collar occupation.

Table 12.10   Elements of Sadistic Rape

Victim stalked	Degrading language
Victim transported	Retarded ejaculation
Use of gags, bondage, handcuffs	Increasing violence with additional rapes
Possible use of blindfolds	Rapist has a rape kit
Possible triolism	Rapist may eventually kill
Victim's clothing is cut	Periods between the rapes will vary
Elements of ritualism	Victims' ages vary

This kind of rapist exhibits a compulsive personality. He demonstrates his compulsiveness in his personal appearance and in the automobile he drives, which is neat, clean, and kept in good cosmetic condition.

This offender is intelligent and probably does not have a police record. He has the ability to escape detection for his offenses, if for no other reason than because he carefully plans his rapes and carries them out within the parameters on his plans. His intelligence, knowledge of the criminal justice system, antisocial personality, and care in the planning and implementation of his rapes make him especially difficult to apprehend.

There is an expressive aim in the rapes of this kind of offender. The aggression component of the rape is not simply for control; he intends to do personal harm to his victim. If this rapist is not apprehended, he will eventually begin to kill his victims (see Table 12.10).

The sadistic rapist uses his well-maintained vehicle to stalk his victims. He takes great care in selecting victims, making certain that he is not seen and taking all precautions necessary to hinder the detection of his crimes and his apprehension. He generally takes his victims to a place where he controls the action, his "comfort zone" (Holmes & Holmes, 2001; Ressler & Shachtman, 1992).

Less to control his victims than to instill terror in them, the sadistic rapist uses gags, duct tape, handcuffs, and other paraphernalia in the commission of his crimes. He may also blindfold his victims, also primarily to increase their fear. He may tell his victims what he plans to do to them, detail by detail, using excessive profanity and degrading language. As he is attacking his victim, he may call her by another name, perhaps his wife's or his mother's.

The sadistic rapist is very ritualistic. Each rape must go according to plan in order for him to experience the feelings he believes are necessary. He may need for his victims to say certain words to him for him to become aroused. Also, he may insist on oral sex as a prelude to coitus.

Biastophilia

Preference for violent rape

Like the power assertive rapist, the sadistic rapist may suffer from retarded ejaculation. This rapist often carries in his car a rape kit (Ressler & Shachtman, 1992). Ted Bundy, for example, carried a kit that included handcuffs, an ice pick, a ski mask, a mask made of panty hose, rope, black garbage bags, and a tire iron.

As he continues his crimes, the sadistic rapist learns increasingly effective methods to stalk his victims and better ways of disposing of the bodies of those he has killed. For this rapist, murder is secondary. As Ted Bundy remarked to the first author during a 1985 interview while he was on death row at Florida State Prison, "A large number of serial killings [are] simply an attempt to silence the victims, a simple but effective means of elimination."

The sadistic rapist is often mildly intoxicated and may be a recreational drug user. He feels no remorse for his crimes and will continue to rape until he is caught. It is not unusual for this offender to escalate his violence to the point where the serial rapist becomes a serial killer.

❖ CONCLUSION

Many people view rape as one of the most despicable crimes that may be committed against a human being. The by-products of rape can include the destruction of the victim's feelings of worth and the victim's internalization of feelings of responsibility for her own victimization. Although recent research on rape has tended to emphasize date or acquaintance rape, and the reported incidence of acquaintance rape has been increasing, the fact is that stranger rape still takes place. We believe that it is important to emphasize this point, in part because many of the kinds of rapists described in this chapter continue to escalate their acts of rape and may move to murder. The investigation and resolution of cases of stranger rape require the concentrated efforts of law enforcement.

We must not forget the possible physical and psychological effects upon the victim. Fear of strangers, fear of being alone, inability to trust anyone, loss of appetite, feelings of anomie, and addiction to alcohol or drugs are all possible effects of a rape and sexual assault. As one victim told us, "I was never the same. He killed my soul."

❖ DISCUSSION QUESTIONS

1. Is rape always a crime of violence? Discuss.

2. How important is it to recognize that there are various types of rapists? What important ramifications does this have for understanding the rapists as well as the investigation of the crime itself?

3. In viewing the various kinds of rapists, which one do you believe is most prevalent? Most dangerous?

4. In discussing the possibility of rehabilitation, which strategies would you undertake in the rehabilitation process for the types of rapists discussed in this chapter?

5. Ted Bundy was a serial killer as well as a serial rapist. Which type was Bundy? Why do you believe that to be so? Give examples for your argument.

❖ REFERENCES

Action Alliance. (2006). *Violence on campuses: Overview. Virginia sexual and domestic violence*. Richmond, VA: Author.

Amir, M. (1971). *Patterns in forcible rape*. New York: Harcourt, Brace & World.

Bachman, R. (1998). The factors related to rape reporting behavior and arrest: New evidence from the national crime victimization survey. *Criminal Justice and Behavior, 1*, 8–29.

Basile, K. (2002). Prevalence of wife rape and other intimate partner sexual coercion in a nationality representative sample of women. *Violence and Victims, 17*(5), 511–524.

Becker, J., & Abel, G. (1978). Men and victimization of women. In M. Chapman & M. Gates (Eds.), *Victimization of women*. Beverly Hills, CA: Sage.

Bennice, J. (2005). Marital rape: History, research, and practice. *Trauma, violence and abuse, 4*(3), 228–246.

Bergen, R. (1998). Wife rape. *Violence Against Women, 5*(9), 989–1085.

Bergen, R. (2006) Marital Rape: New Research and Directions. Applied Research Forum. Retrieved October 17, 2007 from http://www.wcsap.org/MaritalRapeRevised.pdf.

Bureau of Justice Statistics. (2005). *Criminal victimizations 2004*. Washington, DC: U.S. Department of Justice.

Cohen, M., Garofalo, M., Boucher, B., & Seghorn, T. (1971). The psychology of rapists. *Seminars in Psychiatry, 3*, 307–327.

Cohen, S. (2006, February 6). Many rape incidents occur yearly at college. *Dartmouth. Retrieved October 16, 2007 from http://thedartmouth.com/2006/02/06/news/many/*

Crooks, R., & Bauer, K. (1983). *Our sexuality*. Menlo Park, CA: Benjamin/Cummings.

Douglas, J., Burgess, A. W., Burgess, A. G., & Ressler, R. (1992). *Crime classification manual*. Lexington, MA: Lexington Books.

Estrich, S. (1987). *Real rape: How the legal system victimizes women who say no*. Cambridge, MA: Harvard University Press.

Fisher, B., Cullen, F., & Turner, M. (2000). *The sexual victimization of college women*. Washington, DC: Bureau of Justice Statistics.

Foley, L., Evancie, C., & Karni-Karnik, J. (1995). Date rape: Effects of race of assailant and victim and gender of subjects on perceptions. *Journal of Black Psychology, 21*(1), 6–18.

Gaes, G., & Goldberg, A. (2006). *Prison rape: A critical review of the literature*. Washington, DC: National Institute of Justice.

Gardner, T. (1989). *Criminal law: Principles and cases*. St. Paul, MN: West.

Gray, J. (2006). Rape myth beliefs and prejudiced instructions: Effects on decisions of guilt in a case of date rape. *Legal and Criminological Psychology, 11*(1), 75–80.

Groth, N. (1979). *Men who rape: The psychology of the offender*. New York: Plenum.

Haas, L., & Haas, J. (1990). *Understanding sexuality*. Boston: Mosby.

Hagan, F. (1990). *Introduction to criminology* (2nd ed.). Chicago: Nelson-Hall.

Hagan, M., & Gust-Brey, K. (1999). A ten year longitudinal study of adolescent rapists upon return to the community. *International Journal of Offender Therapy and Comparative Criminology, 43*(4), 448–458.

Hazelwood, R., & Warren, J. (1989). The serial rapist: His characteristics and victims. *FBI Law Enforcement Bulletin, 58*(2), 18–25.

Holmes, R. (1983). *The sex offender and the criminal justice system.* Springfield, IL: Charles C Thomas.

Holmes, R., & Holmes, S. (1996). *Profiling violent crimes: An investigative tool* (2nd ed.). Newbury Park, CA: Sage.

Holmes, R., & Holmes, S. (1998). *Serial murder* (2nd ed.). Thousand Oaks, CA: Sage.

Holmes, R., & Holmes, S. (2001). *Murder in America* (2nd ed.). Thousand Oaks, CA: Sage.

Johnson, I. and T. Sigler (1996), Forced sexual intercourse on campus: Crime or offensive behavior. Journal of Contemporary Criminal Justice. *12*(1), 53–68.

Johnson, I., & Sigler, T. (2000). Forced sexual intercourse among intimates. *Journal of Family Violence, 15*(1), 95–108.

Kenney, J., & More, H. (1994). *Principles of investigation.* Minneapolis, MN: West.

Knight, R., & Prentky, R. (1987). The developmental antecedents in adult adaptations of rapist subtypes. *Criminal Justice and Behavior, 14,* 403–426.

Knight, R., Warren, J., & Reboussin, R. (1998). Predicting rapist type from crime-scene variables. *Criminal Justice and Behavior, 25*(1), 46–80.

Koch, L. (1995). Interracial rape: Examining the increasing frequency argument. *American Sociologist, 26*(1), 76–85.

Konradi, A., & Burger, T. (2000). Having the last word: An examination of rape survivors' participation in sentencing. *Violence Against Women, 6*(4), 351–395.

Koss, M., Gidycz, M., & Wisniewski, N. (1987). The scope of rape: Incidence and prevalence of sexual aggression and victimization in a national sample of higher education students. *Journal of Consulting and Clinical Psychology, 55,* 162–170.

Lisak, D. (2006). Rape. Journal of Traumatic Stress. 2(4), 40–52.

Mahoney, P., & Williams, L. (1998). *Sexual assault in marriage: Prevalence, consequences, and treatment of wife rape.* Thousand Oaks, CA: Sage.

Martin, S., & Bachman, R. (1998). The contribution of alcohol to the likelihood of completion and severity of injury in rape incidents. *Violence Against Women, 4*(6), 694–712.

Masters, R., & Robertson, C. (1990). *Inside criminology.* Englewood Cliffs, NJ: Prentice-Hall.

Mayerson, S., & Taylor, D. (1987). The effects of rape with pornography on women's attitudes and the mediating role of sex role stereotyping. *Sex Roles, 17,* 321–338.

Monnier, J., Resnick, H., Kilpatrick, D., & Seals, B. (2002). Patterns of assault in a sample of rape victims. *Violence Against Women, 8*(5), 585–596.

Moriarty, L. and M. Earle (2000). An analysis of service for victims of marital rape: A case study. *Journal of Offender Rehabilitation, 29*(3/4), 23–44.

National Institute of Justice. (2005–2006). *Sexual assault on campus: What colleges and universities are doing about it.* Washington, DC: U.S. Department of Justice.

Nelton, S. (1987). Learning how to cry rape. *Nation's Business,* 67–68, January 7.

Norris, J. (1988). Serial murder: The growing menace. New York: Kensington.

Parke, A. (2006) Personal communication, Louisville, KY, June 21, 2006..

Pino, N., & Meier, R. (1999). Gender differences in rape reporting. *Sex Roles, 40*(11/12), 979–990.

Queen's Bench Foundation. (1976). *The rapist and his crime.* New York: Wiley.

Rada, T. (1978). Alcoholism and forcible rape. *American Journal of Psychiatry, 32,* 444–446.

RAINN. (2006). Statistics [online document]. Retrieved June 21, 2006, from http://feminest.com/rainn.htm.

Rape Relief Center (2006) Personal interview, Louisville, KY., June 20, 2006.

Ressler, R., & Shachtman, T. (1992). *Whoever fights monsters.* Lexington, MA: Lexington Books.

Rodenas, J., Osuna, L., & Luna, A. (1989). Alcohol and drug use by rapists and their victims. *Medicine and Law, 82*(2), 157–164.

Sanders, B., & Moore, D. (1999). Childhood maltreatment and date rape. *Journal of Interpersonal Violence, 14*(2), 115–124.

Saunders, B., Kilpatrick-Dean, & Hanson-Rochelle, F. (1999). Prevalence case characteristics and long-term psychological correlates of child rape among women: A national survey. *Child Maltreatment, 4*(3), 187–200.

Schwartz, M., & Leggett, M. (1999). Bad dates or emotional trauma? The aftermath of campus sexual assault. *Violence Against Women, 5*(3), 251–271.

Schwartz, M., & Nogrady, C. (1996). Fraternity membership, rape myths, and sexual aggression on a college campus. *Violence Against Women, 2*(2), 148–162.

Shook, L. (1990). Sexual glossary. In L. Shook (Ed.), *Investigation of variant sex styles.* Montgomery, AL: Auburn University Press.

Spitzberg, B. (1999). An analysis of empirical estimates of sexual aggression victimization and perpetration. *Violence and Victims, 14*(3), 241–260.

Stevens, D. (1997). Violence and serial rape. Journal of Police Science and Criminal Psychology, *12*(1), 39–47.

Tjaden, P., & Thoennes, N. (2006). Extent, nature and consequences of rape victimization: Findings from the national violence against women survey. Washington, DC: National Institute of Justice.*

Turner, R. (1988). Rape: The myths and realities. *Ebony, 43,* 108.

U.S. Department of Justice Report. (2006). Rape Statistics, 2005–2006. Washington, D.C.

Vicary, J., Klingaman, L., & Harkness, W. (1995). Risk factors associated with date rape and sexual assault of adolescent girls. *Journal of Adolescence, 18*(3), 289–306.

Vinogradov, S., Dishotsky, D,, Doty, A & Tinklenberg, J. (1988). Patterns of behavior in adolescent rape. *American Journal of Orthopsychiatry, 58,* 179–187.

Walker, S. (1988). *Sense and nonsense about crime.* Pacific Grove, CA: Brooks/Cole.

Warren, J., Reboussin, R., & Hazelwood, R. (1998). Crime scene and distance correlates of serial rape. *Journal of Quantitative Criminology, 14*(1), 35–59.

Warshaw, R. (1988). *I never called it rape: The Ms. Report on recognizing, fighting, and surviving date and acquaintance rape.* New York: Sara Lazin.

Wilson, W. (1988). Rape as entertainment. *Psychological Reports, 62,* 607–610.

Workman, J., & Freeburg, E. (1999). An examination of date rape, victim dress, and perceiver variables within the context of attribution theory. *Sex Roles, 41*(3–4), 261–277.

13

Victims of
Sexual Assault

❖ ❖ ❖

Sexual assault brings many images to mind. Some people begin to immediately think of the crime of attempted or completed rape, while others conjure up images of a female victim beaten after some type of sexual encounter. While both these images are correct, the term and concept underlying sexual assault is much broader than that. Some of the crimes committed under the rubric of sexual assault are indeed crimes of a sexual nature and must be punished accordingly. But there are other acts or incidents that are routinely handled as sexual assaults that do not fit the literal reading and spirit of the law. Such was the case when police were called to a Montessori school in Milwaukee in March 2001. In this case, a young man was standing at the top of a stairwell when the young lady in front of him stepped back to open the door to the classroom building. The young man claims that at that time his hand bounced off and accidentally brushed the young lady's buttocks. The young woman complained to a guidance counselor about the incident, and the counselor called the police to investigate. The police came and took statements from both the victim and suspect, placed the youth in custody, and held him overnight. He was released the next day when prosecutors found that they had insufficient evidence to charge the boy (Schulhofer-Wohl, 2001). While it is clear from all statements that the incident was not a true case of sexual assault, the case points out the confusion in our culture about the meaning and definition of sexual assault. It was once considered a serious offense, where true intent had to be discerned, but no longer. This is one of the most important issues of this chapter. That is, clarifying what the elements of a true sexual assault is.

In our sex offenders classes at the University of Louisville and the University of Central Florida, we routinely ask students to define *sexual assault*. The typical answer is some type of assault with a sexual overtone. Then we ask them to identify the elements of this type of crime. Students will routinely say that the victim must have been sexually violated. That answer is not sufficient, because it simply brings in the need to define exactly what a violation entails, which is back at square 1 in effect. It is genital-to-genital contact or oral-genital contact? Does it involve the disrobing of a victim or offender? Does force have to be involved? Does some type of physical injury have to be involved? Can it be some type or form of noncontact verbal harassment with a sexual dimension? Or can it be something as foolish as a high school student walking around and pinching a young female's (or male's) backside?

While there is widespread disagreement of what should be considered a sexual assault, one must remember that, in the mind of the victim, many of the same psychological processes come into play regardless of the type of assault. More often than not, the victim feels violated, may withdraw from social and peer groups, and begin to loose trust in the people and social institutions he or she identifies with.

If we cast a wide net to encompass a wide variety of offenses under the rubric of sexual assault, it is clear that many people are victims of sexual assault and are not aware of it. For instance, if we ask how many people have been in a bar or a crowded place and felt a hand on their bodies where that hand should not have been, the majority of people will respond in the affirmative. While the likelihood that they were in fact victimized depends on their age and involvement in high-risk activities (like frequenting bars or drinking), it is likely that they have unknowingly been a victim of a frotteur. Many young women will admit that they have been the target of a flasher while at the mall or leaving a local movie theater. These victims typically do not ponder very long about their victimization. They may make jokes, call their friends, and have a long laugh about the whole experience as long as the perpetrator turns and either walks, runs, or drives away. The experience would be much more serious if the offender continued to approach the victim.

As one can see, it is easy to talk about sexual assault in very general terms. Sexual assault can take many forms. It involves crimes such as rape, incest, acquaintance rape, sexual molestation, sexual harassment, being the victim of a frotteur or a flasher, or just about any other type of unwelcome sexual advancement. When we start focusing on the real consequences felt by the victims in the more serious types of assault, our attitude becomes much more somber.

It is from this perspective that this chapter is written. While many criminologists and policy analysts in the field are content to talk about the crime rate in abstract terms, distancing themselves from the consequences of victimization, we are not. It is only when society, agencies, and actors within the criminal justice system begin to truly understand how much pain these victims suffer that we can truly begin to understand the full etiology of these offenses.

In order to delineate the problem further, this chapter will be divided into four sections. The first will deal with the incidence and prevalence of sexual assault in the United States today. It is hoped that this section will allow us to see how large the problem is in our society. The second section will discuss the types of victims. The third will delineate the consequences of victimization in American society. And the final section will discuss the role of victim rights groups in helping victims of violent crime and sexual abuse to overcome the experience of their victimization.

❖ INCIDENCE AND PREVALENCE

Most people believe they will never be a victim of a violent crime, and most of them are correct. Despite the local news coverage, official statistics demonstrate our low probability of falling victim to a violent or sexual offender. Probably the most common offense that many people look at when we think about sexual assault is the crime of rape. According to the latest data examining the rate in which rape occurs, the likelihood of falling victim to this type of crime has decreased sharply over the last 30 years.

Other statistics seem to show a declining pattern in the overall rates for violent sexual offenses. For instance, the Bureau of Justice Statistics found in their report on Sex Offenses and Offenders that the number of reported rapes made to the police nationwide in 1995 was the lowest it has been since 1989. It is one thing to report rape as a crime of violence, but rape in many circles can also be called a sexual assault. So in trying to determine the full extent of the problem of sexual assault, one must look

Figure 13.1   National Crime Victimization Survey Number of Rapes of
Victims 12 or Older

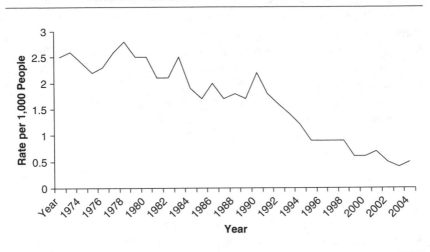

SOURCE: Bureau of Justice Statistics. (2006). National Crime Victimization Survey Violent Crime Trends, 1973–2005. Washington, DC: US Department of Justice.

at the combined figures. Not only must we combine the two numbers, but it may also behoove us to list both the completed and the attempted rapes and sexual assaults, since it is likely that those falling victim to an attempted assault may suffer the same psychological traumas as those who are a victim of a completed sexual assault. One study, which examined just that, was completed by Rennison (1999). This study found that a total of 333,000 persons over the age of 12 were victims of either completed or attempted rapes or sexual assault. Converting these to ratios, Rennison found the attempted or completed rape or sexual assault rate for females aged 12 or over was 2.7 per 1,000 people. And for males, the rate decreased to .2 persons per 1,000 persons for the same age group. These numbers may provide a more accurate picture of the true risk of being a victim of a sexual assault than official government statistics. For instance, the commonly citied statistic on the rape rate published using Uniform Crime Report (UCR) statistics finds that only 34 in 100,000 persons reported being raped in 1998 (Bureau of Justice Statistics, 2001). Further, when official UCR numbers for rape and sexual assault are combined, BJS reports that the official rate for reported forcible rape and sexual assaults was 50.3 per 100,000 residents (Goodman et al., 1993). These ratios—2.7 per 1,000 or 50.3 per 100,000—are drastically different.[1] While Rennison's (1999) study included only victims of attempted rapes and sexual assaults who were over the age of 12, it is easy to see that an individual's risk of victimization may indeed be much higher than the government chooses to report. Studies in the future looking at the incidence and prevalence of sexual assault and sexual violence must be sure to include these combined risks in order to give students and the community a more accurate picture of the true problem.

The Etiology of the Victims of Sexual Assault

Trying to understand the etiology of victims of sexual assault is a difficult task because of the variety of victims and the lack of common traits or characteristics. Understanding why an offender chooses one victim over another requires us to examine the mind of the perpetrators themselves, but the perpetrator is not the focus of this chapter. We can define the types of victims in a crude fashion. For instance, it is rather easy to distinguish between male and female victims, racial majority and racial minority victims, and of course old and young victims. For the most part, male victims are likely to be victimized by other males in particular circumstances. The sexual assault may occur in an institutional setting, where there is a lack of adequate sexual outlets, or the sexual assault may be coupled with the commission of a hate crime against homosexuals. But in most of the cases where a sexual assault is committed, the victim is a female and the perpetrator is a male. As shown in Table 13.1, 85% of all victims of sexual assault are female. Detailing the prevalence of sexual assault, Tjaden and Thoennes (1998) found that 55% of all women in their sample experienced some type of rape or attempted physical assault during their lives. Further, these researchers found that 18% of all women reported experiencing a completed or attempted rape during their life, compared to only 3% of men.

Race of the Victims of Rape and Sexual Assault

One study looked at the victims of both rapists and sexual assaulters and found that 76.4% of all victims of convicted sexual assaulters where white and 20% were black. However, when we look only at the crime of rape, the percentage of white victims drops to 67.8% and the percentage of black victims increases by almost 7 points to 27.6% (Greenfeld, 1997).

Age of the Victims of Sexual Assault

One of the most tenuous distinguishing characteristics of those who have fallen victim to a sexual assault is the age of the victim. The media and popular cultural stereotype tell us that that the most likely victim of sexual assault is a female between 18 and 36 years old. While not

Table 13.1   Victims of Sexual Imprisoned Sexual Assault and Rape
Offenders

| Characteristic | Violent Offenders in State Prison Reporting Single Victims | | |
	All	Rape	Sexual Assault
Sex of Victim			
Male	55.8%	5.5%	15.2%
Female	44.2	94.5	84.8
Race of Victim			
White	64.5%	67.8%	76.4%
Black	29.8	27.6	20.1
Other	5.7	4.6	3.5
Age of Victim			
12 or younger	9.9%	15.2%	44.7%
13 to 17	8.8	21.8	33.0
18 to 24	17.5	25.1	9.4
25 to 34	31.1	25.4	7.7
35 to 54	26.5	10.2	4.3
55 or older	6.3	2.3	.9
Median Age	29 years	22 Years	13 years
Relationship to Offender			
Family	12.9%	20.3%	37.7%
Spouse	2.5	1.2	.6
Child/stepchild	6.1	14.0	25.9
Other relative	4.3	5.1	11.2
Intimate	5.5	9.1	6.2
Boyfriend/girlfriend	5.0	8.8	5.4
Ex-spouse	.5	.3	.8
Acquaintance	34.7	40.8	41.2
Stranger	46.9	29.8	14.9

SOURCE: Greenfeld, L. (1997). *Sex Offenses and Offenders: An Analysis of Data on Rape and Sexual Assault*. Washington, DC: Bureau of Justice Statistics (Table 3, p. 24).

disputing these assertions, we consider more startling the finding that 1 in 3 sexual assaults is committed against a victim under the age of 12. Of these assaults, 43% are against victims under the age of 6, and in all the assaults against children under the age of 12, 34% are committed against children between the ages of 7 and 11 (Snyder & Sickmund, 1999).

Other studies looking at this phenomenon have found somewhat different numbers, but the patterns appear to hold. For example, Greenfeld (1997) reports that 77.7% of all victims of imprisoned sexual assaulters were under the age of 18, and the median age of the victims was 13. In the more serious offense of rape, the victims appear to be older, and only 37% of the victims were under 18.

Physical Location of the Sexual Assault

All too often we think of the crime of rape or sexual assault, we conjure up images of a dark and secluded crime scene. The studies that have looked at the physical locations where these crimes occur found that nothing can be less true. Greenfield (1997) found that nearly 57% of all rapes and sexual assaults occur at the victim's home or that of a close relative or neighbor. Further, this study found that about 10% of these crimes occurred on the streets or away from home and a little over 26% occurred at all other locations (Greenfeld, 1997).

Some victims are chosen because of

- The offender's perception that the risk was low
- The vulnerability of the victim
- The availability of the victim

Victim–Offender Relationship

Probably one of the best places to start examining the etiology of the victims of sexual assault is the relationship between the victim and the offender. Despite the fact that sexual assault continues to represent one of the most rapidly growing violent crimes in America, it is still one of the most underreported crimes. Of all the sexual assaults committed in this country, only 14.9% are committed by persons who are total strangers to the victim. In the crime of rape, this figure increases to almost 30% (Greenfield, 1997).

One of the most striking statistics in the crimes of rape and sexual assault is the relatively large number of victims who are preyed upon by family members. As Table 13.1 shows, 37.7% of all the victims of sexual assault are victimized by family members, with the most prevalent being the victim's own parent or guardian. And about 41% of the victims know or are acquainted with their abuser slightly. This being the case, it is clear that in nearly three fourths of the cases, the perpetrator is not a stranger and does not fit the profile

Some victims contribute to their own victimization by their behavior.

This is not meant to excuse the victimizer, but only to explain why some people are multiple victims while others are never or seldom victimized.

imagined by many, that these beasts are eerie figures that emerge from a dark parking lot or hidden place. They are, instead, those people that we live and interact with daily.

Dispelling another myth, that the perpetrators prey on those unlike the victim, many studies have found sexual assault to be an intraracial crime. While the specifics of this relationship is hampered by numerous studies with small sample sizes, the Bureau of Justice Statistics reports that 8 in 10 sexual assaults that end in murder were intraracial. And of all these cases, 55% were committed by whites, 24% by blacks, the remainder by others. Of those sexual assault/murders where the victim's and offender's races were different, fewer than 2% involved white offenders and black victims, and 15% involved black offenders and white victims (Greenfeld, 1997).

❖ TYPES OF VICTIMS

The primary victims of sex crimes are often truly innocent individuals whose only crime is either being in the wrong place at the wrong time or being born into a maladjusted family. We have already touched on the plight of these victims and the psychological and physical distress that they must be forced to live with as a result of their victimization experience.

But they are by no means the only person that is affected by this experience, there are secondary victims as well. These are the people who are close to the primary victims: fathers and mothers, husbands and wives, sisters and brothers, other relatives, and friends of those who have been victimized and, too often, murdered.

Types of Victims

Primary Victims—those truly innocent persons who were either in the wrong place or born into a maladjusted family.

Secondary Victims—Those close to the primary victims who suffer and also feel victimized.

The Plight of Primary and Secondary Victims

The experience and plight of secondary victims is one that is often overlooked by many actors and agents of the criminal justice system and many laypersons. It is true that being a victim of rape may cause or trigger an aversion to sexuality or sexual contact, but this aversion may also help precipitate the loss of trust between spouses and a loss intimacy that was once enjoyed. This problem can be further exacerbated when the victim is not only married or in a long-term relationship, but when there are children. The victim may retreat from the environment of the family and simply not be able to provide the type of nurturance that a child may need to develop into a well-adjusted adult. When that happens, not only the target is victimized, but also the spouse, children, and anyone else who comes into contact with the family.

It is often the secondary victims who suffer the most from a sexual assault. This is true especially if there is a drastic or violent change in the victim after the sexual assault. While we do not minimize the plight of the primary victims, they can seek help and at least understand what is happening to them. Many secondary victims do not enjoy this luxury. They can console the victim and go with them to counseling, but the healing effects are often outside their control, and they are dependent upon the primary victim to heal herself so that life can carry on as it was before the attack.

Consequences for Secondary Victims

The consequences for secondary victims of sexual assaults may indeed be very dramatic. This is especially true when the case is a homicide. Until recently, little attention has been paid to the widespread secondary victimization that occurs because of such attacks. It has been estimated that about 5,000 victims annually fall prey to serial killers. If this is accurate, a large data set does indeed exist for serious empirical researchers to examine. Few studies have been conducted nonetheless (Friedman, 1982; Lavrakas, 1981).

These proceeding paragraphs detailing the differences between primary and secondary victims are presented here to illustrate a couple of points. First, the actual victims of sexual assault are not the only people who need to be considered as being a victim of a violent and often brutal attack. When anyone is sexually victimized, not only is that person being somehow attacked, but indirectly anyone else with whom that person has intimate or personal contact will also suffer. This is a little-understood, but well-detailed fact that many students of criminal justice and courts need to be cognizant of. It is just too easy to dismiss sexual assault or rape as a crime that lasts only a few minutes. Nothing less true has ever been stated. The long-term impact of sexual victimization can last a lifetime, and the pain felt by both the primary and secondary victims can extend beyond a couple of years and can even be passed from one generation to the next. This idea is important and needs to be brought out in criminal trials and sentencing hearings so that judges and juries can truly assess the amount of damage these offenders have had on the victim, the victim's family, and society at large.

Types of Victims: Assessing Blame

Just as important as understanding the differences between primary and secondary victims is the type or amount of blame that victims share for their own fate. Hagan (1990) developed a typology of victims in terms of their degree of guilt associated with the perpetration of a crime. The victim types are shown in Table 13.2.

Table 13.2   Hagan's Typology of Victims

Type of Victims	Description
The completely innocent	This type of victim shoulders no guilt at all. They are truly innocent and did nothing to precipitate the victimization.
The victim with minor guilt	This type of victim shares some guilt in the experience. Such a case is when a woman provokes a miscarriage and dies as a result. In this case she did not intend to die, but expired as a result of her own actions.
The victim as guilty as the offender	This type of victim, through their actions or deeds, provokes some type of action by themselves or on behalf of someone else in which they end up becoming the victim of the committed crime. An example of this type of offender would be a woman who pleads with someone else to make her crying baby be quiet. While she may not be the person who injures the child, her actions and deed precipitated the violence.
The victim as guiltier than the offender	This type of victim actually provokes the incident in which he or she becomes of the victim of a crime. An example of this type of victim would be a person who wants to kill himself or herself but cannot and pulls a gun on a law enforcement officer, forcing the officer OK to kill him or her. OK
The victim as guiltiest	This type of victim actually provokes the violence on behalf of another and ends up either being wounded or assaulted by self-initiated actions. An example of this type of offender would be a person who provokes a fight with another and is killed in self-defense.
The simulating or imaginary victim	This type of victim is not a real victim at all, but, because of paranoia, senility, or some other mental health problem, believe that they are consistently under attack or being stalked by someone or thing in the environment. An example of this type of victim would be a person who is always complaining to the police that he or she is the victim of electrical anal probes by aliens from another planet.

SOURCE: Hagan F. (1990) *Introduction to Criminology* (2nd Ed.). Chicago: Nelson Hall (p. 217).

Table 13.2 describes the types of victims in the population. While the overwhelming majority of victims that the criminal justice system deals with are completely innocent victims, it is important to note that some victims do retain some culpability for the crimes committed against them. This does not mean a young girl out at a night club in a scantily clad outfit contributes at all to the possibility of sexual victimization, it just means that people should be aware of the contexts where victimization occurs and the risks associated with certain types of behavior. While our risk of becoming a victim of a sex criminal is still relatively low, certain self-protective mechanisms minimize the risk of victimization. The last question that any person wants to ask herself or himself is, "What did I do to deserve this?" and have an answer to the question.

❖ THE EFFECTS OF SEXUAL VICTIMIZATION

Anyone who has fallen victim to any crime undoubtedly knows the shame, embarrassment, and anger that go along with the victimization. They know that when they tell others, some form of stigma will attach to them. In the case of a date rape on a college campus, no one might want to date someone who is in a sense damaged goods. While is the fear is unfounded, a degree of stigma does attach.

In our classes, we typically ask the male students if they would consider dating a female who has been raped. The majority of male students state that it really is not a factor in their decision to ask anyone out. But when we ask them if they would consider getting serious with a rape victim, the answer inevitably changes. Many feel that they do not need this excessive burden of being with someone whom everyone looks at differently. Others state that the victim will always have psychological problems and they simply do not want to have to deal with them. Another group states that if they were dating already, the incident would not cause them to break up with their partners, but if they were just thinking about asking the young girl out, the rape itself might cause them to think twice. Luckily, 30% of students remain who continue to say it doesn't matter.

While it is easy to chastise the male students who state that they would not date or consider getting serious with a rape victim, we would be ignoring a fundamental truth. That is, rape victims may indeed carry a great deal of psychological trauma from the assault. This trauma more often than not manifests itself in psychological mechanisms long after the 5–10 minutes in which the crime occurred. According to many victims, the criminal event is the easy part, the real trauma occurs in the next 2 years as the victim tries to reintegrate himself or herself into mainstream society.

The stigmatization effect is one of the primary contributors to female victims' unwillingness to come forth and report either rapes or other serious sexual assaults. The victim knows that she will be looked at differently and will be vilified if the offender is a well-respected classmate, celebrity, or community or family member. In an effort to avoid being vilified, the victim may choose to tell no one, wishing to contain her emotions inside, exposing to the outside world only that reality that she chooses. This choice, however, is dangerous, since many people, not just women, who undergo a traumatic experience such as this have a difficult time adjusting after the victimization experience.

Whether or not a victim decides to come forth, many experience similar feelings of guilt, shame, embarrassment, and responsibility that often cloud the fact that they truly are not whom to blame for the attack. Many victims will begin to assume blame for the attack, believing that it was their fault for dancing too long and close with the stranger, taking that last drink, dressing too provocatively, or going back to his apartment after the party. They may believe that they simply didn't try hard enough to stop it before the assault started, or that they somehow wanted the assault to happen.

Photo 13.1   Mike Tyson, former heavyweight champion and convicted rapist.

SOURCE: © Matt Campbell/AFP/Getty Images

Of course, these explanations are all ridiculous to most of us in a calm rational state. For instance, when boxing legend Mike Tyson was accused in 1991 of raping beauty pageant contestant Desiree Washington, the Indianapolis jury didn't buy his claim that it was consensual sex nor his assertion that, if she didn't want to have sex with him, what was she doing in his hotel room in the late night hours? Very few people doubted his guilt, but a few out there felt that Ms. Washington shared some of the blame. She probably should not have placed herself in that type of situation, but that does not excuse the type of crime that Tyson was accused and convicted of.

Another common feeling expressed by many victims after a sexual assault is fear. Pervasive fear can affect victim's perceptions about their world, their relationships, and their self-image. Once a victim has been attacked, the person knows that there are some people in this world who truly are monsters. And with that knowledge comes the fear that these monsters can be around every corner and just waiting for an opportunity to offend. This fear is a product of violent crime with personal, social, and economic consequences (Sheley, 1979).

The Personal Consequences of Fear: Withdrawal and Retreat

Sheley (1979) claims that fear of crime and victimization influences the thoughts and actions of almost every citizen in organized society. Individuals experience crime and learn to fear crime or it may become a contagion: people hear about a victimization experience of a fellow worker and they become fearful about becoming the next victim (Skogan, 1986). One of the most common responses to this fear is social withdrawal and retreatism. Various surveys reported by Sheley (1979) indicates that 43% of urban populations and 16% of the nation as a whole remains off the streets at night from fear of a criminal attack. In many large, industrialized cities, some people make efforts to not leave their homes at night and totally withdraw from community life, especially in the twilight hours.

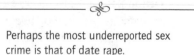

Perhaps the most underreported sex crime is that of date rape.

Others may take self-protective measures such as purchasing a gun, barring up their windows, or installing a burglar alarm. The extant literature seems to suggest that the aggregate level of fear is depends on the location of residence, prevalence of influential cases in the news, and whether the individual has ever been a victim of a crime (Greenberg, 1985).

While many of these responses may seem a little dramatic, it is important to understand how dramatic fear of falling a victim to a violent or sex crime can be. Not only may people withdraw or retreat from society, but they may also believe that they cannot trust anyone other than themselves. These are the social consequences of fear.

Social Consequences of Fear

Just as people can begin to fear the city or the neighborhood at night, they also are likely to develop a fear of other people whom they do not know. In this case, Sheley (1979) emphasizes that fear of crime is primarily fear of strangers. And when people begin to distrust each other, it is highly unlikely, if not impossible, to bring forth the proper treatment to reacquaint individuals with others and the social world to prove to them that not all people are criminals. This is a cycle that must be stopped before all people become shut-ins and refuse to participate in their communities. In fact, most of the current research stresses the fact that the more people participate in their communal functions, the better they feel about themselves, their city, and others as well (Skogan, 1986; Taylor & Covington, 1993).

Economic Consequences of Fear

There are also economic consequences caused by citizens' fear of crime. This cost is estimated to be in the billions of dollars each year. These costs take a number of forms: for example, the expenses borne by the American people each year to invest in burglar alarms, the local mall's cost in paying a security force to make sure that rowdy teens to not congregate on corners intimidating shoppers, the purchase and acquisition of guns or other weapons for self-protection. While there is no way to accurately count the true cost that crime, especially violent crime, has on our society, it is obvious that people are not only mystified by violence in our culture, but are also accurately aware of it and shift patterns of behavior in response to it. Further, when we examine the effect of violent and sexual crimes with a wide-angle lens, it is clear that not only are the primary victims and secondary victims injured, but so is society at large.

The economic consequences of victimization may also fall on the individual victims and their families. Many victims are harmed or even murdered during their most productive years or when their most productive years lie ahead. Some have families and other dependents who suffer great financial loss because of the sexual victimization. This is true not only of those who die as a result of a sexual assault, but also often of those who have suffered at the hands of a sexual offender and have not been able to reach their former or potential level of productivity. Lauder (1985) quotes one victim:

The man who murdered my husband is in prison. . . . Taxpayers are paying for his room, board, and medical and psychiatric help. My husband was my only means of support. I'm now destitute, very ill, and have no financial means. Meanwhile, the murderer has 600 acres of valuable property. Why should the man who ruined my life be able to keep and return in a few years to that, while I have nothing? (p. 169)

According to Holmes and DeBurger (1988, p. 143), there are issues of fairness in dealing with the needs of primary and secondary victims. The fairness issue must somehow be balanced with the financial resources available to address the wider financial and economic issues.

Lauder (1985) offers a critique on the economic aspects of secondary victimization. He states that it is a shame that the state covers all the expenses of the perpetrators but provides very little assistance for those who need it most, the victims and their families. These, he states, are the truly innocent and most deserving of state help, instead of those who intentionally prey on and victimize the innocent taxpaying civilians. Lauder's points are provided in Table 13.3 below.

It is important to understand the types of victims and the fact that offenders injure not only the victims and their families and friends but society as well; it is just as important to understand the individual emotions that take over an individual who has fallen victim to a sexual offender. Feelings of hurt is one. It typically arises from the victim's not being able to understand why a person would be motivated to do such a thing, and the pain is turned inward. Anger is another effect. Anger is directed outward, and it may be a better psychological reaction than hurt, because the feeling is directed toward someone other than oneself.

Morale and Mental Health Consequences

Sexual assault is not only a problem for mature single women, but also for children. The impending physical and psychological processes that the victim may endure should be construed to apply not only to teen and adults, but to child victims as well. In fact, the impact on the psychosocial development of child victims may be more traumatic than that on older victims.

Recent studies have shown that men who have been sexually abused are more likely than those who have not been to use drugs and commit sexual offenses as a way of self-medicating their victimization. While there is evidence that women undergo the same emotional processes, the pattern in them is not quite as clear. One study by CASA (1999) found that women who have suffered sexual abuse as children

Table 13.3   Lauder's Critique on the Economic Aspects of Secondary
Victimization

Points	Description
Point 1	It is a travesty of justice that, while the costs of defense are often paid fully by tax funds, through a public defender service, victims or survivors in states without crime compensation laws get nothing.
Point 2	Federal laws should require that profits reaped by celebrated murderers from films, books, and so forth about their lives must be placed in a fund for restitution to survivors or the community. Only a small incentive amount should be excluded from this requirement.
Point 3	If states are willing to pay the bill for psychological or psychiatric counseling of the homicidal criminal, why are so few willing to foot the bill for counseling the victim's surviving spouse or children?
Point 4	If states are willing to fund the extensive costs of defense counsel and related expenses for a perpetrator of homicidal violence, then they should also fund the costs of a survivor's suit for wrongful death against the convicted killer. In the event hidden assets are uncovered or the killer is paroled to productive work, payment of any award to the survivors would be enforceable by the court.

SOURCE: Lauder, R. (1985). *Fighting Violent Crimes in the United States*. New York: Dodd, Mead (pp. 165–170).

are more likely than nonabused women to abuse alcohol and suffer long-term psychological trauma.

Sedney and Brooks (1984) looked at the effect of early childhood sexual experiences and found that of the 13% of college-age women in their sample had been a victim of incest, most reported sleep disorders (51%), had severe bouts of depression (65%), had nervous or anxiety attacks (59%), or had nightmares about the incident (30%). Sedney and Brooks concluded that women with early childhood sexual experiences had significantly more problems with depression and anxiety and were 2½ times as likely to consult mental health practitioners or be hospitalized because of their experience.

This being the case, it is easy to see that while males may generally direct their frustration outward from a victimization experience, women may suppress their true feelings. As a result, they retreat from society, need psychological treatment before their lives can return to normal, and lose the ability to trust others for years, or even never regain it.

The impact of sexual victimization on secondary victims can be great; it may indeed be fatal. Domestic problems, too often leading to marital dissolution or breakdowns in interpersonal relationships, are often the result of rape. In cases involving serial murder, the primary victims are often not found for weeks or months—sometimes even for years. Many are never found. This certainly has an impact upon the morale and the health, both mental and physical, of the secondary victims.

Consider the cases of four families of primary victims of Ted Bundy—the Laura Aime, Debbie Kent, Denise Naslund, and Georgeann Hawkins families.[2] Laura Aime, an 18-year-old victim, was killed by Bundy in 1974. Her father was hospitalized for depression after Laura's death. There appears to be little doubt that his depression was at least exacerbated by the victimization of his daughter. As he stated as he drove by the mountain parkway, looking toward the spot where the police found Laura's body, "My little baby was up there all by herself and there was nothing I could do to help her." Mr. Aime died in 1987 of heart problems, and no doubt the stress of his daughter's death contributed to his condition. A Mormon family, the Aimes found little consolation in their faith (authors' files).

Belva Kent is the mother of Debbie Kent, who was murdered by Bundy in 1974. In a personal interview, Mrs. Kent said that Debbie's body has never been found, but that a kneecap was found in 1989 that they believe belonged to Debbie. The Kents held a memorial service for Debbie, alongside the headstone they erected for their daughter. Billy, Debbie's younger brother, was killed in an automobile accident in the mid-1980s. Mrs. Kent and her husband have since divorced. Mrs. Kent said that the media originally badgered her family, appearing interested only in selling newspapers and raising TV ratings. She said that the media actually believed that Debbie was a runaway and a troubled youngster and would not consider the possibility of foul play until much later. As the case developed and time passed, Mrs. Kent believes the media have become more sensitive and appreciative of the feelings and emotions the survivors endure. Also devout Mormons, the Kent family found solace within their religion.

Denise Naslund's mother has not changed her daughter's bedroom since the day Denise went with her friends to Lake Sam in 1974. Constant concern about what her daughter had to go through on the day of her death is always on her mind.

The father of Georgeann Hawkins, another Bundy victim, stated, "You just want to reach out and do something. . . . But you can't. You get so drawn out. You waste so damn much emotional effort trying to transfer your hate and bitterness. You get over the loss, then you keep getting reminded of it" (Michaud & Aynesworth, 1983, p. 313).

These cases are not unusual. The mother of one of Jerry Brudos's victims, Mildred Slawson, stated that she was so upset with a book written about the serial killer and what the author said about the killing of her daughter that she went into the hospital for a week. Mrs. Slawson said that the author had never interviewed her about her daughter, a point about which she is quite bitter. She was additionally upset that the author of the book had access to police information that she, as the mother of a primary victim, was denied. In an interview, Karen Sprinker's mother also said that she disapproved of a book being written about the murder of her daughter. She was somewhat unnerved that an author could profit from a crime like this, a fact that actually contributed to her grief as a secondary victim. She also suffered further because of hearing from others some of the content of the book, including what her daughter suffered before her death. She stated that she had not read the book, and ended the interview by asking, "Why do people write things like this?" These killings occurred in the late 1960s, but the pain still persists in the minds of these secondary victims.

Physical and Psychological Processes of Sexual Assault Victims

Reactions and adjustments to a sexual assault are often similar to those a person might experience after another life crisis. Of course, they vary in duration, frequency, and intensity from one person to another. They will also vary with the support system the victim has—family, religious, and social supports—as well as the type of attack.

Victims pass through particular phases of adjustment. Table 13.4 lists some common ones, but they vary from one victim to another. There is no one "right" way to adjust. While it would be incorrect to attempt to clinically diagnose any phase a person is in after an assault, the patterns hold across the majority of cases.

The first phase that victims of sexual assault typically undergo in called shock. This is called Phase 1 because it is the phase that typically immediately follows the victimization. In this phase, the individual simply cannot believe that this actually happened to them. While they may try to go on with their lives, they will experience periodic episodes of hysteria and anxiety attacks and begin to blame themselves for the attack and suffer from acutely low self-esteem. While there is no way to determine how long victims will stay in this phase, they usually progress to phase 2 within 60 to 90 days.

Table 13.4   Stages of Victims Reponses to Sexual Assault

Stage	Description
Stage 1: Shock	During this period the victim may experience acute anxiety, pangs of guilt, episodes of fear. In this stage, many victims exhibit behavior that runs the gamut from hysteria to behavioral numbness.
Stage 2: Denial	During this period the victim may make a concentrated effort to put the entire episode of the sexual attack behind her. She may feel it is "time to forget" the attack. She may attempt to suppress the feelings that came to the psychological surface in Stage 1. She will probably discuss the attack as little as possible, and she will try to return to her regular daily routine.
Stage 3: Integration	Despite the psychological attempt at restoration, many victims discover that sexual attacks have more impact upon them than they initially realized. Nightmares, breakdowns in interpersonal relationships, employment difficulties, and the like often continue to be problems in the adjustment process.

The second phase is that of denial. In this phase, individuals realize the source of the attacks and try to put the whole incident behind them. While the victim may choose to not discuss the incident with significant others and act as if she is no longer bothered by the incident, nothing can be less true. She may still experience the fear and panic attacks found in Phase 1, but those feelings come less frequently and the victim is often able to hide her reaction to the incident better. Just as in the first phase, there is also no timetable for which the victims to move from this phase to the next. It may begin as early as 30 to 60 days after the incident or anytime later. Its duration is variable as well. It may last for a couple of months, or after a more ferocious attack, extend several years.

The final phase is that of integration. In this phase, the victim has finally come to grips with the incident and has accepted the experience as an unfortunate, but nonetheless learning, experience that life has dealt them. It is important to note that the boundaries between all these phases are permeable. That is, because the fact that a person has come to grips with the assault does not mean there will not be routine or periodic setbacks. Even victims in the final phase of reintegration may experience sudden, even severe, panic attacks as environmental stimuli remind them of the incident. While their treatment may be over, many still have a fear of confined spaces and, when they encounter situations where they feel trapped, may relive the experience.

❖ HELPING THE VICTIMS

Those who work with sexual assault victims and those who are close to victims of such an attack, must help move the victim from a feeling that the culpability rests with them to the realization that the blame rests rather on the perpetrator. There are several ways to do this. While speaking with a sex crime victim, one must allow her to express feelings in the way she finds most comfortable. It is vital for the victim to ventilate and talk out feelings of concern. Some of the distressing issues that may surface and that must be dealt with include the victim's fears about having contracted a disease in the attack, about death, about unwanted pregnancy resulting from the attack, about the stigma from others learning about the attack, and about being victimized again.

The setting for a professional interview must be considered carefully. It must be private and secure from interruptions. Unwanted or clamorous persons must not be permitted to invade this physical or psychological space. It is also imperative that family members or friends of the victim encourage their loved one to seek outside help, whether it be support from victims' groups or professional mental health treatment. You must let the individual know that not everyone who seeks mental health treatment is mentally ill or weak. Victims need to understand that they, like many others, just need support and someone who will listen to them and their fears without passing judgment.

Society's Responses and Victims' Rights Groups

Not only must the victims of sexual assault rely upon friends, family, and mental health practitioners to help them overcome this experience, but they can also seek help from peer groups of people who have been touched by this type of crime. While there are many types of victim support groups across the country, most form in reaction to a serious or critical event. While the longevity of some of these groups is short, others gain a life of their own as the families and friends of the surviving victims dedicate themselves to this cause in memory of a lost loved one. Such was the case in the formation of the group Citizens and Victims for Justice Reform in Louisville, Kentucky. This support and legal action committee was formed after two 16-year-old male high school students were abducted at gunpoint. Their bodies were found later that evening. Both boys had been bound, and one had been sodomized. Both had been shot in the head. Less than 8 hours later, two men were arrested and charged with their murders.

The Stephanie Roper Society was founded by her parents after this young college-aged woman was abducted beside her disabled car. She was taken to an abandoned house, where she was repeatedly raped, then burned and shot in the head. Her killers were apprehended within a week of the crime.

It is not surprising that organizations such as the two mentioned above have arisen in recent years to deal with the problems confronted by victims, both primary and secondary. These groups have often voiced their dissatisfaction with the operation of the criminal justice system and have offered a variety of services to victims of all types of crime, not only those that involve sex as a motivating factor.

This concern for victims' rights has emerged as one of the most significant issues in the last two decades. The first victim compensation program in this country began in California in 1965, and today all 50 states, the District of Columbia, and the Virgin Islands provide some type of financial assistance to victims of nearly every type of violent crime, including rape, robbery, assault, sexual abuse, drunk driving, and domestic violence (Office of Victims of Crimes, 1998). The programs pay for a certain portion of the expenses of victims, including medical, mental health counseling, lost wages, and, in cases of homicide, funerals. The payout for these programs to crime victims depends on the amount of injury done and the limits and maximums for that state. The typical payout for such a claim is a little over $2,000 (National Association of Crime Victim Compensation Boards, 1997; Parent, Auerbach, & Carlson, 1992). What they do not cover is lost, stolen, or otherwise damaged property. This loss is the responsibility of the individual or their insurance company.

In Kentucky, for example, a victim may receive up to $25,000, but he or she must demonstrate evidence of financial need, report the crime to the police within 2 days of its occurrence, and file a claim within 12 months. Other states have other eligibility requirements. Generally, the requirements that the defendants must report the crime to the police within 72 hours, cooperate with the police and court officials, submit a timely application to a compensation program (usually within a year of the event), and provide information about the event to the local boards. Claimants are not eligible if they by their own actions or deeds contributed the criminal victimization. While some of these requirements are firm, others can be waived if the victim is a child or incapacitated for a period of time (National Association of Crime Victim Compensation Boards, 1997).

Table 13.5 gives typical services provided by victim assistance agencies.

Table 13.5   List of Typical Services Provided by Victim Service Agencies

Service Provided	Description
Personal advocacy	Helping victims receive all the services to which they are entitled by both social service and criminal justice agencies
Referral	Recommending or obtaining assistance other than that given by the programs
Restitution	Urging judges to order (or probation authorities to collect) restitution, and helping violent crime victims fill out the proper papers necessary to receive compensation
Court orientation	Helping victims and witnesses understand the criminal justice system and their participation in it
Transportation	Providing victims with rides to and from court, to social service agencies, and, if necessary, to shelters
Court escort	Escorting witnesses to court and staying with them during the proceedings
Emotional support	Giving victims support during their time of greatest need and with the processes of the criminal justice system that lead to a formal accusation or trial

SOURCE: Samaha, J. (1997) *Criminal Justice* (4th Ed.). Minneapolis: West Publishing Company (p. 100).

❖ CONCLUSION

Any discussion of sexual assault must include the wide variety of offenses that fall under its legal and sociological definitions. Sexual assault in many circles includes almost any uninvited sexual advance. Sexual assault has both primary and secondary victims who are traumatized. There is an large incongruence between the incidence and prevalence rates reported by researchers and the federal government. Society has made great strides in the past 30 years in setting up and implementing victim assistance agencies and support networks to help these victims lead productive lives soon after the victimization. It is hoped that as we enter the 21st century, more programs will come on line to help these victims, their families, and the communities that suffer from these horrendous crimes.

❖ DISCUSSION QUESTIONS

1. Compare and contrast primary and secondary victims of crime.

2. With the readings in this section, consult the *Sourcebook on Criminal Justice Statistics* to get the latest data on victimization rates in the United States. Also check the *Uniform Crime Reports* for their data. Compare the two. How similar and different are the statistics?

3. How can some victims become "career victims"?

4. Have you or a member of your family been victimized? Explain the psychological consequences of the victimization.

5. If you have been victimized, has this changed you? In what way(s)? Explain.

❖ NOTES

1. Using the same ratio, Rennison's (1999) risk of actual or attempted sexual victimization is 270 persons in 100,000, while UCR numbers would have us believe that this rate is only 50.3 per 100,000 persons. Rennison's reported rate is more than 5 times that of official government figures.

2. The authors would like to thank James Massie for the information used in this chapter on the families of the victims of Ted Bundy and Jerry Brudos.

❖ REFERENCES

Bureau of Justice Statistics. (2006). National Crime Victimization Survey Violent Crime Trends, 1973–2005. Washington, DC: US Department of Justice.

Bureau of Justice Statistics. (2001). *The number of crimes reported to police and crime rates since 1960, U.S. Totals and by state from the FBI's Uniform Crime Reports.* Retrieved March 19, 2001, from http://www.ojp.usdoj.gov/bjs/dtdata.htm#index.

CASA. (1999). *Dangerous liaisons: Substance abuse and sex.* New York: National Center on Addiction and Substance Abuse at Columbia University.

Castleberry, V. (1982, August 1). The pain of survival. *Dallas Times Herald,* pp. 1, 6, 7.

Federal Bureau of Investigation. (2000). *Crime in the United States, U.S. reports 1999.* Washington, DC: U.S. Department of Justice.

Friedman, K. (1982). *Victims and helpers: Reactions to crime.* Washington, D.C.: National Institute on Crime.

Goodman, G., Batterman, J., & Kenney, R. (1993). Optimizing children's testimony: Research and social policy issues concerning allegations of child sexual abuse. In D. Cicchetti & S. Toth (Eds.), *Child abuse, child development, and social policy: Advances in applied developmental psychology.* Norwood, NJ : Ablex.

Greenberg, S. (1985). Fears and its relationship to crime, neighborhood deterioration, and informal social control. In J. Byrne & R. Sampson (Eds.), *The social ecology of crime* (pp. 47–62). New York: Springer Verlag.

Greenfeld, L. (1997). *Sex offenses and offenders: An analysis of data on rape and sexual assault.* Washington, DC: Bureau of Justice Statistics.

Hagan, F. (1990). *Introduction to criminology* (2nd ed.). Chicago: Nelson-Hall.

Holmes, R., & DeBurger, J. (1988). *Serial murder.* Newbury Park, CA: Sage.

Lauder, R. (1985). *Fighting violent crimes in the United States.* New York: Dodd, Mead.

Lavrakas, P. J. (1981). "On Households." In Lewis, Dan A., *Reactions to Crime.* 67–85, Thousand Oaks, CA: Sage Publications,1981.

Michaud, S., & Aynesworth, H. (1983). *The only living witness.* New York: Linden.

National Association of Crime Victim Compensation Boards. (1997). *Crime victim compensation program directory* (No. 1). Washington, DC: Author.

Office of Victims of Crimes. (1998). *New directions from the field: Victims' rights and services for the 21st century* (No. 172829). Washington, DC: Office of Justice Programs.

Parent, D., Auerbach, B., & Carlson, K. (1992). *Compensating crime victims: A summary of policies and practices* (No. NCJ 136500). Washington, DC: Office of Justice Programs.

Rennison, C. (1999). *Criminal victimization 1998: Changes 1997–1998 with trends 1993–1998.* Washington, DC: Bureau of Justice Statistics.

Samaha, J. (1997). *Criminal justice.* St. Paul, MN: West.

Schulhofer-Wohl, S. (2001, March 3). Contact in school hall leads only to confusion: Boy, 12, accused of sex assault held for a day. *Milwaukee Journal Sentinel.* [Online]. Available" www.jsonline.com/mews/mtero/mar01/kid03030201a.asp.

Sedney, M., & Brooks, B. (1984). Factors associated with a history of childhood sexual experience in a nonclinical female population. *Journal of the American Academy of Child Psychiatry, 23,* 215–218

Sheley, J. (1979). *Understanding crime: Concepts, issues, decisions.* Belmont, CA: Wadsworth.

Skogan, W. (1986). Fear of crime and neighborhood change. In A. Reiss & M. Tonry (Eds.), *Communities and crime* (pp. 191–232). Chicago: University of Chicago Press.

Snyder, H., & Sickmund, M. (1999). *Juvenile offenders and victims: 1999 national report.* Washington, DC: Office of Juvenile Justice and Delinquency Prevention.

Taylor, R., & Covington, J. (1993). Community structural change and fear of crime. *Social Problems, 40,* 374–392.

Tjaden, P., & Thoennes, N. (1998). *Prevalence, incidence, and consequences of violence against women: Findings from the National Violence Against Women Survey.* Washington, D.C.: National Institute of Justice.

14

Treatment of
Sex Offenders

❖　❖　❖

The previous chapters in this book have looked at the variety of people who commit sex crimes and the personal consequences for the victims. These are important issues. But there is one topic that we have left until this final chapter. That is, what does a society and the criminal justice system do with those who commit sexual crimes? If you ask a cross section of people this same question, you inevitably get a variety of answers, but there is some consensus of opinion about these offenders' relative worth. Most will imply that the criminal justice system should punish them severely; some will even go as far as suggesting castration. Others will say put them to death, and a minority will claim that we should treat them. Over time, society has at one point or another undertaken all these approaches. What is interesting about the role and status of sex offenders in society today is that even in the eyes of those who are incarcerated, the offenders occupy a unique social caste in society (Vaughn & Sapp, 1989).

Not only do incarcerated inmates believe that most sex offenders are of little worth, but that opinion is shared by a majority of the population. This opinion has been further bolstered by the recent rash of media attention on the crimes of these offenders.

In order to illustrate this effect, an example may be called for. In fall 2000, two children got off a school bus in an upper-middle-class suburban subdivision near Orlando, Florida. As they walked to their home, a Hispanic man aged 25–35 approached them and grabbed the younger of the two children. The older child spoke up and told the man to leave her sister alone, which he did, and grabbed the eldest child. The perpetrator reached in his pocket, pulled out a bag and rubbed fecal material over the older child's face and head. He then stepped back, took a picture, got in his pickup and drove away.

While the details of this incident were never made public, news spread quickly. Notes went home from the school telling the parents that about "an incident," and soon word of mouth filled in the details. Immediately afterward, parents began searching the sexual predators database of the Florida Department of Law Enforcement and located 3 convicted sex offenders who lived near the affected school. Flyers were then printed and posted at the local grocery store, surf shop, cleaners, liquor store, dance studio, and karate gym, with pictures of these offenders, their addresses, and criminal offending history.

Castration

The physical removal of the male testicles through surgical procedures

---

While these targeted offenders were not responsible for this offense, the hysteria created by this incident shook this child-rich community to its core. The local women's group encouraged its members to call the police when they saw a suspicious car. Neighborhood members began stopping and questioning anyone they felt didn't belong. Members of the local sheriff's department stepped up patrols and began giving community talks to the residents about ways to keep their children safe from sexual predators and offenders.

About six months later, a Hispanic man matching the physical description given by the children was caught in a local convenience store spraying the shoppers and clerks with a squirt gun. The contents of the squirt gun was his own urine. While these two crimes were never linked, the residents of Orlando will never be the same because they realize that there are people out there who engage in these types of criminal paraphilias.

❖ PERCEPTIONS OF SEX
  OFFENDERS AND CRIMINAL REMEDIES

Just as the people in Orlando were shocked by the weird nature of these crimes, they were also perplexed about the type of person who would engage in them. Surely, this individual was in need of treatment, but many wondered if he could even be treated. What was it that makes a person smear fecal material on a child's face or spray innocent people with urine? Treatment in this case did not seem like enough. This person had to be punished. After all, he had committed such an atrocious offense that many felt that he was not deserving of state-sponsored mental health treatment, at least until after he had completed receiving punishment.

While the crimes may differ from jurisdiction to jurisdiction, the feelings of animosity toward these offenders is invariant. When a critical case involving a sex offender is solved, very few citizens are concerned with what motivates the individual or what can make the individual stop. Most people just want to make sure the offender is punished for the crimes and make sure he never has the opportunity to reoffend.

As shown in Table 14.1, in 1998, the arrests for rape and other sex offenses constituted 1% of all arrests in 1998 (Bureau of Justice Statistics, 2000). Still, although there may not be many sex offenses actually occurring in this country, the heinous nature of the crimes that we are aware of is not only enough to scare us, but often enough to make us change our daily patterns of behavior.

What is interesting is that while the police do not make many arrests for these types of offenses, offenders who are convicted or rape or sexual assault comprise just under 5% of the total correctional population in the United States (Greenfeld, 1997a). Other researchers, who have defined sexual assault using more liberal terms, claim that the figure may be as high as 25–30% (Welch, 1988). This problem is further aggravated by the fact that, since 1980, the number of prisoners sentenced for violent sexual assault other than rape increased 15%. This increase is reported to be faster than that of any of the other reported violent crimes (Greenfeld, 1997b).

Table 14.1   Estimated Number of Arrests in the United States for Selected Offenses, 1998

Type of Offense	Number of Arrests in 1998	Percentage of All Arrests (14,528,300)
Rape	31,070	0.2%
Other sex offenses (excluding rape and prostitution)	93,600	0.6%

SOURCE: Federal Bureau of Investigation. (1999). *Crime in the United States, 1998.* Washington, DC: Government Printing Office, p. 210.

The problem of what to do with these inmates, how to keep them away from the general population to protect them, and how to provide efficient yet cost-effective treatment is aggravated because they are a heterogeneous group (National Institute of Corrections, 1988; Welch, 1988). They come from backgrounds that reflect all socioeconomic classes; some are aggressive, some are not. Although many races are represented, most are in their 20s and 30s, many are married, and they are predominantly white.

Despite our distaste for many of these offenders and their offenses, many politicians and professional correctional administrators realize the importance of treating them. While correctional ideologies change with the wind, perhaps no one is more deserving of treatment than these individuals if we take the perspective that anyone with a sexual interest in children, or who has come to associate sexual pleasure with violence, is truly mentally ill.

Whether or not these offenders deserve to be treated or are the class of offenders most in need of treatment is an open question. But we can all agree that society and all people (men, women, and especially children) must be protected. If change occurs within the personality of the offender, this is well and good, but above all society must be protected. But how does this occur? Either the sex criminal must be locked away for the rest of his life or change must happen—the sex criminal must be "treated" and "rehabilitated."

❖ WHAT IS TREATMENT?

Rehabilitation is often mistaken to be synonymous with treatment. *Treatment* is an action word; treatment entails processes carried out so that rehabilitation can be realized. *Rehabilitation* is a result of a process of treatment. It is indeed a noble goal to effect rehabilitation for everyone. There are some, however, who would argue that there are persons who are not amenable to treatment. For example, Rizzo (1981, p. 45) states, "It is my conviction that there are persons beyond the scope and reach of modern behavioral science's ability to rehabilitate." And Welch (1988, p. 7) has said, "No responsible person would say that we cure sex offenders. . . . We give them the tools to control their deviance."

There is also a problem with the word *rehabilitate.* In the medical sense, rehabilitation may be what we wish to

---

Rehabilitation

The process by which offenders are changed through treatment to once again become normal, functioning members of society

accomplish with the sex offender, but the medical model has lost a great deal of its luster in the past few years. We do not want simply to make the person what they *used to be*; we want to change them so they will *not* become as they were. *Habilitation*, then, might be the better word. But since *rehabilitation* is the commonly used term, and since we now know the difference between rehabilitation and habilitation, we will continue to use *rehabilitation* here.

In rehabilitating sex offenders, one notion that must be kept in mind is that not all sex criminals are alike. The National Institute of Corrections (1988) states that incarcerated sex offenders can be divided into two main types: child molesters and rapists. And under these two main types there are a variety of offenders who choose their victim based on either situational elements or victim preferences.[1]

This typology was composed mainly for incarcerated inmates. Thus, what it ignores is the variety of other offenders who commit less serious offenses such as exhibitionism, voyeurism, and scatophilia. These offenders are less likely to be found in prisons unless their offense was committed in conjunction with a more serous one. These less serious offenders are more likely to be found temporarily housed in local jails and are often referred to outpatient or private residential treatment facilities.

Habilitation

The process by which offenders are changed through treatment to become normal functioning members of society

If we want to discuss the variety of offenders using meaningful categories, it might be best to classify them into three categories based on their propensity to reoffend or our ability to provide effective treatment. According to Welch (1988) there are basically three types of sex offenders. These three can be found in Table 14.2.

Classifying offenders in this way gives us a glimpse of who the offenders are, what motivates them, and what their chances for rehabilitation are. For instance, we know that most *first offenders* are just beginning to express their paraphilias in public ways. They may be individuals who have just undergone a life-threatening or life-changing event and choose to act out in these ways as a way of self-medicating for their pain. An example of this type of offender would be a man whose wife just left him and he may go out and inflict pain on other women for the pain inflicted upon him by his former spouse. He may physically assault women he comes in contact with not for the pleasure of it, but because it is his way of self-medicating for his deep-seated emotional problems. In this type of case, if correctional or other treatment officials intervene quickly to discover the root cause

Table 14.2   Typology of Sex Offenders, Based on Propensity to Reoffend

Type	Description
First offenders	These individuals typically have no previous record and blame their offense on recent life stressors or substance abuse.
Controlled chronic offenders	These individuals are the serial offenders. They are the coldest and most calculating and antisocial offenders. Typically with each new offense, the severity of the crime also increases to add additional thrill.
Chronic offenders	These offenders are inept, possibly mentally slow and very impulsive. They have much larger problems than that which can be treated using standard treatment techniques.

SOURCE: Welch, R. (1988). Treating Sex Offenders. *Corrections Compendium, 13*(5): 7

of this animosity, then his future chances of recidivism may decrease significantly.

On the other hand, we have the *chronic offenders*. These offenders are often mentally ill, slow, socially inept, and easily agitated, and they may have some condition that can be dealt with through medication. These people are everywhere, and there generally is one or two in every academic program in universities across the country. Just because they exhibit these indicators does not mean that they are sexual offenders in waiting, but if they did have a propensity to engage in these types of behavior, there would be little holding them back from acting on their impulses. This type of offenders is different from the first type of offenders and may also call for a different type of treatment approach.

The third type described by Welch (1988) is the *controlled chronic offenders*. These offenders are cold, calculating individuals and are sometimes called serial offenders. They often relive their fantasies with each new crime and the level of shame and humiliation they impose on their victims increases with each new episode. These offenders may be the least amenable to treatment because of their deceptive nature. Note, we are not saying that these offenders cannot be treated, but since we know that in order for treatment mechanisms to work, the person must want to change, officials have no way to know whether these offenders are undergoing treatment for personal betterment or just to decrease their sentence and accelerate the time for them to recommence their offending behavior.

Classifying offenders allows us to understand when and what types of therapeutic or institutional treatment may best serve the individual or society at large. And if the final goal in corrections is to return these individuals to society, where they may function normally, then the classification of offenders and likelihood of treatment success is a basic or fundamental principle upon which any discussion of treatment or rehabilitation must proceed.

Rehabilitation and Recidivism

The literature on the success of various treatment programs, modalities, and facilities is typically contradictory. Some of the older studies found that sex offenders seldom were reported to have committed new sex crimes and were considered not to be a danger to themselves or others (Amir, 1971; Groth, Longo, & McFadin, 1982; Sturup, 1968; Tappan, 1971).

Other research reached contradictory conclusions. Furby, Weinrott, & Blackshaw's (1989) widely publicized and cited paper claimed that sex offenders could not be treated. Some have doubts about the methods they used and the reliability of their data, but then, in their conclusions they stated only that the evidence was inconclusive on whether psychological treatment was effective in preventing recidivism for sexual offenders. Unfortunately, some did not read the paper well, and many politicians and those working for mass media outlets began citing Furby as conclusive evidence that sex offenders could not be treated or rehabilitated.

Since that time, numerous studies have been conducted and researchers have been able to locate some support for treatment programs for sexual offenders. For instance, in a meta-analysis of sexual offender treatment programs, Alexander (1999) found that nationwide, the majority of sex offender treatment programs report

Table 14.3   Estimated Costs of Treatment and Maintenance for Sex Offenders, 1993

Institutional Type	Cost per Day	Cost per Month	Cost per Year
In correctional institutional settings	$210	$6,300	$75,600
In mental health facility	$77	$2,310	$27,720
In residential outpatient treatment center	$56	$1,680	$20,160

SOURCE: Office of the Legislative Auditor. (1994). Sex Offender Treatment Programs (94-07). St. Paul, MN: .

more positive results than negative. In fact of the 12 major meta-analyses done on the variety of these programs, 9 reported positive findings, 3 found that they could make no determination, and none concluded that it had no effect (Alexander, 1994). Table 14.3 presents the twelve studies and their findings.

While this meta-analysis does not allow us to examine the strengths and weaknesses of each program, their outcome criteria, or their individual methodologies, the evidence presented in the more than 356 studies included seems to indicate that treatment may indeed have some positive impact on the offenders. What we do not know is what effect it did have, and how motivated the respondents were to participate in these therapeutic sessions. These are critical elements in an evaluation of voluntary treatment programs.

It is often apparent that some treatment programs are more effective than others. At the Oregon State Hospital, for example, the rate of recidivism for sex offenders over a 6-year period was 10–14%. At the Western State Hospital in Washington, the rate of recidivism over a 17-year period was 28.7%. Does this mean that the Oregon State Hospital program is better than the one in Washington? Not necessarily. Many details affect the final success rate of a program; these details can differ widely. The time frame that is used to measure the rate of success as well as type of offense committed are two considerations in the measurement of recidivism. Success may be measured by whether the subject reoffends by committing another sex crime or by committing any type of crime, sexual or not— this clearly will influence the measured rate of recidivism. Controlling intake is another method of influencing the rate of success. If a program admits only minor sex criminals, that program's chances of having a high long-term success rate are better than if the program admits more hard-core offenders.

Meta-analysis

An analytic technique in which researchers study the results of a series of studies and make generalizations about the likelihood of a social theory or proposition

As shown in Figure 14.1, Alexander (2001) found that on the average, treated sex offenders recidivated in 11% of the cases, whereas untreated sex offenders recidivated 17.6% of the time. For incest perpetrators who have once been victims, no one in the treated sample recidivated within 5 years, but 5.3% of those who did not receive treatment abused their own children within this same 5-year time frame. And finally, child molesters who received treatment reoffended almost 18% of the time rather than the 25% found in those who did not receive treatment (Alexander, 2001).

Figure 14.1   Recidivism Rate for Selected Offenders Over a 5-Year Period

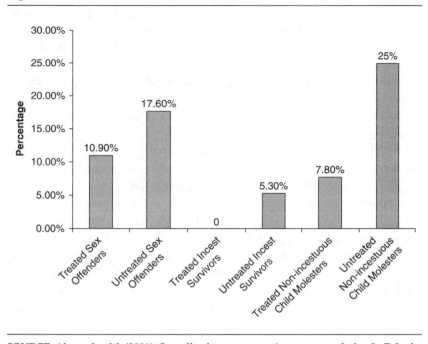

SOURCE: Alexander, M. (2001). Sex offender treatment: A response to furby. In E. Lotke (2003) *Issues and Answers: Sex Offenders: Does treatment work?* [On-line] http://www.igc .org/ncia/sexo.html.

Figure 14.2   Recidivism Among Treated Male Sex Offenders Before and After 1980

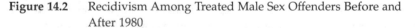

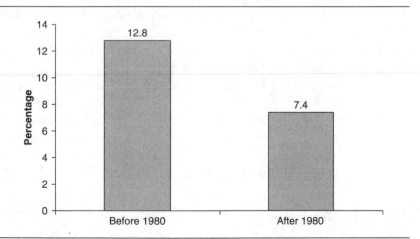

SOURCE: Alexander, M. (2001). Sex offender treatment: A response to furby. In E. Lotke (2003) *Issues and Answers: Sex Offenders: Does treatment work?* [On-line] http://www.igc .org/ncia/sexo.html.

What is interesting about these numbers is not just that any kind of treatment appears to have some effect, but that contrary to public perception, different types of sex offenders respond differently to treatment. So it may not only be differences in individuals or treatment modalities that precipitate the likelihood that a person will succeed in treatment, but it also may be a function of the type of fantasies that these offenders entertain and have decided to carry out.

Moreover, in looking at the effectives of treatment across time, Alexander (1999) found evidence to support the notion that as we learn more about the problem, our ability has to treat these individuals has also gotten better. This evidence is presented in Figure 14.2.

Romero and Williams (1985) conducted another study that examined different types of sex offenders and their propensity to reoffend. They analyzed outcome data from 231 adult males who were exhibitionists, pedophiles, or sexual assaulters. They found that exhibitionists were arrested on sex-related offenses twice as often as were sexual assaulters. Sexual assaulters were found to have committed as many nonsexual offenses as sexual offenses. The crimes of the sexual assaulters (rapists) were usually linked with an overall pattern of violent behavior. Exhibitionists and pedophiles studied had lower rates of non-sex crimes and higher rates of sex crimes than did the sexual assaulters. In their conclusion, Romero and Williams (1985) call for long-term analysis of the recidivism rate of sex offenders and the discovery of undetected crimes, both sex crimes and non-sex crimes.

Other studies looking at the recidivism rates for various types of sex offenders have reached similar conclusions. Researchers from the State of Vermont found that treatment appears to cut the risk of recidivism in half for exhibitionists and child molesters. Yet they found little difference in a rapist likelihood of recidivism when we compare the rates for those who have undergone treatment and those who have not. (Vermont Department of Corrections, 1995).

While we have not covered all the studies that have been conducted on the efficiency of treatment for sex offenders, the preponderance of the evidence seems to support the notion that treatment can reduce recidivism for some offenders better than for others. While we are sure that it does good things, there are many obstacles that often prevent these offenders from receiving the treatment they need.

Obstacles to Treatment

In order for effective treatment to begin, those in the criminal justice and state political system must not only find the need for treatment but also provide resources so that treatment can be undertaken. Many legislators and citizens are concerned that sex criminals are "coddled," and that too much tax money is spent on these undeserving individuals. Others believe that incapacitation is the answer, and that any type of treatment program is a waste of time. The impediments to

Incapacitation

A goal of corrections in which offenders are locked away for extended periods of time to protect the public

effective treatment fall into four broad categories: societal obstacles, political obstacles, criminal justice system obstacles, and financial obstacles.

Societal Obstacles

There is a general belief in society that people are to be held personally responsible for their own actions. This appears to be a return to the "classical school of criminology," in which individuals are considered to have free will and deterrence to crime is gained through swift, sure, and public punishment. Many believe that treatment programs designed for the rehabilitation of sex offenders constitute an unrealistic approach. The real answer lies in punishment, including incapacitation of the offenders and retribution (Federal Bureau of Investigation, 2000; Fogel, 1975; Irwin, 1988). According to this view, treatment programs do not belong inside prison walls, and therapy should be extended only to those persons who are able to pay on their own once they have "paid their debt to society."

Societal rejection of sex offenders creates low status for such offenders and a negative treatment environment in prison. Society is reluctant to appropriate funds for the treatment of persons who perpetrate such despicable crimes (Vaughn & Sapp, 1989). When an increase in funds for such treatment is

Retribution

A goal of corrections in which individual offenders are made to pay for their crime physically, financially, or in emotional strain.

appropriated, it typically goes into community-based treatment programs rather than prison programs (Cox, 1984). Because of this pervasive attitude, in-prison rehabilitation may not be a viable process for changing the lives of many sex offenders.

Political Obstacles

With too many politicians, it seems that the main concern is reelection. Reflecting the main concerns of their constituents, politicians who are judged to be "soft on crime" certainly are at risk at election time. Maintaining a hard line against sex criminals almost ensures a popular response from the voters. But this may have a deleterious effect on fiscal maintenance for programs in institutions as well as community-based treatment programs.

Viability of a program depends on financial maintenance, and such maintenance requires legislative support. An elected member of state or federal government earns an ill-deserved reputation for being "soft on crime" when he or she has voted in support of treatment programs for sex criminals, and that vote may become an insurmountable problem at election time.

Criminal Justice System Obstacles

The criminal justice system has the main responsibility for the treatment of sex criminals. With the pendulum swing back to custody and incapacitation, treatment and rehabilitation are again taking a backseat. It is true that almost every penal institution has some type of treatment program, and some are more advanced than others, but the reality at most institutions is custody.

Jails do not offer treatment as such, although some maintain psychologists or social workers on staff. This is probably just as well because of the short time the sex criminal is usually in the jail setting. Prisons, however, do offer treatment, although the quality of that treatment in prison can be of questionable value. In prisons, just as the turnover rate of security personnel is extremely high, so is that of treatment personnel. Salaries for treatment personnel are often so low that they fall below the poverty line for a person with a family of four. In many states, a correctional officer with a spouse and two children may qualify for food stamps. This is hardly an incentive for dedicated and professionally prepared persons to stay on the job.

Professional administrators in prisons may find it very difficult to allocate resources, both human resources and financial support, to administer a sex offender's treatment program. Because of the low status of sex offenders and their likelihood of being victimized by other inmates, they are often segregated from the general prison population; this segregation further isolates sex criminals and limits their treatment participation and personal movement (Cotton & Groth, 1982; Vaughn & Sapp, 1989).

The clients themselves often pose serious obstacles to the treatment process. Sex offenders have gone about their business on the outside by being manipulative and thwarting attempts at change. They naturally bring these attitudes into the therapeutic situation, and this certainly impedes the process of attempted change. As Figure 14.3 shows, sex offenders are typically at the bottom of the status hierarchy of prison inmates, and their status may pose a further impediment, as many sex offenders are reluctant to identify themselves as such because of the

Figure 14.3   Correctional Status Hierarchy

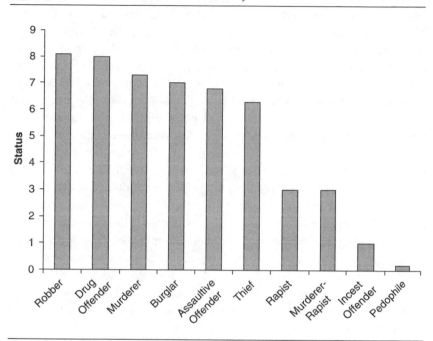

SOURCE: Vaughn, M., & Sapp, A. (1989). Less than utopian: Sex offender treatment in a milieu of power struggles, status positioning, and inmate manipulations in state correctional institutions. *Prison Journal 69*(2), 73–89.

ramifications it may have in their dealings with others inside the prison walls (Akerstrom, 1986).

So, inside the system itself, the problems are manifested on all levels: the administration, the custody staff, the treatment personnel, and the sex offender. The criminal justice system itself must now decide what course it will take with this very serious problem. The criminal justice system's relationship with state and national government leaders is crucial; as government leadership can change every four years, program stability is an ongoing concern.

Financial Obstacles

Similar but related to the aforementioned obstacle to treatment is the financial burden that accompanies individual treatment for sex offenders. Any type of individual level treatment is expensive, and all the more so psychological counseling. If these treatment costs are extended to the already burgeoning costs of holding an inmate in custody, it is easy to see how fast the cost of holding and attempting to implement and design individual treatment programs for sexual offenders.

With the growing number of offenders in the system for sex and drug offenses, many states have been forced to build additional space. The cost of adding an addition cell is approximately $55,000. In addition to construction costs, the average maintenance fee for each cell is approximately $22,000. While not all sex offenders may get a "new cell," it is clear that many states and correctional officials have to be cognizant of these costs and the problems associated with housing these offenders. Not only must the facility house these offenders and provide basic services for their upkeep, but it is often prudent to keep these offenders segregated from the rest of the population for their own safety. Thus, any estimated costs for housing an inmate can be doubled or tripled if the inmate is a sex offender and runs the risk of being victimized by another inmate.

Knowing the costs of building new cells, their maintenance, and how these figures may only be conservative estimates if the offender is a sex offender, is only half of the equation. Because many of these individuals are in need of individual treatment, the costs of rehabilitation programs for these inmates is also much higher than that of the typical inmate. Counselors often need to work with these offenders one on one in order to understand and treat the psychological malady that plagues them.

A low-cost alternative to housing these offenders and providing them treatment in secure facilities is to provide outpatient treatment. Many believe that because of the risk of victimization in prison and the low likelihood of recidivism behavior while the offender is under close scrutiny, intensive supervision probation programs are a lower-cost alternative. The costs of these programs, including treatment, range from $5,000 to $15,000 per year. A full year of treatment costs far less than an additional year of prison.

For many officials, residential treatment programs, coupled with intensive supervision, remain a viable alternative for those sex offenders who are not considered an imminent danger to society. The numbers presented show how residential treatments remain a viable option, given the relatively low rate of recidivism for offense-specific behavior. When these costs are viewed not only in fiscal year cycles, but in comparison with the case in which no treatment or ineffective treatment was provided in a institutional setting, it is estimated that their care may cost the state more than $22,000 per year for as long as the offender remains under supervision. Treatment is therefore an essential means of protecting the community at an affordable cost (Office of the Legislative Auditor, 1994).

While many are not in favor of allowing sex offenders to live in residential areas, some have suggested that we house these offenders in mental health facilities. One study conducted by the State of Minnesota found that this also was not a viable economic alternative. The daily cost of housing an inmate in a mental health facility, including treatment, was

$210 per day, $6,300 a month, or $75,600 a year. When these costs are compared to correctional institutions, the comparative figure drops to $77 a day, $2,310 a month, or $27,720 a year. And finally, when compared with the cost of housing and treating these offenders in the community, the numbers drop slightly to $56 a day, $1,680 a month, and $20,160 a year. A full breakdown of these numbers can be found in Table 14.4 (Office of the Legislative Auditor, 1994).

Table 14.4   Estimated Costs of Treatment and Maintenance for Sex Offenders, 1993

Institutional Type	Cost per Day	Cost per Month	Cost per Year
In correctional institutional settings	$210	$6,300	$75,600
In mental health facility	$77	$2,310	$27,720
In residential outpatient treatment center	$56	$1,680	$20,160

SOURCE: Office of the Legislative Auditor. (1994). Sex Offender Treatment Programs (94-07). St. Paul, MN: Author.

If we look at treatment costs alone, the cost of treating an inmate in institutional settings was less than that of outpatient programs ($7,200 vs. $4,500). However, the research tends to show that residential treatment programs work better than those conducted in either an institutional setting or a mental health facility. So any capital saved in the short term may be offset by future recidivism. In sum, treatment costs comprise between 11% and 50% of the total annual cost per offender at state correctional facilities (Office of the Legislative Auditor, 1994).

❖ TYPES OF TREATMENT

The previous discussion of the expense of treatment may be a little premature. While any type of inmate treatment is an additional burden placed on the coffers of criminal justice institutions, the type of treatment that an inmate receives is just as important as where this treatment in received, if not more so. In general, there are three types of treatment programs that are available to sex offenders under state supervision: behavioral, cognitive, and medical treatments.

Behavioral Therapy

Behavioral therapies typically utilize rewards and punishments to influence client behavior. In sexual counseling, the rewards and punishments are used to change sexual patterns and scripts of behavior. In one treatment therapy, for example, a sex offender may be shown slides of erotic scenes while the extent of his physical and psychological arousal is monitored by a penile plethysmograph; when he begins to become aroused by the materials, he may receive negative reinforcement in the form of a dose of ammonia administered through plastic tubing fastened under his nose. Other methods of behavior modification may include encouraging the offender to talk about his favorite sexual fantasy and then administering ammonia if he becomes sexually aroused by his deviant fantasy.

Cognitive Therapy

In this approach, a sex offender is encouraged to change the basic perceptions of his own sex life and the world around him as it pertains to sex and his interactions with others. These perceptions typically revolve around sex, education, skills, relationships, and so on. Through instruction, an attempt is made to help the offender relearn the world and his roles as they interact with the world. For example, the offender is taught skills that will help him appropriately express not only affection but anger and hostility.

> Offenders may re-enact their crimes on video, then show those videos to their group and to their spouse and outside friends. In an attempt to teach them empathy, they will read books and see videos from the victim's point of view, and perhaps meet with the victims or victims' counselors, or write letters to their own victims. (Welch, 1988, p. 9)

In this approach the offender is taught to recognize the steps or stages that have led him to commit his crimes. By becoming aware of his own personal danger signs, he may be able to divert himself from situations that in the past would result in some type of sexual victimization.

Medical Treatment

Medical programs typically use drugs, such as Depo-Provera, to lower sex criminals' testosterone levels. It is believed that the manifestation of sexual aggression is based on some type of hormonal imbalance. The administration of the drug does not alter the sexual preference of the offender, but it does decrease his physical urges to act them out and makes it easier for him to control those urges (Melella, Travin, & Cullen, 1989).

Depo-Provera was initiated as a drug of treatment for sex offenders in 1966 at Johns Hopkins University (Bradford, 1983). It is a synthetic progestin that inhibits the release of androgen, a male hormone, from the testicles. After stopping the administration of the drug, erectile and ejaculatory capacity usually begin to return within 7 to 10 days (Callan, 1985).

A repeat pedophile's wish for a sentence allowing him to serve his time in the community was partially granted yesterday.

Justice Robert Desmarais handed down a punishment that will gradually reintegrate the sex abuser into society.

Judge Desmarais said he believed Peter Graham, 36, wants to get better and is prepared to do whatever it takes to curb his heterosexual pedophilia.

However, to send a message to child abusers and to protect society until a drug program could be started, the judge said he had to send Mr. Graham to jail for a time.

The judge's sentence has a large component of rehabilitation that puts Mr. Graham on a leash for five years. The leash will be a tight one at first, but if Mr. Graham fulfils his obligations, it will loosen.

Mr. Graham is to serve nine months in jail, most likely at a facility in Brampton that specializes in sex offenders. There, he will get started on a "chemical castration" drug to reduce his sexual impulses, and take intense counseling.

After this, he will be on a 15-month conditional sentence under house arrest at his aunt's home in old Ottawa South.

During this time, he will be under a doctor's care and must follow all recommended treatments. He must stay inside for the hour before school starts and the hour after it ends.

After this, he will be on probation for three years, with the same treatment and school-hour conditions.

He is also banned for life from parks, playgrounds and arcades that draw children. There is a lifetime ban on any job that involves children.

If he breaches any of these conditions, he can be charged and further sentenced.

Mr. Graham's latest convictions are for sexual interference and sexual touching.

Last summer, he moved in with a woman and admits to several occasions of sexual behavior toward her daughter. On July 23, he took off her dress and threatened to kill himself if she told her mother. Later, he interfered with her sexually though he never penetrated the girl.

In 1990, Mr. Graham was convicted of sexual interference of a three-year-old girl. In 1991, he was convicted of invitation to sexual touching with a five-year-old girl.

(Continued)

(Continued)

> Yesterday's sentence came as no relief for the mother of Mr. Graham's latest victim. The woman, who was in court yesterday, said she is angry because Mr. Graham's mother and aunt, whom she has known for seven years, knew of his sexual tendencies but never told her. "I had no idea," she said. "This has caused my daughter a lot of pain and grief."
>
> Earlier at his sentencing hearing, Mr. Graham made a pledge to the community to go beyond what the law requires in sentencing and to never stop dealing with his sickness.
>
> "He is up to the challenge," his lawyer, Michael Crystal said. "Today is the first day of his new life."
>
> SOURCE: Rupert, J. (2001, March 24). Pedophile Gets Chance at "New Life": Chemical Castration Part of Sentence. *Ottawa Citizen*, p. C3.

It may be that Depo-Provera is best suited for those sex criminals for whom fantasy plays a prepotent role: pedophiles, exhibitionists, and voyeurs. The use of Depo-Provera is controversial. There are some indications that long-term effects may include diabetes, gallstones, thrombosis, and cancer. Short-term effects may include deep depression, high blood pressure, dramatic weight gain, and fatigue (Callan, 1985). Despite these causes for concern, many states and jurisdictions offer the use of this drug as a treatment alternative and as a way in which a convicted sex offender may decrease his sentence. In fact, 7 states now authorize the use of this drug to inhibit sexual desires. And 2 give offenders the choice of undergoing chemical castration or the actual physical removal of the testes as a condition of release or in lieu of a prison term.

The effect of this drug lasts only as long as they are taken, but many politicians and uninformed people support the use of them to gain political capital and show the people they are tough on crime. In a recent letter to a Maryland state task force, a Maryland delegate urged prison authorities to study castration as a "post-release management technique" for sex offenders (Montgomery & Mosk, 2001).

❖ THE FUTURE OF TREATMENT FOR SEX OFFENDERS

How treatment will evolve and how society will perceive sex offenders in the next century is an open question. While the two are separate questions, they are intricately linked. The more that we learn about sex offenders, the more that we come to accept that there typically is something distinctly different about them. We are not suggesting that they look different or come from different backgrounds, races, or any other traditional sociological indicator, but there is something different inside their psyches that causes them to behave in ways that are not in line with mainstream society. While it may be a pretty good guess that sex offenders, as a population, will never—at least in our lifetimes—be accepted into mainstream society, the future of treatment is less certain.

It is fairly apparent that behavioral, cognitive, and medical treatments will continue. As more research and evaluative studies are conducted on these programs, it is clear that we soon will have a better understanding of the best practices of the most successful programs. While we do not see any treatment approach as being better than another for all people, the research generally supports the notion that the time under treatment is a key indicator of success. Thus, while sentences for these offenders may get longer, it is sure to involve more treatment than incapacitation and retribution.

Regarding treatment, it is also clear that as state expenditures for criminal justice services increase, while legislative appropriations remain relatively constant, prison officials are going to have to focus their efforts on lower-cost treatment mechanisms that provide the best benefit for the offender, society, and state coffers. As discussed earlier in this chapter, this may involve housing offenders in halfway houses or residential treatment facilities for trial periods and releasing them back into the community after an extended adjustment phase. That does not mean that they should be released without restrictions. We also expect to see the use of high-tech monitoring devices such as ankle bracelets, house arrest, and other contemporary probationary surveillance methods to keep these offenders away from primary targets (schools, Little League fields, and other places where their targets of choice regularly assemble).

In addition, we are also likely to see additional jurisdictions begin to investigate modern medical methods of inhibiting sexual desires and proclivities. While some of the next generation of antiandrogen drugs do not have the same side effects as those used in the past, their use is a risky proposition, since we often do not know the long-term effects of medication until 5–10 years after a cohort of people have been on the drugs. If there are serious potential side effects to these medications, the state and drug companies could be looking at a very lengthy and expensive settlement.

In any event, while we would like to say that the future looks bright for the prevention and reduction of recidivism of sexual offenders through modern treatment mechanisms, it is a difficult to say how far we will go, especially since the topic is so politically charged. A single proposal that garners political and public support, such as the physical castration of all violent sex offenders, can set behavioral and cognitive treatment modalities back 10 years. The best we can hope for is that researchers and clinicians will be able to identify the best treatment mechanisms and match these with the types of offenders for which they are most likely to succeed. If such a study or report could be conducted, that landmark study might help shape the future and direction of sex offender treatment for the next 20–30 years.

❖ CONCLUSION

There is growing concern about the protection of society from those persons who present a clear and present danger to its law-abiding members. Incapacitation may be an answer, but it is only a short-term answer. The changing of the sex offender's sexual value system and propensity for violence directed toward others must be dealt with. Also, we must learn more about early identification of those persons who may become sexually violent as they age into adulthood. There is no doubt that protection is a right; the issue becomes how to accomplish it. We must give serious consideration to identification, isolation, and effective change of those who are dangerous.

❖ DISCUSSION QUESTIONS

1. Why do you believe that despite contemporary studies, many people still believe that sex offenders cannot be treated?

2. In discussing treatment options for sex offenders, why is it so important that we consider the political ramifications of increasing funds for treating these special classes of offenders?

3. Why do you believe that convicted sex offenders are consistently harassed by people both inside and outside prisons? How does this knowledge affect the way prison administrators and state criminal justice officials have to house and hold these offenders?

4. Why do you believe that residential treatment programs appear to work better in decreasing recidivism than treatment programs in mental health facilities or in correctional institutions?

5. Discuss the three variants of treatment options for sex offenders and give an example of innovative programs for each.

6. Go to your local library, run an electronic search, and count the number of incidences of sexual violence against children this year in your community. Now compare this number to that of 10 years ago. Has the prevalence of these reported crimes increased or decreased? If there is a difference, what do you believe explains the difference?

7. Why do you believe that the recidivism rate for sexual offenses is so different across the types of offenses committed? What types of offender do you believe are the most and the least likely to commit a similar crime after undergoing treatment? And why?

❖ NOTE

1. A prime example of a preferential offender is a child molester who will prey on youth only between ages of 12 and 15. A situational offender will act on opportunity. The victim of a situational offender may be known but will be chosen mainly at random.

❖ REFERENCES

Akerstrom, M. (1986). Outcasts in prison: The cases of informers and sex offenders. *Deviant Behavior, 7*(1), 1–20.

Alexander, M. (1994, November 11). *Sex offender treatment: A response to Furby.* Paper presented at a meeting of the Association for the Treatment of Sex Offenders. Chicago, Il.

Lotke, E. (2003) Issues and Answers: Sex Offenders: Does treatment work? [On-line] http://beachildshero.com/doestreatmentwork.htm

Alexander, M. (1999). Sexual offender treatment efficacy revisited. *Sexual Abuse: A Journal of Research and Treatment, 11*(2), 101–116

Alexander, M. (2001). Sex offender treatment: A response to furby. Paper presented at the association for the treatment of sex offenders. (1994, november 11). In E. Lotke (Ed.), *Issues and answers: Sex offenders: Does treatment work?* http://www.igc.org/ncia/sexo.html.

Amir, M. (1971). *Patterns in forcible rape.* New York: Harcourt, Brace & World.

Bradford, J. (1983). The hormonal treatment of sexual offenders. *Bulletin of American Academy of Psychiatry and Law, 11,* 159–166.

Bureau of Justice Statistics. (2000). *Sourcebook of criminal justice statistics, 1999* (No. NCJ 184989). Washington, DC: U.S. Department of Justice.

Callan, J. (1985). Depo-Provera for sex offenders. *Corrections Compendium, 5*(2), 6–8.

Cotton, D., & Groth, A. (1982). Inmate rape: Prevention and intervention. *Journal of Prison and Jail Health, 59*(2), 47–57.

Cox, G. (1984). Values, culture, and prison policy. *Prison Journal, 15,* 22–27.

Federal Bureau of Investigation. (2000). *Crime in the united states, us reports 1999.* Washington, DC: U.S. Department of Justice.

Fogel, D. (1975). *We are the living proof.* Cincinnati, OH: Anderson.

Furby, L., Weinrott, M., & Blackshaw, L. (1989). Sex offender recidivism: A review. *Psychological Bulletin, 105,* 3–30.

Greenfeld, L. (1997a). *Sex offenses and offenders* (No. NCJ-163392). Washington, DC: Bureau of Justice Statistics.

Greenfeld, L. (1997b). *Sex offenses and offenders: An analysis of data on rape and sexual assault.* Washington, DC: Bureau of Justice Statistics.

Groth, A., Longo, R., & McFadin, J. (1982). Undetected recidivism among rapists and child molesters. *Crime and Delinquency, 3,* 450–458.

Irwin, J. (1988). Donald Cressey and the sociology of the prison community. *Journal of Criminal Law and Criminology, 34,* 328–337.

Melella, J., Travin, S., & Cullen, K. (1989). Legal and ethical issues in the use of antiandrogens in treating sex offenders. *Bulletin of the American Academy of Psychiatry and Law, 17,* 223–231.

Montgomery, L., & Mosk, M. (2001, March 29). For the worst sex offenders. A radical proposal. *Washington Post,* p. T-02.

National Institute of Corrections. (1988). *Questions and answers on issues related to the incarcerated male sex offender.* Washington, DC: National Institute of Justice.

Office of the Legislative Auditor. (1994). *Sex offender treatment programs* (No. 94–07). St. Paul, MN:

Rizzo, N. (1981). Can everyone be rehabilitated? *International Journal of Offender Therapy and Comparative Criminology, 25*(1), 40–46.

Romero, J., & Williams, L. (1985). Recidivism among convicted sex offenders: A 10 year followup study. *Federal Probation, 49*(1), 58–64.

Sturup, G. (1968). Treatment of sexual offenders in Hertedester, Denmark. *Acta Psychiatria Scandinavica, 44,* 1–45.

Tappan, P. (1971). Some myths about the sex offender. In M. Wolfgang & L. Radzinowicz (Eds.), *The criminal society.* New York: Basic Books. 32–36

Vaughn, M., & Sapp, A. (1989). Less than utopian: Sex offender treatment in a milieu of power struggles, status positioning, and inmate manipulations in state correctional institutions. *Prison Journal, 69*(2), 73–89.

Vermont Department of Corrections. (1995). *Facts and figures: Legislative presentation.* Montpelier, VT: Vermont Department of Corrections.

Welch, R. (1988). Treating sex offenders. *Corrections Compendium, 13*(5), 1–10.

Glossary

Abnormal sex: generic term encompassing all criminalized or disvalued sexual behaviors, with the exceptions of adultery and fornication

Acmegenesis: orgasm

Acrophilia: sexual arousal from heights or high attitudes

Acrotomophilia: sexual preference for amputees

Adultery: sexual intercourse between two people when at least one is married

Agonophilia: sexual excitation from a pretension that one's partner is involved in a struggle to be free

Agoraphilia: sexual arousal from open spaces or having sex in public

Agrexophilia: sexual arousal from others knowing the person is having sex

Algolagnia: sexual satisfaction derived from the anticipation of inflicting or suffering pain

Anthropophagolagnia: rape with cannibalism

Arachnophilia: sexual arousal from spiders

Axillistic rape: rape of the armpit

Bestiality: sexual activity with an animal

Biastophilia: preference for violent rape

Brachioproticism: insertion of the arm into the rectum of another person for sexual pleasure

Bug chasing: the deliberate attempt to be infected by the HIV virus

Buggery: anal sodomy

Catheterophilia: sexual arousal from the use of catheters

Clap: gonorrhea

Coitobalnism: sex in a bathtub

Coitus a mammilla: insertion of penis between breasts

Computer sex: the use of computers for sexual games, communication, and erotic photography

Concubinage: use of female slaves as sex partners; living with sex partner without being married

Coprography: writing obscene words or phrases, usually in public toilets

Coprolagnia: arousal from feces

Coprolalia: arousal from using obscene language or writing

Coprophagy: the consumption of feces

Coprophilia: arousal from playing with feces, also called scat

Coproscopist: arousal from watching a person defecate

Cross dresser: a person who wears the apparel of the opposite sex

Crurofact: leg fetish

Cunnilingus: oral sex on a woman

Cynophilia: arousal from sex with dogs

Dacnolagnomania: lust murder

Dacrylagnia: arousal from seeing tears in the eyes of a partner

Dacryphilia: person who is aroused by seeing their partner cry

Date rape: use of force to gain sex from an unwilling woman during a mutually consensual social encounter

Dildo: artificial penis

Drag queens: gay men who dress in female attire

Dungeons: rooms that are decorated for sadomasochistic play

Dysmorphophilia: arousal from being with or around mentally impaired individuals.

Electric shock: using electric shock for sensory enhancement

Enonism: transvestitism or cross-dressing

Entomophilia: arousal from insects or using them in sex play

Eproctophilia: arousal from flatulence

Erotica: sexual literature and photos

Erotolalia: deriving sexual pleasure from talking about or listening to talk about sex

Erotomania: a compulsive interest in sexual matters

Essayeurs: men who were hired by bordellos to become sexual with women so that timid clients would follow their lead

Eugenics: belief that only the fittest should impregnate women

Eunuchs: castrated men

Exhibitionism: the deliberate exposure of the body in inappropriate situations to nonconsenting people for sexual arousal

Felching: inserting animals into the anus or vagina

Fellatio: oral sex on a male

Female impersonators: men who dress in women's clothing, often for pay

Fetish: inanimate object to which one attaches sexual connotations

Fisting: inserting a fist or hand into the vagina or anus

Flagellation: striking a person with an object

Flasher: exhibitionist

Folkways: the normal, habitual ways of doing things

Foot fetish: podophilia

Formicophilia: sex play involving insects which nibble or eat upon body parts that have been sweetened with a substance

Frigidity: inability to respond to sexual stimulation

Frottage: rubbing one's body against partner or object for arousal

Frotteur: one who practices frottage on an unwilling person

Gay: person who prefers a same-sex lover

Gerontophilia: sexual attraction to a partner who belongs to an older generation

Golden shower: practice of urinating onto a partner's body for sexual pleasure.

Hebephilia: sexual attraction (of a man) to teenage boys

Hedonism: unusual degree of indulgence in pleasure

Hetaera: highest-class Greek prostitute or female companion

Homosexuality: sex drive oriented toward personal and sexual gratification with the same sex

Homoeroticism: sexual arousal from person of same sex

Impotence: inability to achieve enough tumescence to penetrate a partner with one's penis

Incest: sexual relations between persons who are too closely related by blood to marry

Incubus: spirit believed to lie on top of women and have sex while they slept

Infantilism: dressing as a young child for sex play

Infibulation: torture of one's own genitals

Inspectionism: voyeurism

Jack gagger: husband who procures men to pay for sex with his wife

Kleptolagnia: sexual arousal from stealing

Kleptomania: compulsion to steal

Kleptophilia: sexual arousal from stealing

Leptosadism: mild form of sadism

Lesbian: woman who prefers a female lover

Lewd: legal term used to describe criminal, depraved, disvalued, and perverse sexual behaviors

Mammagymnophilia: arousal from female breasts

Masochism: ability to transfer emotions caused by pain to erotic feelings

Mastix: female sadist

Mastofact: breast fetish

Mazophallate: rubbing penis between breasts

Mores: those behaviors that, if violated, would result in the destruction of the society

Mysophilia: arousal from filth, soiled clothing, or foul, decaying odors

Narratophilia: sexual gratification or stimulation from listening to sexual stories; this may also apply to the passive partner in obscene telephone calls

Nasolingus: arousal from sucking nose of partner

Nasophilia: nose fetish

Necrochlesis: sex with a female corpse

Necrocoitus: penetration of corpses

Necrophagia: cannibalism of corpses

Necrophilia: sex with corpses

Necrosadism: sadism or mutilation of corpses

Nudomania: arousal from nudity

Obscene phone callers: people who become aroused by making phone calls and using vulgar language, or trying to elicit a reaction of shock from the other party

Obscenity: anything disgusting to the senses; it may or may not be sexual

Ochlophilia: arousal from being in a crowd

Oedipus complex: repressed desire to have sex with the parent of the opposite sex

Ophidicism: use of snakes, sometimes for sexual purposes

Ophidiophilia: arousal from snakes

Orgies: group sex

Osmolagnia: arousal from odors

Oxygen regulation: regulating intake of oxygen for sexual arousal

Pederasty: anal sex

Pedophilia: sex with minors

Peeping Tom: voyeur

Pictophilia: deriving sexual satisfaction from erotic pictures

Podophilia: arousal from feet

Polyandry: practice of one wife having multiple husbands

Polygamy: practice of having multiple marriage partners

Polygyny: practice of one husband having multiple wives

Polyiterophilia: arousal only after having sex with a series of partners

Pornography: anything deliberately fashioned to arouse erotic feelings

Proctophallism: anal sex

Pyromania: eroticized igniting of fires

Rape: nonconsensual sex involving coercion, empowerment, or anger

Raptophilia: inability to be aroused except by raping a victim

Red light district: area with bordellos and perhaps street prostitutes

Renifleur: person aroused by smell of urine or by sniffing underwear

Retifism: shoe fetish

Rhabdophilia: arousal from being flagellated

Rimming: penetration of anus with tongue

Roman shower: vomiting on partner, usually after drinking urine or wine

Sadism: empowerment and arousal derived from injuring others

Saliromania: sexual gratification received from the destruction or defilement of nude statutes or paintings of women

Sapphosadism: lesbian sadism

Satyriasis: (in a man) uncontrollable desire for sex

Scatolophilia: sexual gratification from making obscene telephone calls.

Scoptophilia: arousal from looking at sexually stimulating scenes

Short eyes: prison term for child-sex offenders

Sodomy: sexual penetration of any orifice other than the vagina

Statuophilia: sexual attraction to statues

Stigmatophilia: arousal from partner who is stigmatized (i.e., having tattoos, piercings, scars)

Succubus: female spirit believed to lie underneath men and have sex with them while they slept

Swinging: group sex or wife swapping

Tea room: slang term for public restrooms used for impersonal sex

Telephone scatophilia: arousal from obscene phone calls

Toilet training: urinating or defecating on a partner as a form of slavery

Toucheurism: touching a stranger for arousal

Transvestite: person who is aroused by cross-dressing

Transvestophilia: arousal from cross-dressing

Traumaphilia: sexual arousal from wounds or injurious trauma

Tribadism: lesbianism; sex by rubbing

Triolism: sexual gratification associated with seeing oneself or others in sexual scenes

Tyrannism: sadism

Undinism: sexual attraction to urine

Urolagnia: arousal from urine

Vampirism: sexual gratification from the drinking of blood

Vincilagnia: arousal from bondage

Whipping: striking or flagellating a partner for sensory enhancement

Zoophilia: arousal from animals

Zooerasty: sexual gratification achieved with animals by stroking, petting, or kissing, but without sexual intercourse

Index

Note: In page references, p indicates photos, f indicates figures and t indicates tables.

Bordan, T., 78
Boscredon, J., 87
Boucher, B., 235
Bourgeois, M., 190
Bourget, D., 195–196
Bourguignon, A., 187
Bowker, A., 177, 178
Bowman, H., 73
Boys *See* Children
Brachioproticism, 182
Bradford, J., 105, 121, 188,
    195–196, 289
Brain dysfunctions, 123
Briggs, F., 111
Brill, A., 182
Brislin-Slutz, J., 159
Brooks, B., 264
Brown, D., 55
Brown, G., 104
Brown, J., 104, 195
Brown, R., 112, 113
Browne, K., 113
Brownmiller, S., 18, 163
Brudos, J., 75, 205
    consequences of
        victimization and, 266
    fantasies and, 20
    necrophilia and, 186
    sadism and, 188
    sexual symbolism and, 22
    transvestitism and, 79
    triolism and, 72
Bruess, C., 81, 190
Bryant, C., 149
Buggery, 182
Bullough, V., 85
Bundy, C., 206, 214
Bundy, T., xiii, 1, 3
    compulsion and, 26
    consequences of
        victimization and, 265
    lust murder and, 206, 214
    necrophilia and, 184, 186, 187
    nuisance sex behaviors and, 64
    rape and, 243, 244
    sadism and, 188
    standards and, 18
    vampirism and, 209
Buono A., 206
Burdiit, T., 142

Bureau of Justice Statistics:
    arrests and, 275
    interracial sexual assault and, 256
    prisons and, 63
    rape and, 218, 223, 227, 228, 233,
        251, 252
Burg, B., 122, 182
Burger, T., 232
Burgess, A., 88, 120, 121, 122, 190,
    193, 209
Burgess, A. G., 235
Burgess, A. W., 235
Buttell, F., 178
Byrne, D., 157

Calef, V., 185
Callan, J., 289, 290
Call girls, 70
    See also Prostitution
Campbell, R., 83, 86
Campus rape, 233–234
Candaulism, 73
Candib, L., 102
Cannibalism, 209
    dangerous sex crimes and, 181
    fantasies and, 20
    necrophilia and, 186, 187
    pedophilia and, 120
    rape and, 241
Canter, D., 114
Cargan, L., 73
Carlisle, A., 116
Carney, M., 178
Caron, S., 158
Carpenter, R., 187
Carter, D., 158
Caruso, B., 102
Castration, 9, 104, 274, 289, 290, 292
Catheterophilia, 84
Celibacy, 27, 58
Cerebrotonia, 41, 43t
Cesnik, J., 192
Champagne, F., 113
Chang, D., 104
Chastity, 59
Chat rooms, 149, 160, 162, 167,
    168, 171, 176–177
Chatterjee, B., 171
Cheit, R., 113
Chemical imbalances, 44–45

Sexual pleasure *See* Pleasure
Sexual predators *See* Predators
Sexual standards, 13–18
  See also Standards
Sgroi, S., 120
Shachtman, T., 243
Shame:
  erotic asphyxia and, 192t
  exhibitionism and, 77
  klismaphilia and, 85
  pedophilia and, 127
  sadism and, 188
  serial offenders and, 278
  sexual assault and, 259
  victims of sexual assault and, 260
Sharma, K., 168
Sharp, E., 71
Shaver, F., 72
Shawcross, A., 210
Sheehan, W., 191
Sheldon, W., 41, 42, 43
Sheley, J., 261, 262
Shelp, E., 89
Sheridan, P., 104
Shock probation, 117, 130
Shoham, S., 39
Shrum, W., 76
Shuster, S., 209
Sickmund, M., 254
Siegel, L., 44
Siegel, S., 159
Sigler, T., 218, 224, 230
Sigurdsson, J., 113, 115, 208
Silberstein, J., 189
Silva, J., 190
Silverman, I., 104
Simon, L., 115
Singer, S. D., 212
Sivaloganathan, S., 194
Skogan, W., 261, 262
Sleep disorders, 264
Smallbone, S., 111
Smith, A., 68
Snyder, H., 254
Sobel, L., 154
Social issues:
  behavior and, 14–17
  child pornography and,
    138, 145, 150

consequences of
    victimization and, 263
  current sexual
    standards and, 58–59
  families and, 49–59
  fear and, 261–262
  homosexuality and, 8–9, 11, 13
  incest and, 97, 101, 104, 105
  killing and, 5–6
  lust murder and, 207
  manners and, 4
  moral judgment and, 145
  mores and, 3, 5, 15, 16
  norms and, 3, 7, 8, 13, 30
  pedophilia and,
    110, 127, 128
  pornography and, 156, 163
  protection of, 276, 286
  pyromania and, 198
  rape and, 6
  secondary victims of sexual
    assault and, 257
  sex offenders and,
    30, 290–291, 292
  sexual assault and, 251
  treatment and, 270,
    274–275, 279. *See also*
    Treatment
  victims of sexual assault
    and, 259, 261
  See also Culture; Standards
Social skills, 68, 113–114
Social workers, 284
Society for the Second
    Self (TRI-S), 79
Sodomy:
  definition of, 11
  important dates in the gay
    liberation movement and, 10t
  incest and, 96
  laws and, 10t, 11
  legal degrees of, 221–222
  necrophilia and, 182
  pedophilia and, 114
Soeken, S., 158
Somatotyping theory, 41, 42, 43
Sonenschein, D., 128
Specht, F., 111
Spitzberg, B., 217

About the Authors

Stephen T. Holmes is associate dean and an associate professor of criminal justice at the University of Central Florida. Prior to this position, he was a social science analyst for the National Institute of Justice in Washington, D.C. He has written 8 books and more than 15 articles dealing with policing, drug testing, probation and parole issues, and violent crime. He received his doctorate from the University of Cincinnati.

Ronald M. Holmes is professor of justice administration at the University of Louisville. He is the author of several books, among them *Profiling Violent Crimes, Sex Crimes,* and *Serial Murder.* He is also the author of more than 50 articles appearing in scholarly publications. He is vice president of the National Center for the Study of Unresolved Homicides and has completed more than 500 psychological profiles for police departments across the United States. He received his doctorate from Indiana University.